NUCLEAR WEAPONS
and the
BLUE-EYED PEOPLE

A Sociobiological Analysis

NUCLEAR WEAPONS
and the
BLUE-EYED PEOPLE

A Sociobiological Analysis

Richard R. Peppe

Glassworks Publishing

Richard R. Peppe is a practicing attorney in Pembroke, New Hampshire. He is a graduate of Tufts University and Suffolk University Law School, and he has an MBA from Northeastern University.

Glassworks Publishing
P.O. Box 208
Pembroke, NH 03275

Interior design: John Culleton
    http://wexfordpress.com

Cover design: Ellen Connor-Stahl
    http://www.hollisgate.com

ISBN 0-9749853-0-9.

Library of Congress catalog card number: 2004101486

Manufactured in the United States of America

To the memory of my parents, with love

CONTENTS

Peasant Societies as Learned Behavior

One can only speculate on the details of the mechanisms by which the epigenetic rules of valuation and decision making lead to such manifestations as economic conservatism and cultural neophobia.

E. O. Wilson[1]

Probably no one plants in the spring simply because he then harvests in the fall.

B. F. Skinner[2]

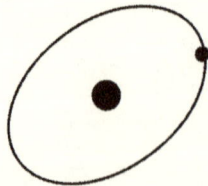

Learning theory is a superior platform to analyze traditional peasant behavior for two reasons: It is inevitably more parsimonious than its competitors, and it deals with "how" rather than "why" questions.

I use "biobehaviorism" for that space in human sociobiology that can be profitably treated by behaviorism. It is an attempt to carry B. F. Skinner's philosophy to a specific place: the peasant village.

In various places Wilson suggests that the revolutionary task of sociobiology was to challenge, across the board, behaviorism as an explanation for large scale, replicable human behavior. Well, he really did not mean it; and there is an enormous area in the peasant societies where behaviorism and sociobiology, Skinner and Wilson, can complement each other.

The phrase, "the Wogs begin at Calais," is helpful here. It is not literally true, because it could never have been directed at the Germans: they share too much with the English. The English can trace their King, much of their language, some of their free and independent political structure, their religion, and, partly at least, their good looks, directly to Germany.

Given the marriage prohibitions which tracked both American and British expansion in the west, in the east, and in the south, one may conclude that, aesthetics, no doubt, is the central message. But it is not the only message. The blonds really do share fundamental familial and social behaviors that are completely at odds with a peasantry.

Biobehaviorism accounts for the fit one sees between the peasant and his environment as a demonstration of behaviorism as taught by B. F. Skinner, modified by some tenets of sociobiology. It is an enormous physical space that has supported a very large fraction of human activity. It can explain many important elements of the economic activity of the peasant, perhaps the largest category of human activity ever on the planet.

Wilson is partially right. Because of its methodology and claims it was inevitable that behaviorism would be forced to yield to the ambitions of other, more biologically grounded, theories and methods.[3] But the need to scale back the behaviorist's claims did not necessitate their denial.

The blond intellectual, the essence of the non-peasant, the anti-peasant; views the peasant's thinking, even more than the peasant's looks, as the problem. The power relationships are disturbing; but the thinking is even more foreign. "False consciousness" must be what acute foreign observers from Germany and England have been reporting to their diary for hundreds of years: The peasant's thinking fails to conform to his objective reality.[4] The blond report back home has sounded the same for centuries. The blonds were always cultural anthropologists, and always had the intelligence to know that the first task of the great anthropologist was to get a great fighter out in front.

The blond intellectual opines that the struggle for a free intelligence, and therefore freedom, is and was a struggle between mentalities: literal on the one hand, ironic on the other.⁵ Irony plays a key role in the challenge to authority. Also creative, so long as the community does not need the authority.

A behaviorist's account would sidestep the issue of the behavior inside the skull and highlight the behavior one sees. That, plus the related issue of the time that the peasantry took to develop the behavior. For most of the immense beginning, virtually all is hidden. There is evidence of rice being cultivated in Asia 15,000 years ago, or more. Forget the human story. How to begin the rice story?

First, the peasant's perspective on the behavior. What was at issue was not simply good manner. It was a way of thinking. He was doing the only thing fitting and proper.⁶ Very different from irony.

From the first world, the blond world, the peasants' villages are like Spiro Agnew's slums: They all look alike. They are poor and dirty, and seemed to be chained to one of a series of dominant and curiously similar orthodoxies about personal behavior. The blonds see the very big, visible, power relationships which characterize the traditional peasant societies, have always characterized them, and see the relationship as at least a mistake, and probably evil.

Wittfogel's account might be seen as an early, impressive, but pre-sociobiological narrative; an attempt to place the peasant's creation in an analytical, positivist, history.⁷ His attempt to make the intrusiveness and severity of the "dictator" a kind of dependent variable in the ditch-digging story opens up what otherwise would be a white and black morality play.

Wittfogel saw the powerful as the central lever in a very long operational chain. The ecology of a given area, chiefly the availability of water, plays off a variety of repressive governments to create a kind of political scaling of exploitation.

Skinner and Wilson, as blonds and as scientists would share the same abhorrence of controls. Wilson does not deal with it at length, but it would appear that he shares Wittfogel's historiography on the political issues: The controls, which are a very characteristic mark of peasant societies, entered history from the top down. Wilson tells us that agriculture began with families on small tracts, got larger, were egalitarian, "politics" entered, inevitably with an expanding population, and hierarchies began to form. Tribal chiefs and later "states" required agricultural surplus, and rulers and priests took control.⁸ The familiar blond history. The Vikings thought the same.

But Wittfogel, Wilson and the blond convention must be wrong. To get the fit right, the controls must somehow operate very close to home. Maybe not as fine a fit as genetic structures, but the next best alternative. The kingdom could not have created the hydraulic system. Great sections of it must have been built, ditch by ditch, family by family, village by village, for millennia, before anyone had any idea about what could be done with that spectacular series of ditches one sees as one flies into Asia.

Skinner was closer to the truth but failed to see the implications of his theory for a real, a biologized, peasant world. In his writings, authoritarian controls are never reviewed as anything but a problem. He tells us that democracy was a countercontrol that operates to solve the evils of manipulation.[9]

The usual approach to the peasantry is through economics; assume that the behavior is about very large aggregates of people and a demand for "more" by certain powerful participants along the food chain. Economists make that assumption all the time.

Ditch digging is a very unpleasant activity to take on for really long periods of time. Outsiders, like Wittfogel, assert that the entity that compels people to dig is big, political and harsh. Economists are very likely to assume the mantle of political scientist: The man with the spade is driven by the man with a club.[10]

But a peasantry with water up to its collective chin does not have the capital to support really large club wielding officialdoms. Moreover, it is the economics profession that tells us that the inefficient must inevitably lose ground to the efficient over really long time periods. Surely it would be more efficient to move the club inside the peasant, and thereby theoretically free up all those men with clubs to pull weeds themselves.

It is more than interesting that from the simplest biological test, sheer numbers, the most successful peasant/weed puller did not have a heroic or militaristic image to represent itself. The ancient Chinese character for the people of the Central Nation was simply a man with bare hands and bare feet.[11] One can not imagine the blonds with such a modest coat. The people to the east of the Chinese were depicted by a character suggesting a big man carrying a bow, and people to the south by a character which might be the image of a campfire with dogs on guard. Did the Chinese notice something about themselves and their neighbors at a very, very early stage of development?

For sociobiology, the central fact has to be the amount of territory the ditch-digger appropriated in the teeth of a very hostile human and natural environment. Not just in China, but as Wittfogel, and other historians tell the story, in much of the Globe. There is a great exception where the blonds were established, but the record is impressive enough.

Perhaps the most telling commentary on the thesis, Man Is A Hunter, is the fact that the peasantry advanced precisely at the expense of the hunter. Not everywhere, but one can have a pretty good record without batting a thousand. When one considers the diversity of the locales where the peasant did succeed, and the undeniable behavioral constants within that success, one begins to doubt the universality of the concept, "Culture." The behavioral reality just could not have been that plastic. The issue does not revolve around motivation, it revolves around a kind of replicable order, what one encounters throughout the peasant's world. "Idiocy" misses the larger issue; the peasant did not start work in an otherwise empty planet.

The characteristic behavior can be not easily connected to what the peasant actually does, certainly not by the peasantry, a collection of illiterates. That fit was not at a direct genetic reality, but took place at a behavioral edge. The controls did not begin with the king, the despot, or the aristocratic nobility. None of them knew that much.

The social scientist, initially at least, is responsible for his own vision. Skinner was right: The scientist carries the lamp of parsimony as far into the night as it lights. The sort of fit that exists between the peasant village; the carrying capacity of the environment, given a certain style of agriculture, could not have been planned. The rationality of the peasant's behavior must have been beyond the comprehension of the peasant. The question then can be improved from "Why?" to "How?"

Assume that reports about culling cattle by sex in India are correct; male calves are killed where draught animals are not required, and females are destroyed where there is an intense need for draught cattle.[12] All the participants, whether they cull males or females, express a sincere abhorrence of killing cattle. There is no suggestion of a collective effort to influence ratios of surviving cattle by sex.

Marvin Harris glides past the curious fit between the behavior and the society, and focuses on the relationship between the presumed man inside the skull, and the man we see. He sees fraud: The peasant is not telling us the real story. Harris calls for an operational bifurcation between thought and behavior, a division that can be approached from either the peasant's perspective, or that of the social scientist. "Objective" accounts can be generated for each.[13] The social scientist trades in testability and replicability. The peasant follows certain mental realities. He uses the term "emic" to label the activity of the native: It is adequate insofar as it generates statements the native finds informative and meaningful. An "etic" analysis is more demanding. It generates data and theories that are useful to the scientists seeking "sociocultural" causation.

Now, he offers a kind of summary which displays the salient possibilities: Emic/behavioral, the male calf should live; emic/mental, calves have a right to life; etic/behavioral, male calves are starved, and etic/mental, when food is scarce the males should starve.[14]

Harris tells us that anthropology did not have a Skinner.[15] Well, it did. The anthropologists were not listening.

Harris asserts that a complete anthropology would deal with the mental life of the peasant. A research agenda that is designed to deal with both the emic and etic experiences is simply more complete than a strategy that focuses on one at the expense of the other. The promise is seductive. Could it be successful?

Well, who knows? The risk is that granting the mental experience its own integrity inexorably requires the assumption of a kind of logic structure that may not exist for the performance of the behavior at issue. At least not operationally, not outside and not inside. Maybe all one needs is a kind of social relationship, inside and out.

Harris would appear to believe that, at some inside level, the peasant is aware of what he is doing when he starves the calf. He notes that the method of death; they just are not fed, is ambiguous enough to avoid an outright condemnation.[16] Moreover, he tells us that people can be misled or confused about their own thought, as well as their behavior. He suggests that the man inside has an unconscious or "nonsalient level of attention."[17]

While the discipline, human sociobiology, will be characterized by a great deal of diversity, very different from behaviorism; learning theory will remain a major consistent theme in both. Now, starving the calf is a long drawn out process. One would think it would cause a major amount of problems for the Hindu peasant if he believes he is participating in a great evil.

One does not have to find a solution for every peasant. It is enough to find as simple a solution as possible for some peasants. Behaviorism is not incompatible with parts of Harris' "cultural materialism." Both Harris and Skinner see the void between the doctrine and the deed. Skinner discounts it. Harris seems to resort to an inner structure, awareness, and repression. The possibility is there. Is that complexity required?

I do not think so. If a peasant moved from an area where he culled males to an area where males were in short supply, he could feed them.

Biobehaviorism would move the control inside the peasant, where it would be most effective; but it would get there through an experience rather than a mentality. The real education would be transmitted through a dense, intensely social experience, in which no one really knew "why." They were simply doing what they should do.

Two points. Everyone would concede that one might act, without knowing, fully, what has led to the act. The second point has to do with parsimony. To the degree that one can track biological advantage to non-mentalist events, choice begin to recede. The key is the relationship between the behaviors. I am arguing that in peasant societies the relationships between act and behavior reflect a biological reality that is not seen, spoken, or intended.

Where the peasant expresses rational culling behavior, one may assume that someone taught him. The father is the obvious nominee. The fact that the behavior was taught along with the general prohibition makes the problem more difficult, but it does not require a new geography. There is no need to make the problem more complex by postulating new structures, with their own terminology. Emic and etic, like all arbitrary classification schemes, perpetually carry the threat to substitute for an operational analysis.

This is an answer that could be tested. Assume that a camera followed the peasant father with his son, each time they approached a cow standing with a calf of the "wrong" sex. The camera may reveal that the father teaches the son through his actions. Tone of voice, body language, gestures and touches, probably below the neck, maybe on the legs where they could be most easily ignored by both, in a continuous and consistent pattern, could effectively convey the "information" without any need for a troublesome mental superstructure. His posture and handling of the calf could be charted. Neither the father nor the son would have to mention the unmentionable. In fact neither would have to be aware of it. The father could have learned the appropriateness of the behavior in certain phases in the economic cycle from his father. And so each generation, and each region, could feel their way through horrific threats.

It would be best, given the nature and extent of the threat, for the father to have a certain type of relationship with the son. The more attentive the son, the better.

The mentalist alternative has to involve a kind of conspiracy. All those fathers pursuing a hidden agenda with their sons, always careful not to let the neighbors know. And of course, given the rationality of the overall pattern, all the neighbors are doing the same.

A step away, the conspiracy theory poses two insuperable problems. First it requires that the father know that he is supposed to commit bovicide on a massive scale in the teeth of a gigantic and terrifying orthodoxy which teaches that it is a monstrous crime. Second, the fit between the animal population and the real world setting would require an understanding that the dogma would be violated, without anyone reporting it.

Wilson's dictum that the brain operates on meaning[18] must be correct, part of the time. But the peasant has to use what is available. To first establish the prohibition, and then break it, he needs a range of behaviors given to him by a society. He does not need a continuous cost benefit analysis operating in his head. He needs to explain something to himself when he culls cattle, but he does not have to explain to himself that he is culling cattle.

The peasant lives at the end of a number of control points where he makes "correct" decisions, without knowing how correct they are. Wilson makes numerous allusions to the peasant's rationality from a biological perspective. The fact that the behavior is as appropriate as it is provides support for his formulation of a gene culture coevolution, a condition of which is the observation of a link between practice and biological fitness.[19] Well, who can object? The risk is that, because it is so powerful, a presumed genetic formulation will foreclose a research strategy into environmental causation.

For example, Wilson discusses the behavior of certain Mediterranean populations and favism as an instance of the "link" between culture and biology. There is a high incidence of a certain gene in some Mediterranean populations as a result of selection pressure caused by malaria; an ancient, widespread, and virulent disease in the basin. While the gene confers heightened resistance to malaria, it also presents a health hazard of its own because it is sometimes associated with enzyme deficiencies. The consumption of fava beans exacerbates the deficiency, sometimes causing illness or death. Wilson notes that while the people in the area have not made any direct correlation between the bean and the disease, the bean has been interwoven into rituals, taboos and legends for centuries.[20]

I think Wilson offers the observation as a kind of example for his "culturgen," a behavior that has been placed under direct biological influence. Now, he presents evidence, which nearly everyone accepts, that such traits as extroversion, introversion, depression, hearing acuity, etc., are also subject to genetic influence. And he goes higher on the scale to include number ability, spatial ability, and word fluency.

But I have a great reluctance to assume that something like fava bean behavior should be added to the list. It looks too much like a great deal of the peasant's behavior generally: too much like cattle culling. It combines too many specific and detailed movements.

Fasts may be a candidate for biobehaviorism. They are an unmistakably biological part of the hydraulic order, and they are counter-intuitive. Why would a population, which is perpetually close to the minimal subsistence level, deny itself food?

Biobehaviorism would favor an approach that begins at home, and serves some very important physical ends. Their appearance on the yearly calendar might hold some clues. Do they tend to appear at certain periods in the planting/harvesting cycle? Is there a scaling operating: harsher in drought areas, milder where the climate is more forgiving? What affect do they have on birth and death rates? Do they assist in the maintenance of an age cohort for the population?

Fasts and food handling rituals generally can also begin at very low behavioral levels. The controls are introduced one village at a time, and slowly make their way across the environment, emerging centuries later with a great shout, and a religious/political rationalization by the mighty, who, finally, come from the same village, and think the same thoughts.

Biobehaviorism offers itself as a solution, specifically for a peasantry, partly because of the reported similarities in the peasant's behavior across political and ethnic lines. The variations are there: but the consistencies are there too, and may be part of the larger story. The role of women, the pace of the family, the emphasis on order, the space between the father and the children, have all been noted time and time again.

Primitive medical practices may be mediated by biobehaviorism. A patient suffering from smallpox in India has a special status as a worshiper of the mother goddess, Sitala, and must not be touched.[21] It really is not necessary for biobehaviorism to determine if the behavior preceded the custom, or vice-versa. The behavior does not really need the goddess. In fact, the goddess may be a convenient peg for the man to explain the behavior to himself. Here the brain's great size and strength create their own problem and inefficiencies. It requires the man to make up a long, involved, and more or less logical story.

"Amoral familism" is an observation the blonds would have made for centuries, perhaps millennia, and not just in southern Italy. The density and size of the peasantry suggests its effectiveness.

I believe there are two main reasons why so many peasant populations look behaviorally so different from the blonds and so similar, by contrast, with each other. Catholic Mediterranean societies, the Arab world, China, much of the Slavic world; virtually all of the hydraulic world, have a father who is very effective at mining child labor.

The second is their long experience of existence in relatively isolated, closed agricultural villages. The periodic but unpredictable year when the crops would fail required that the village protect itself from the threat of children without adult males to feed them. Economists and anthropologists who attempt to understand the village without the insight that the village needed a balance, will miss the true story of the "moral economy."

One of the clearest demonstrations of this balance is found, repeatedly, in the pattern of distribution of family held land. The dimension and the spread of the pattern suggests a truth which was learned again and again, in places as far removed as China, Southeastern Asia, the Mediterranean, and parts of the Slavic world. These societies exhibited different land tenure systems, and were not even internally consistent within ethnic groups. Yet the consistent pattern of maintaining family plots for basic sustenance in extremely small individual plots, curiously distant from each other, strongly suggests adaptation.

Generations of land division in Tonkin created so may small, dispersed family plots which required so much inefficient work, that some estimates projected an increase of 10 percent in rice production, with the same labor force, had the family plots had been integrated.[22] One educated outside observer in Southern Italy viewed the pattern as chaotic.[23] In one southern Chinese villager, peasants walked over three hours to work on different family plots.[24]

The advantage of small-dispersed plots, trivial to the outsider, crucial to the peasant, is that a crop failure in one place because of insects, flooding, or plant disease, does not condemn the family to starvation. The extensive energy expended on maintaining the scattered plots are insurance premium payments.

Clearly the travel to the plots, and the work to maintain them, are not directly under genetic control. Nevertheless the behavior is widespread enough that one is justified in asking whether the fit between the man and the dispersion reflects learned behavior. For that to have occurred, one does not need to be able to articulate its advantages. One needs a history sufficiently long and sufficiently intense to establish the orthodoxy. Alternatively, there may once have been villagers who "saw" the advantages of dispersed plots, one grim year, and decisions were made which later became behavior, and left the decision behind. It is similar to, but a little less complicated than culling cattle. Here, there is no need to mediate in the teeth of a taboo.

Dispersion of family plots, culling cattle and fasts are counterweights to the anecdotes provided by more traditional observers who feature power relationships and political structures. Wittfogel is identified with the argument that large, coordinated, disciplined groups of workers are required to safely handle and control the tendency of water to accumulate into larger bodies. He theorizes that in the beginning there were farmers who were able to farm without irrigation systems, but banded together to exploit arid plains, and voluntarily submitted to a central authority.[25] The theory fits with mentalism and with the blond intellectual's certitude that people can choose, and that they always choose. It assumes a goal driven economic structure, a compact, which, has evolved into a type of society which somehow balances an intense familism, and an all-powerful central authority.

The account simply can not be an accurate reconstruction. One's choice of a theory of learning is crucial. Neither the peasantry nor the nascent autocracy had ever seen a hydraulic society.

If, in the beginning, there was a bond strong enough to enable the individuals to subordinate themselves to a central authority so severe that the outsider identifies it as despotic; one wonders why the blond intellectual consistently reports a familism which is directed against the central authority. Moreover, if the initial step was a decision by diverse individuals, one wonders why there should be so many consistencies among the peasantry in so many different places.

I would begin the story inside the family. Child labor is a very familiar feature of the peasant village. Throughout the hydraulic world there is a universal commandment: The child owes his family labor. Perhaps this is an area where the hunter/gatherer was at a decisive disadvantage vis-à-vis the agriculturist.

The peasant could call on his entire family to participate in the economic life of the family. Wittfogel locates the decisive quality of the hydraulic societies in water; a sociobiological alternative would find it in blood, albeit through a control system which was not dominated by the genes in a direct way.

For Wittfogel the initial impulse toward the control system might be identified as opportunity: irrigation. It is an interesting contrast that at least one Chinese alternative presents the system as a protection against an ever present danger: flood.[26] And as the Chinese account presents it, the danger of flood and risk of death was so high, that outside social control would not be effective. The peasantry had to internalize the need to work for a common goal.

Biobehaviorism sees the stronger argument in the small tradition, with the village and family. This suggests that for substantial projects, irrigation functions probably, but maybe not necessarily, preceded flood control work. Family units of less than 50 people and a village of three hundred or less could not make much of a difference in battling floods. An almanac, in its list of greatest natural disasters, leads off with 3,700,000 deaths in China as a result of the flooding of the Huang He River in August 1931.[27] It caused, by far, more casualties than any of the earthquakes, tidal waves, tornadoes, blizzards, or other disasters listed.

As Wilson developed the theory of sociobiology, it emphasized the direct application of evolutionary biology to human social behavior.[28] But an emphasis does not preclude other possibilities from making an appearance.

The control of water for both irrigation and flood prevention must have played a central role in much of the peasants' efforts to prevent starvation for millennia. Religions, at the beginning, must have been affected by this social reality.

The practice of interval planting of rice fields in Indonesia is a really startling demonstration of the peasant's behavior, mediated by religious authorities through symbols and rites, leading to a rational result; without any evidence to support a belief the peasantry knew what it was doing. For a thousand years or more rice growers in Bali have, in fairly large geographical areas, spaced the planting of rice fields, according to instructions from the religious authorities. The complex, engineered, terraced system had provided food for over a millennium without self-defeating ecological damage.[29] The rice paddies are controlled by "subaks," cooperative associations that may direct production for hundreds of acres.

Western experts entered the arena, armed with new rice strains, and advised switching to hybrid rice, which matured faster than traditional types. Pesticides and fertilizers were subsidized and promoted. Westernization, and rationalization, also brought the end of staggered planting within the subaks, as each farmer was free to find his own optimum return. The temples lost control of planting schedules. Each paddy began to be farmed without regard to the overall pattern.

Unexpectedly however, instead of the boom predicted by the scientists, the villagers found that the crops were failing due to an increase in pests and viruses. Upon closer examination, scientists found that if farmers plant at the same time, and harvest at the same time, the demand for water overwhelms the supply. If the villagers vary planting and harvesting, but in a random way, water supplies would be adequate, but pest infestation would become severe. Indeed, a computer model for 172 subaks showed that when the associations independently scheduled their planting and harvesting, eventually pests would destroy the entire crop. The computer also showed that the schedules promulgated by the temple system were the most efficient.

How could one account for this curious serendipity? Behaviorism is indispensable here. People can learn in the same way that animals learn.

There is a middle ground between the genes working directly on the thoughts or the behavior of the peasant; and the position that biology plays no role at all. I focus on controls, but mimicry may play an equally decisive role in the overall pattern in the village. One would think that in a very small, intensely familistic setting, mimicry would have an excellent opportunity to develop. What Skinner would call the resulting topography could fit within a sociobiological analysis of the village. It did not evolve directly, but it is more defined by biology than the simple observation that the organism can do what it does.

There are other examples. One writer, arguing that some peasant practices are simply silly, or even dangerous, cites the practice of peasant women in the foothills of the Himalayas giving birth in cow sheds, and remaining there a week or two after the event. They act as if cow urine has beneficial properties. Figures on mortality suggest the reverse.[30] However, the fact that there may be better ways of handling a problem does not demonstrate that the cow shed does not have its advantages. The real trick is to find the charm of the shed, and then to imagine the "how" of the social behavior.

Barash discusses the ability of the snow monkeys in Japan to separate wheat from sand by dropping handfuls of the mixture into water.[31] The wheat, which floated could then be scooped from the surface and eaten. One monkey may have dropped a handful of the mix; others would see the result and followed suit. Could the initial drop have been "planned?" One would think not.

The subak was once a small village. People may have noticed what happened when nearby villages planted their rice at the same time the home village planted. Mimicry, one generation after the other, ensured the survival of the rational behavior. The first rough optimum schedule could have been in place generations before the priesthood developed an explanation for it.

Is such behavior within the field of sociobiology? The grain feeds the monkey. The rice feeds the man. Mimicry is part of the behavior. If the grain changes the size, say, of the troop that can be supported in a given area, one could say that biology has monkey behavior, the size of the troop, on a string. Definitions are not true or false, but more or less useful for a given situation. I suppose the way one feels about extending behaviorism into "sociobiology" is almost an aesthetic judgment.

The assumption is that social behavior; social rules and evolution all fit together. How to approach the issue? My argument for putting behaviorism into sociobiology is that it may be another way to understand the "how" of certain consistent peasant behaviors.

Barash highlights various advantages that accrue to disparate species across a series of categories such as territoriality, parenting, mating, protection, etc. Learning seems to have the same status as other behaviors and is an area where social existence confers advantages. Mimicry is the characteristic that is the backdrop for the behavior of the snow monkey.

Learning is the category that has the potential to be a link between a strictly biological (animal and human sociobiology?), and a cultural (strictly human?) sociobiology. Social learning, Barash tell us, is strictly cultural, while the capacity to do the social acts is biological, both in terms of physiological structures and the "tendencies" within social organizations which are the behavioral back-drop of the behavior.

In the long term, I believe that sociobiology will drain all advantage from the storage bag labeled "cultural."[32] If the behavior is old, and resonates across different ethnic groups engaged in somewhat similar behavior, its genesis probably was biological. Life was on too thin of a margin for too long for that not to have been the case.

The first human agriculture could have merged in a very similar way as wheat sifting in snow monkeys. Harvesting would have been delayed from the time the planting was accomplished. But people have bigger brains than monkeys, and a man might remember what he threw in that moist dark area a few months ago. A whole series of practices, some rational, some not, which reflected an intense absorption with the food source might have arisen. At first they were spread by mimicry, and later, controls. The subak seems beyond comprehension because of what is hidden: the immense time that the schedule took to develop.

Wilson's ambition for sociobiology is nothing less than the reformulation of the social sciences from a biological perspective.[33] The ambition requires that the social scientist approach human behavior with some of the fundamental as-sumptions one would use to investigate animal behavior. The first assumption, that life is a struggle, leads directly to the great emphasis on replicable patterns. It may not be an iron law, but in the working out, once one finds the pattern, an attempt at a formulation of its contribution to biological fitness is not far behind.

One would expect historians or economists, and not sociobiologists, to use words like "apathy" or "underdevelopment." They assume a simpler, rational, world, rather than the dense, biological/behavioral world that exists.

Economics is a social science that has progressed through greater abstraction and quantification. The key assumptions have involved the primacy of the market, and the rational profit maximizer. These assumptions evaporate in the teeth of the fit one sees between the peasant and his world.

Economics counts stuff, sociobiology counts people. Until very recently, the human animal, like every other animal, was not far from the margin of life. Survival, for oneself, for one's progeny, was not for free. One would assume that the patterns people developed to survive had an adaptive value, as with all other animals under the threat of starvation. It is very difficult to account for the Bali rice fields if the central character in the story is an economically rational peasant. If one is willing to let the man do what he does without knowing why he does it, the story is not about maximization but about adaptation.

Number of children

One very obvious, very biological, fact about peasants is the number of children that they have. The first step in moving away from the familiar is to call the behavior biological.

Perhaps the most congenial straightforward sociobiological assumption would be to assume the peasant had as many children as he could. Once he supported them to an age when they could support themselves, they would spread the parents' genes. The position has more to support it than simplicity. Some authorities do state that the evidence suggests that in pre-modern societies, the typical couple is not able to have as many children as they would like.[34] Certain experts claim that women were having children approximately up to their biological limits as recently as the 19th century.[35]

Wilson and Lumsden tell us that the first principle of sociobiology is that social behavior is shaped by natural selection[36] The number of children people have would certainly seem to be a very basic behavior, and thus subject to selection process. Yet that number changes very rapidly when the peasants leave the village. Is there an explanation that would also be compatible with sociobiology?

Animals limit their densities. The failure of some to reproduce is a genetic loss for those individuals, but could be a net gain for the survivability of the group. Studies of the ways populations limit their densities can be as sophisticated as any in biology and clearly out of reach for the layman. Still, the layman knows in a general way that it happens.

Physiological events within the organism can select out certain individuals. One biologist argues that degenerative cardiovascular disease may have conferred advantage to the primitive group by selecting out middle age men who had completed the task of raising their young.[37] The argument makes heavy use of dietary data. Early man, the argument runs, was a generalized carnivore, who traveled in small bands under intense competitive pressure. The social bands that survived must have been characterized by a membership that was active and vigorous, and not handicapped with older men who consumed resources that they could not produce.

As societies evolved, the adaptation was masked as man developed agriculture and began a diet that was heavily weighted toward grain consumption, and relatively little meat. But once industrialization and increased wealth allowed people to resume their preferred diet, heart attacks reappeared to weed out the participant who could not contribute to the fitness of the carnivore band.

Could social forces operate to produce a certain population level? What forces might have moved the peasantry toward an optimum population mix?

The sanctions that certain peasant societies imposed against marriage for the youngest son until the parents died and the family farm became available, could be seen as attempts to limit the population.[38] This possibility is somewhat at odds with the view that the peasant woman was essentially having children up to her biological capacity.

Learning issues are the nutritious variables for the most important "how" question here. Labeling them "cultural" does not help.

One must see an agricultural population on a finite space with a limited technology trying to avoid overshoot and collapse. The biological imperative has been softened, and the raging impulse of the individual has been subordinated to the needs of the group.

It has a charm to it, and may be right. Still, these are all illiterates, who have not read much anthropology, and want to have sex. Assume that the people in the village never saw a collapse. How do they behave rationally?

When I travel from New Hampshire to New York City, the impression of crowds of people all around is simply overwhelming. It is exciting certainly, but an outsider wonders about the interminable nature of it. At 4 o'clock in the morning all those people and that roar are still there. How do they get used to it? I suppose a Third World slum would make the point even more dramatically.

If "crowding" triggers population-limiting behavior in people, one would think that the giant cities we see would not have been possible. One looks at the New York skyline and assumes that there are no mechanisms to prevent collapse in human populations, because there is no mechanism to flag an overshoot. The term remains perpetually abstract.

At the level of the individual, one of the behavioral characteristics of urbanized industrialized population everywhere is a clear intent to limit family size. The phenomenon tracks the move from the peasant village to the city consistently, without much regard for religious tradition, or ethnicity. The dominant assumption seems to be that it reflects a rational weighing of advantages.

But what is there about the village, or the peasantry that establishes a high birth rate compared to the rate in the slum? One may assume that the key mechanics revolve around the same concept one applies in the slum: choice. That could be a mistake.

I believe that it is instructive that reports from China state how much difficulty the central authority has in implementing a one child per family policy in the village, but not in the newly burgeoning cities.[39] Why?

Some claim that there is a "rather long delay" between the commencement of the social and educational forces that force modernization, and the behavioral changes that are associated with industrialized societies.[40] But birth rates do not respond like that. They appear to change as soon as the peasant family enters the slum.

The biobehavioristic model would prefer a virtual instantaneous change in preference. The peasant woman, with a very restricted range of social contacts in the village, and no friends outside the village, should desire that number of children which "makes sense" for the village environment. Her peers and her family teach her that number. Given the age and durability of the village in a fiercely difficult and risky environment, one should not assume that a behavior this basic, this biological, would be completely outside village social control. To say that, is not to say that there has to be a genetic directive to have a given number of children, or that people in the village have to know what that number is. It is something like culling cattle. A given behavior works, and people can learn to do it without knowing that they do it.

That responses from peasant women from places as diverse as East Asia and the Mediterranean basin, on questionnaires concerning the preferred number of children, tend to cluster near 5 is intriguing.[41] Have social scientist just assumed that this represents some sort of biological limit; or, alternatively, that it reflects economic rationality? One would think that very different types of agriculture, or very different environments might produce very different numbers.

Is there another place to look that is more compatible with a biobehaviorist analysis? Assume that pre-agricultural Neolithic man, lived to about eighteen, and women to about twenty, and that they required about six or seven children to maintain the species.[42]

Hunter-gatherers probably adopted agriculture in a discursive, non-linear, tortuous schedule lasting generations. The true peasant was centuries in the making. That transformation was characterized by tremendous competition by populations exhibiting different behaviors. The populations which reproduced on a proper schedule; not too many, not too few, possessed a very basic biological advantage. It is not surprising that controls could have developed to maintain that advantage. A model with just individual preference reflecting a presumed economic advantage does not adequately handle the tremendous amount of consistency one sees across very widely dispersed, behaviorally diverse populations.

My hypothesis is that the magic of the number six reflects an ancient behavioral reality, and that the village is a control mechanism that keeps that number in place. Villages that did not maintain the number lost ground to those that did. The argument does not expand "evolution" to include villages; it does allow social organizations to influence basic behaviors.

Once one sees this possibility one is less willing to defer to the garbage bag labeled "culture." Certain behaviors, such as taboos on intercourse during lactation, do limit fertility. Applying these rules properly allows for the "rational" number of children, without consciously recognizing a desire to limit fertility.[43]

The peasant does restrict the birth rate in response to adverse conditions.[44] Moreover, even for pre-industrial populations, technology is an important variable in determining the population a given land area will support. Holland and Venice are dramatic demonstrations of the fact. Also, extra village influences can affect the birth rate. Apparently some Russian landlords imposed fines on unmarried serfs.[45]

Overall, the central sociobiological reality for the peasant was that he would have to provide for between five and six children, in good year after bad, century after century. The speed with which peasant women, removed to the slum, change their behavior on a very basic behavior suggests that more than individual preference is at stake. While it is commonplace to decry the problem of overpopulation, some analysis claim that the rate of decline in fertility takes place much faster now than it did in Europe's demographic transition.[46] Putting the control inside the village, rather than the woman's head, would also fit with survey data which found that the education of the wife, and the wife's non-farm work experience, were the two most important core modernization variables in lowering fertility.[47] "Cultural variables," including those facts, religions, and processes that were peculiar to individual countries, were much less important.

The claim that one can predict fertility from a matrix of biological and socio-logical factors, and that biology and society combine to make a decision on the number of children couples should have, is consistent with biobehaviorism.[48] Biobehaviorism goes beyond that to offer an answer to the "How?" question.

The fact that it is women's experience which seems to dominate the really dramatic downward shift which occurs when the village weakens, may sug-gest that the control is in the sex which is characteristically presented as the "victim," rather than the perpetrator. Maybe American women intellectuals see themselves perpetually as daughters-in-law, rather than mothers-in-law. One wonders how the preference for number of children compares for women and men, inside the village.

It is not necessary for women to leave the village, to have the control dissipate. As the village school becomes bigger, the ancient behavioral peasantry becomes smaller and weaker. What was crucial to learn; knowledge about life and death issues becomes an amusing anecdote in the school and the slum.

The fears that compulsions will be required to limit population growth are probably misplaced as villagers move to slums. Functionally a very specific historic number, 5 to 7, gives way to another number, 2 or 3. No large urban metropolitan urban area could match the detailed pressure point by pressure point of the isolated 1500 person familistic agricultural village. Reports out of China suggest that the controls of the central government to limit births are in line with what city dwellers wish to do anyway. In one precinct of about 40,000 people in the city of Shenyang in northeast China, not one child was born outside state quotas between 1980 and 1987.[49]

The earlier Russian experience was a precursor of the Chinese experience. In the early years of the 20th century ethnic Russians were overwhelmingly rural and had traditional large families. By the beginning of the 21st century they were largely urbanized and had a low birth rate, but the rural Muslim population in the former Soviet Union continued to have large families.

The solution involves more than knowledge; it involves behavior. The tenacity of the rule, 5 or 6 children within the traditional peasant village, across cultural fault lines, becomes understandable once one sees it, not as poverty; but as a biological success story within a relentlessly biological world.

Periodically one reads of attempts to quantify major historical trends by extrapolating past trends. The trend, of course, eventually leads to disaster. Readers over 50 may have forgotten the prediction in the early 1970's that the world would have 7 billion people by the year 2000, but they will remember the book that made the prediction. [50]

Skinner himself did not see behaviorism operating on the birth rate within the village to support a certain number. His seems to have shared the conventional view. High birth rates are a mistake; they threaten human prosperity and happiness, they require correction by changes in public institutions like schools, legislation, and medicine.[51] His last book stated that the solution for overpopulation was for governments to give people reasons to have fewer or no children.[52]

Poverty stricken people have poverty stricken governments. Inevitably. Economics is like that. The right answer to the problem is to crack the structure that teaches the people what they need to know.

The village was right for millennia. With the coming of industrialization, the village became wrong. When the despot's school and the urban slum combine to create not just a new man, but more important, a new family, the change to smaller families is irreversible.

Scarcity/Security

The first fact about the peasant society is the first fact about agriculture. It provided an enhanced security and wealth over hunter-gatherer societies. The peasantry looks poor compared with industrial workers, but they are the beneficiaries of incredible wealth compared with the societies they replaced. However, the wealth and enhanced densities, leashed to the reality of five or six children per married woman, means there will be a continuing tendency with a given technology, to breed up to the carrying capacity of that land.

Peasant agriculture is a very high-risk occupation. It has been more risky for more people than any other occupation. The image of the peasant as a man living his life in water up to his chin understates the drama, and the potential horror.

The image fits in an average year. But the peasant knows that some years are worse than average. Much worse. Run enough years together and water over the chin is inevitable.

Weak technology agriculture has been the most exciting adventure for the biggest number of people up to the advent of nuclear weapons. In 7, or 12, or 20 years, men, wives, parents, and children will see the water go over their heads. Everyone in the village knows that.

A major assertion of peasant biobehaviorism is that major adaptations; adaptations involving deep, widespread, and basic patterns of thought and behavior; make sense through the lens of that exciting year when the crops fail. That these behaviors might have had some grounding in reality has been unexamined in the blond English speaking world for various reasons. One is that they are tough to document.

Another is the way the blond English speaking world, regardless of class, has always felt about what was not them. Journals and reports by foreigners as early as the 1400's remarked consistently about two characteristics of the English: their impressive wealth, and their hatred of foreigners.[53]

Prior to 1500 the word "peasant" was used exclusively to apply to foreigners, and was used within a context of describing poverty.[54] The Mediterranean, France and Italy specifically, were reported as being impoverished, lacking basic materials and having a diet characterized by vegetables and fruits, compared to the Englishman's meat, fish, and general abundance.[55] The general impression of English speaking visitors was consistent for a long time. The relative size of people and animals between Englishmen and much of the peasant world might be seen as a probe into a very different past.[56] The anecdotes about what the blonds encountered in much of the peasant world outside of Europe are remarkably consistent. In Turkey,[57] and Algeria,[58] they found poverty unknown at home.

Iurii Krizhanich, a seventeenth century Croat who had traveled in Russia as well as Western Europe, makes a number of telling comments about the difference in living standards among different peoples which he had visited. The Russian peasant was seen as living better than peasants in Greece or Spain, where they could not afford meat of fur. But England, Germany and France were polities where single cities were seen as having more wealth than the entire Russian nation, excluding the Tsar's holdings.[59]

Bakunin, a Slav writing in the nineteenth century, reported the same story within the blond world: great wealth and a passionate dislike of foreigners. [60] An observer reported in the nineteenth century that there were many years in which the Russian peasant had bread for less than 6 months. [61]

Marvin Harris saw peasant children in Brazil wearing just one sneaker. After investigating, he found that the children shared a pair of sneakers because the family was too poor to buy more than a singe pair.[62] In the province of Palermo children dragged their own chair to school because the public system was too poor to supply chairs to all.[63] As recently as the 1960's urbanized sophisticated Chinese college students were surprised to learn that there were Chinese peasants who were too poor to buy sandals or mosquito netting.[64]

The relative richness of the blond diet, even in pre-industrial times, may have been more pronounced when the comparison was with Asians than with other populations in Europe.[65] As recently as the 1960's meat was prohibitively expensive for the Chinese peasant. The sale of a brood, about ten half-grown piglets, brought almost as much as a half-year's wages for an adult male.[66] In most of Southeast Asia, peasants have been able to barely meet minimum standards of diet, clothing and shelter, plus just enough to invest in the next year's crop.[67] It was not uncommon for Chinese peasants, in the slack season, to request permission from officials to enter the cities to beg.[68] Poverty in pre-Communist China, in the 1930's was so severe some years that some parents were required to sell their daughters into slavery, a separation that would never be ended, in order to preserve the rest of the family.[69]

One frequently sees references to "capitalism" promoting and enforcing certain virtues, such as thrift. But when one compares the savings rate of the blonds, the people who created capitalism, with the traditional peasantry one sees that it might be more accurate to say that in the first instance capitalism required a certain margin to waste money.

The extreme poverty of the classic peasantry was coupled with a delayed entrance to industrialization. The agricultural population represented a very large percentage of the Russian nation until relatively recent times. Some estimates claim that as much as 90% of the Russian population could be classified as peasants in the early 19th century. [70] The percentage classified as urban increased from 39% to 59% between 1950 and 1972.[71] A Russian text reported that about 25% were collective farm peasants in 1970.[72] As late as 1940, the eve of World War II, 60% of the Japanese labor force was employed in agriculture; the highest of the major world powers.[73] In 1947, well after the end of the war, half were still employed in agriculture.[74] In 1956 Japan attempted to join with Mexico, in a bracero program to furnish unskilled agricultural labor to the U.S.[75]

In 1958 peasants accounted for about 60% of Korea's population, with an annual income below $80.00.[76] Agricultural products comprised over 45% of India's domestic economy in 1975.[77] China had about 80% of its population employed in agriculture in the 1980's.[78]

The sheer mass of the population pulling weeds is enormous. In terms of absolute numbers the peasantry will remain a major presence for a very, very long time. In China the peasantry expanded from about 450 million to 800 million, between 1956, and 1978.[79] The rural agricultural village, then, not the independent farmer, is the locus of much of history, outside the blond world, right to the twentieth century. Economic historians, who rely on numbers for comparisons, rather than behaviors, miss the point. The fact that post World War II Germany went from a diet of a pound of meat, and a half pound of butter, to one of the richest economies in the world within the space of a few years, does not provide much information than can be related to the peasantry.[80]

The difference does not revolve around a market, free or controlled. Germany had already created a basically open, industrialized, self-aware, literate society.

They had been relatively open, wealthy, self-aware and literate for a long, long time. National decision makers did not have to contend with the determination and resolve of a peasantry that had successfully dealt with basic survival issues for hundreds, perhaps thousands of years, and, as a collective, generated and enforced rules that had been successfully tested for generations. Rules that were at odds with the requirements of industrialization and modernization.

The village and the authoritarian family had provided a vital role in collecting and investing very scarce capital. Where could the modernizing state, communist or fascist obtain capital?

Just as peasant agriculture enjoyed an advantage over hunter-gatherers because of child labor, so an industrializing society generates an enhanced productivity partly through an increase in hours worked. One of the unremarked differences between an agrarian and an industrialized work force is the inevitable enforced idleness which accompanies a primitive agriculture during parts of the year. In Algeria, in the 1950's the peasant worked sixty-five days a year.[81] At about the same time, in a rural town in Sicily, the average farm worker, who probably headed a household, worked about seventy days a year,[82] and landless peasants in rural Mexico worked between 100 and 194 days.[83]

In Russia it was not unusual for the peasant to divide his labor between his own farm and the landlord's holdings.[84] The poverty and low productivity of Russian agriculture associated with Russian agriculture provides some reason to believe the serf also experienced considerable enforced unemployment. Average grain yields for European Russia were less than half the rate for Western Europe.[85] Figures for the first half of the nineteenth century point to a death rate more than one-third above that of slaves in the American South, and approximating that of Caribbean slaves.[86] A report, written in 1888, stated that the average Russian peasant received only one-third of his livelihood from his own land.[87] The rest came from day labor. Moreover, there was a large percentage of the peasantry, perhaps one third, who had no land of their own.[88]

Apparently Russian agriculture was perceived as particularly backward well before the Communist took power. In 1911 the 5.5 bushels an acre harvested in the Russian wheat belt was unfavorably compared with the 20 bushels an acre in Argentina.[89] The authors blamed poverty, ignorance and political oppression. Russia's ability to export wheat despite low productivity was attributed to the ability of an autocratic government to force the peasantry to eat rye instead of wheat.[90]

The Chinese government's policy to allow increased movement from the village to the cities was one of the most positive economic steps that it could have taken.[91] As recently as 1979, China had about 95 million non-agricultural workers, out of a population of 950 million people. The unemployed totaled approximately 20 million.[92] By 1995, about 100 million Chinese were a "floating" population, and rural workers made about one-fourth of the city dweller.[93]

The traditional advice of the blond intellectual; raise rural productivity with free markets misses the point. It assumes that top heavy governmental structures are behind the details of the village life. The village is its own teacher.

The city is not the foe of increased village productivity; it is its fiercest exponent. The city is the indispensable engine for increased village wealth. The city builds the school that breaks down the controls that define the village; define the village because they have worked.

The visible formal statistical reality "unemployment" is not the issue. A society moving from agriculture to industrialization is finally a behavioral matter. Even in a place as sophisticated, educated, and wealthy as 19th century Massachusetts: In good times, about one-third of the work force was unemployed three or four months a year. In harsh times, two-thirds of blue-collar employees would be unemployed.[94]

Sixty-year olds, who were youngsters in Massachusetts as late as the 1940's, can remember dairy farms in large numbers. Similar farms were the source of labor for an expanding industrialized work force, a century and a half earlier. Given the virtually universal history of the human race, there is no alternative to building the skilled work force of tomorrow from an agricultural base. But the specifics of the unemployment and deprivation were significantly different between the blonds and the peasantry.

Consistent features about planting and harvesting in all agricultural societies mandate labor surpluses in certain seasons and shortages at others. Even classic China may have had labor shortages at times, given the reality that direct human effort was the major productive input. But once school and industrialization enter the equation, one sees that the way to more food is not more people and more work.

Two generations after an agricultural Japan considered exporting its excess agricultural labor to the United States, the Chinese government offered to send its excess agricultural labor to Japan, which, by the 1990's, had a labor shortage.[95] The tendency of peasants to increase their numbers inevitably necessitates more land, more labor, or better technology. From the bio-behavioral perspective, peasant agriculture is less a sector of an economy, and more a part of a biological loop. Attempts to abstract out rules to develop the peasant village are likely to miss the deeper behavioral realities. The traditional game involves a dynamic which promises consumption will remain consistently, and continually, perilously close to starvation levels. Given the technology and the age old, successful, birthrate of between 5 and 6 live children, the issue was never, "How to develop China?" The essential task from the peasant's perspective was always to find more land.

Land Ownership

Economic studies on the traditional peasant societies often prominently feature statistics concerning land ownership. They announce that a very small percentage of the population owns a tremendous majority of the nation's land. It is understandable. But the important issues are not about equity, they are about land use.

What is grown? What is not grown? What is the ratio between consumption, and investment back in the land? Which capital investments are made?

The peasant believes that if only he had just one more tract of land, this season, life could change for the better. One assumes that one reason Communist organizers succeeded in societies like Russia and China is that the Communists held a trump card no other party could match: Come victory, we will kill the landlord. With that card, they were able to turn a marginal economic issue into the central issue of the struggle. Who owns the land? became the pivot around which the entire society revolved.

Within the populations that the blonds saw as peasants, there was a considerable diversity on land tenure systems. Japan may always have has less of the peasant look to the blonds then some other Asian states. For several centuries the central government, which was regarded as the owner of all the land, assigned rights to families who were to put it into agricultural use and pay taxes on it. The Japanese appear to have followed the Chinese model in much of their political structure.[96] Later, a pattern of decentralization developed, and the peasant began to resemble the European serf.[97]

China, the classic Asian rice peasantry, apparently had developed an intensive agriculture over four thousand years ago.[98] The country was divided into territories that were administered by chiefs appointed by the central authority. Princes regarded the collective peasantry in their areas as another exploitable resource.[99] While there is debate on the issue, some scholars feel that a looser system, which allowed for some private ownership, was in place thousands of years ago.[100] In certain areas, a large plot, owned by the government, was communally farmed by family groups, that would be permitted to farm their own plots after communal obligation were satisfied. An alternative system simply required the peasant family to pay a proportional tax to the central government, based on the success of the harvest.[101]

In more modern times, the Chinese system recognized extended family, or clan, rights to agricultural holdings. After the death of the parents, the children would donate a portion of their estate to the clan, and would divide the remaining property among themselves, with the eldest sons taking a slightly larger share, and unmarried daughters, less than a full share.[102]

Mao recorded the poverty the peasants shared in 1927. The rich peasants were ten percent of the total; the middle, twenty percent; and the poor, seventy percent. The "middle" peasants were those who were not in immediate danger of starvation, but who had no surplus assets. Some of the poor had some land, but not enough to support themselves, and a substantial fraction of the total peasant population were without any land.[103]

An investigation of a southern Chinese village with a population just under a thousand surviving on five hundred acres, just prior to the revolution, revealed that 80 to 85 percent were classified as poor and lower-middle peasants.[104] The poor owned virtually no land while the lower-middle had some land, but were forced to provide field labor for others, or to lease their land to survive. In the whole village there were only two landlords, and five "rich peasants," families who hired labor, or leased out serious holdings.

Vietnam is another example of traditional peasant agriculture. Villages typically included three hundred to a thousand persons, and, in pre-colonial times, considerable pressure was exerted to keep land ownership within the members of the village. Outsiders had fewer rights than natives to own village land and this disability could continue for several generations.

In Tonkin and Annan, the central area, at least one-fourth of the land was controlled by village authorities and divided among the membership periodically.[105] Sixty percent of the land was controlled by less than seven percent of the families.[106] In parts of Cochinchina, the most southerly district of Vietnam, seventy to eighty percent of the populace owned no land at all prior to the coming of the French.[107] The central government, however, acted to ameliorate the condition of the poorer peasants by requiring village authorities to place communal land at the disposal of the poor.[108]

It is interesting that different areas of Vietnam experienced very different standards of living. The regions that were able to rely on rainfall farming enjoyed the highest levels of consumption, and experienced the least intrusive political structures.

India presents another image of Third World poverty in a series of dirty, isolated, small, agricultural villages. The high density of the population would appear to guarantee a high rate of poverty in a virtually exclusively agricultural economy. In Bihar, one of the poorer Indian states, in the 1960's, there were over 5,000 people for every 1,000 hectares of cultivated land. Barely 20 percent of the families owned almost 80 percent of the farms.[109] At the other end of the scale, over 40 percent of the holdings were for less than half a hectare, about 1.2 acres.[110] In the Punjab, a wealthier region, with a better record of agricultural development, over half of the holdings were for 2 hectares or less.[111]

The Indian village, like the Vietnamese village, discouraged the free alienation of land. Prior to the British invasion, caste forces operated to prevent the sale of land to strangers.[112]

From the other side of the ethnic street, poverty and inferiority are twins. The Germans have always seen the Slavs as very different from them: poorer, inferior, and a threat. A 60 year old remembers the mid-century American determination to keep ahead of the Russians in the nuclear arms race by limiting access to sensitive nuclear technology. He then reads in his 60's that Charlemagne issued an order prohibiting the export of the Frankish sword to Slavic tribes.[113] Twelve hundred years of ethnic military conflict become compressed in an anecdote about technology and secrecy.

The Slavs were the greatest victors in the Twentieth Century: At its end the Russians were able to cook the Germans, but the Germans could not cook the Russians. The Russian nuclear weapon program terminated the greatest confrontation between two different ethnic groups in the history of the planet.

Kolchin's attempt to draw parallels between Russian serfs and African slaves in the American South misses the really critical difference of behavioral controls. One group had been doing the same thing, basically on its own, long enough to get the controls, and the behavior right. The other group was taught in a very brief period to deal with one foreign object, cotton, with another foreign object, the white man's whip.

One sees many of the same patterns with the Slavs that one sees with the Vietnamese and Indian peasant: a communal village arrangement with a fairly rigid hierarchy, and an impressive concentration of power. The numbers can be dramatic.

Kolchin presents some dramatic figures. One nobleman owned 73,500 male serfs in 1763.[114] A general required 38 kennel keepers to look after 673 hunting dogs.[115] However, the larger reality was more modest: Three-quarters of the nobility possessed a hundred serfs, or less.[116]

Serfs, the overwhelming majority of the Russian population, had no legal right to own land directly, but they did hold traditional communal "rights."[117] The right and the "knowledge" to essentially run their own village is a critical behavioral demarcation between the peasant and the American slave.[118]

Blond intellectuals probably always exaggerated the degree of control exercised by the central authority in peasant societies. The task of subduing and cultivating the land is central in the development of any peasantry. In Russia, the family that brought virgin land into cultivation was entitled to enjoy the harvests for a certain number of years. Their rights continued as long as they farmed the property until the village authorities determined that they had received a fair return on their investment.[119] While the system is most closely identified with the Russians, it may have been a common pattern among all the Slavonic populations, except for those few tribes that had been heavily influenced by Western influences.[120] The reasons given for the low productivity of Russian agriculture stayed consistent for centuries: a very long winter,[121] and a politic that did not promote economic rationality.[122]

The blonds seem to have viewed the Russians in a very characteristic way for a long, long time. One sees that the word "slave" and "Slav" have the same root in German. The blonds have been monitoring the Slavs for a long, long, time from a very specific perch.

Aesthetics were implicated, but so was behavior. The German disdain is understandable. In the sixteen hundreds, a century or so before the development of the first industrial cities, a blond traveler found the Russians very limited occupationally, and socially.[123] In 1888 over 80 percent of the Russian work force was still engaged in agriculture; virtually unchanged since the 17th century.[124] The Emancipation Act of 1861 that abolished the legal status of the serfs did not terminate distinctive systems of land tenure. Justification was argued in terms of communality, not productivity. The behavior within the village: authoritarian, familistic, with very different gender roles remained constant. Industrialization underlined and exaggerated the differences between the blonds and the Slavs; differences the blond intellectual saw clearly. Those differences preceded industrialization and Communism.

The Mediterranean peasant had much more in common with the Slav peasant, than with the blonds. Peasants in central Italy often owned some land, but also farmed large estates.[125] In southern Italy the more common arrangement was characterized by family ownership of small-scattered holdings, whose members also provided labor for large landlords. In parts of the southern Italy, the relative weight of the village and the large private estate was similar to the Russian experience. In Russia the village was part of, and belonged to the estate. In parts of Sicily the village was smaller and weaker than the large estate that surrounded it.

There have been many attempts to track southern Italian social behaviors to the economic structures which had evolved over centuries. But while the low level of social participation, familism, and limited social morality is dramatically visible in the blond part of the continent, these characteristics are very similar to what prevails in traditional peasant societies everywhere.

This is not news to intellectuals; not to the blond intellectuals, or to the non-blond intellectuals. One Latin American writer puts it simply; the Anglo-Saxon farmer always existed in a very different economic category, and he was the seed for the evolution of a very different political structure.[126] A Venezuelan, who traveled to the United States in the 18th century, remarked on the existence of contiguous, individually owned farms.[127]

Present day agriculture in South America presents a case study of how fast agricultural can improve once the village gets small and the slum gets big. In 1875 Argentina did not produce agricultural products for export. By 1887 it exported over 8 million bushels of wheat and over 14 million bushels of corn.[128] Brazil, at the end of the 19th century had a largely illiterate work force engaged in a mono-agriculture, coffee, manned by illiterate peasants. As late as 1940, coffee still accounted for three fourths of all Brazilian exports.[129] By the 1980's

Brazil was one of the four or five biggest exporters of agricultural products in the world.

The European and Japanese emigrant who went to Argentina or Brazil had much more favorable natural conditions than he faced in Europe, or Japan. The Argentines who developed the beef industry faced a very different ratio of animals to land than they faced in the Mediterranean basin. In the early decades of the 20th century, it was estimated that 25,000 acres of pastureland could be maintained by 10 to 12 men. Put the land into cultivation and 1500 acres would require forty to fifty persons to develop and maintain it.[130]

Some estates were very large indeed. Around the beginning of the 20th century, Argentina had about a hundred estates of more than 120,000 acres; roughly 1400 were in excess of 24,000 acres. A European visitor found the land tenure system very different from the farms of North America; where holdings averaged less than 100 acres, and the average of all agricultural properties was about 140 acres.[131] While there were some private and public efforts to allow the peasantry to buy their own farms, the more common pattern featured tenant farmers paying a fixed rent, or a portion of the yearly profit.[132] The size of the holdings, and the distance between the tenant and the landlord suggests classic Russia, or the Mediterranean, or even Asia. It was a very different agriculture than what prevailed in North America.

Argentina in the 19th century gave the impression of extreme poverty to foreign Europeans and North Americans. In 1888 wages for a sugar factory worker were $18.50 per month.[133] Practically none of the workers could read, and there were no public educational facilities.[134] In parts of the country virtually all agricultural work was done by laborers, who had no chance to own their own land.[135] Over a quarter of the houses in Buenos Aires Province, and over 70 percent in the province of Cordoba, were 1-story adobe houses with thatched roofs.[136]

However, once the processes of industrialization took hold, the peasant had the opportunity to become a farmer, via the slum. In the 1940's the size of the average farm in Brazil, 198 acres, was not too dissimilar from the United States, 158 acres. This suggests modernization, but the breakup of enormous family held agricultural holdings does not necessarily lead to the blond social structure. And an agriculture characterized by very large holdings does not require a authoritarian political structure. Blond democratic Australia averaged 665 acres per farm. [137]

Modernization everywhere has meant more food produced by fewer people. Inevitably the peasantry becomes expendable and redundant. Most of the time, John Henry loses.

As the city grows big, and industrialization destroys the village, market forces squeeze both ends of the traditional order: The five-acre citrus grower and the dilettante land baron are forced out. But, more critically, the forms and effect of agriculture as an economic activity just become less important.

The character and size of land holdings cease to be anything but an interesting anecdote, as two different social realities become very, very big: the slum and the school. Operationally they destroy the millennia old home of the peasant, the village.

The Young Peasant

The steel chain that linked production and consumption in the village allowed for only a brief balance at a given population level, it promised danger sooner or later. Critics of child labor in factories miss the main message. Insofar as the child was drawn from the peasantry the child was doing what the child had always done; had done what everyone assumed they had to do: Work.

The morality of child labor is irrelevant. Given a tight enough squeeze, the societies that engage in it will survive; the rest are only of academic interest. Whatever the merits of Freudian psychology, behaviorism, sociobiology, or Christianity, it is certain that the society that needs child labor will develop the morality for it. One is not surprised to read an analysis of French peasant folklore that cites instances of condemnation of children who will not work, but who demand the right to eat.[138]

The peasantry faces its economic challenges that terrible year, with the strength of its children. When there is work to be done, the nature of peasant agriculture is that everyone available must work. If parts of the year are slow, other parts of the year require a very intense, continuous, focused effort. One hundred years ago, small children in Russia were expected to work when work was available.[139] In Sicily, children as young as 5 would help with harvests.[140] Ten and twelve year olds worked a full day in stone quarries to help their families survive.[141] In India, although schools recently became free, there were rural villages where children would not attend because they could not afford food and proper clothing and were required to work.[142] In China 14 year olds were recognized as full time members of agricultural work teams.[143]

The imperative to work when it had to be done extended to pregnant women. In Russia it was not unusual for prospective mothers to work so long that they had miscarriages.[144] The same experience was reported in rural China.[145] In southern Italy, pregnant women would collect grain right up to the time of delivery.[146]

There is an interesting split among the blonds concerning the peasant's attitude toward work. Generally, the image in the blond world is lassitude: Mexican Joe, the Slav and the Latin peasant are typically presented at siesta time. That is one of their redeeming bits of charm. The picture of a man asleep is a convenient and understandable accounting of the poverty. The other image is at the completely opposite pole: the peasant works so hard for such a small gain that it borders on the irrational.[147]

What the peasant takes for granted in child labor becomes a scandal in the blond world. Marx' attacks on child labor were effective: Children working 12 hours a day or more attract sympathy.

The young peasant's early companion in his labor is infection. It is clear that the close relationship between parasite and child is consistent across ethnic boundaries in every form of primitive agriculture. From the Mediterranean to China, young peasants live in close proximity to animals, and until recently, without adequate footwear or medical care.[148] In the early years of the twentieth century, three quarters of the peasants in Costa Rica were afflicted with parasites.[149] In parts of Vietnam, hookworm incidence was 50 to 55 percent; liver flukes were common.[150] In the Italian south, as recently as the 1950's, there were regions where 90 percent of the agricultural labor force may have been infected with intestinal parasites, and over one tenth of the children were affected by polyparasitism, with some affected by as many as six parasites.[151]

Tropical lands were some of the worst areas for unskilled agricultural labor. The United Fruit Company reported that malaria was the source of 90 percent of the sickness in its camps, and that every laborer who worked on the tropical coast in Central or South America, would eventually contact the disease.[152]

Even in the United States, as recently as the early 20th century, parasites were a serious problem in areas that practiced traditional agriculture. A survey of Southern rural counties revealed that hookworm infected almost 40 percent of poor white children.[153] There was some concern that publicizing the problem would cause Northerners to use it as an occasion of humor.

The young peasant is ignorant. The most dramatic difference between the blond and the peasant mentalities concerns education. One sees the blonds educating their young at a very, very early stage, hundreds of years ago; setting the table for the feast that would follow.

The first modern industrial city was Manchester, England, and 1780 is probably as good a year as any to begin the industrialization clock.[154] "Literacy" is too plastic, and too dependent upon local definition, to serve as the term that separates the behavioral past from the behavioral present. At certain places and times, anyone who could write his or her name was considered literate.[155] Still, given that caveat, it is interesting to compare published observations on what the educational situation was among the blonds, compared to the peasantry prior to 1780.

David Hackett Fischer's celebrated study of the early, and continuing, influence of certain specific British groups in the formation and present day functioning of America is a riveting account of the durability and constancy of group behavior.[156] It might be seen as the impressive visible part of a behavioral realty that preceded the formation of not merely of the United States, but even Britain.

Fischer's history highlights differences among four British populations that greatly affected America. It is the persistence of these differences that strike the reader with the force of a hammer, and mark the book as a reference for sociobiology.

What is really interesting on the issue of education, is how different the four were (and the Germans?) collectively, from the peasant populations that surrounded them. New England, from the beginning, had a deserved reputation as a place of learning. The first free public school system in the country was established in Massachusetts. Parents were legally responsible for teaching their children in 1642. By 1647, only about a generation from the first landing at Plymouth, settlements of at least 50 families were required to support a teacher, a ratio not much changed in the next 350 years.[157] Two-thirds of adult men in the 1600's were able to sign their own name, compared to about one-third in England itself prior to about 1640, roughly a century before industrialization.[158] In 1660 over one-third of the women were able to sign their own wills in the Massachusetts Bay Colony; the figure rose to 50 percent by 1760.[159]

Anyone who has put a fair amount of time researching real estate title in southern New Hampshire has likely confronted the problem of reverters on schoolhouse lots. That is, private citizens would convey land to a school district as long as the property was used for educational purposes; if the use changed title to the property would revert to the grantor or his heirs. Some of these districts predate 1800. In one northern Massachusetts town, school classes were held in private homes until the first schoolhouse was built in 1718. Approximately 80 years later, there were 12 district schools in that town.[160]

Virginia, settled primarily by people from the south and west of England were somewhat less literate than New Englanders; just as their forbears were somewhat less literate than the populations from the east of England, the ancestral home of the Puritans. In the seventeenth century about half of the male property owners in Virginia could write, the figure was 40 percent for tenants and laborers.[161] The pattern of literacy in Virginia was similar to that group's area of origin in England.

A third founding group, the Quakers from the North Midlands of England and Wales, the site of the world's first industrial center, settled in the Delaware Valley. Literacy rates were less than for the Puritans, but higher than for Virginia. In the early 1700's about half of the adults were able to sign their own names.[162] In the 1830's, a few years after the establishment of the factory system, about one-third of the working children were able to read and write.[163]

The fourth and final of Fischer's founding populations came from the border country of North Britain. They were largely from Scotland, Ireland, and northern England and were most numerous and influential in North and South Carolina, Georgia, Kentucky, Tennessee, and parts of Virginia, Maryland and Pennsylvania.[164] Literacy rates varied in the back country, more so than in the other areas of British North America.[165] This may reflect a group that was somewhat more literate than the populations in the north of England at the time. A study, cited by Fischer, estimated that 36 percent of the laborers there were literate in the period 1700 to 1770.[166]

The differences among the four groups should not obscure how educated they were for their time. When about a third of the American backwoodsmen were unable to read or write comparable figures for Italy or Spain were 70 to 80 percent.[167]

A study concentrating on New Hampshire in the 1600's supports Fischer's conclusions. One estimate, based on research of probate records, petitions, and other documents found that the literacy rate was about 75 percent.[168] Now, keeping in mind the caution that precise measurements are not possible; it is worthwhile to compare the level of literacy among the blonds at, or before, the advent of industrialization two to three hundred years ago, with literacy among the peasantry in the twentieth century. Before 1949, over 80 percent of Chinese adults were illiterate.[169] Estimates of literacy rates during various periods in the 20th century for India, Pakistan and Turkey, were 36, 25, and 55 percent, respectively.[170]

In 1950 less than half of India's children were in school. According to one report in 1990, literacy in India, nationwide, was about 52 percent. One sees how different the classic, isolated peasant village is from the blond experience, when one sees that in some Indian villages, well after automobiles, jet travel, and television were fixtures in the West, literacy rates were often below 40 percent, and rates for women did not exceed 10 percent.[171]

In 1954 in parts of Islamic Algeria, only one boy in five was attending school, and only one in sixteen among the girls.[172] Approximately 25 percent of the Muslim population was literate in Arabic.[173] In Moslem Turkey in the late 1960's the rural literacy rate of married women aged 20–44 was 15 percent, in rural Morocco it was only about one percent.[174] Out of a village of almost 1,000 in southern China about the same time, about 5 had been to high school.[175]

In Japan, the first Asian country to reach a rough parity with the blonds, only about 45 percent of the men, and 15 percent of the women, were literate in the middle of the 19th century.[176] In 1854 in one small Latin American town only one or two people were literate.[177] In parts of urban Brazil as late as 1920, about 44 percent of the foreign born Europeans were literate and only 27 percent of the native born.[178] In certain areas of neighboring Argentina in 1905, only one child in three was able to read or write.[179] In one survey of the Santa Fe colonies about 30 years earlier, only about one-third of the school age children were in school.[180]

In Mediterranean Europe, the educational situation was somewhat better, but still very different from the blonds. In Palermo, as recently as 1950, among one sample of 78 children, 33 were in school and 45 were not. In only two families of the older generation from the sample, were both parents literate.[181] One rural agricultural village in Sicily was so poor that children were required to bring their own chairs for classes.[182] It was estimated that the literacy rate in Portugal, as late as 1977, was only about 77 percent.[183]

Eastern Europe and Russia shared the very low levels of literacy common among the peasantry, and demonstrated the dramatic gulf between northwestern Europe, and every place else. In portions of Poland in the late 1920's, 60 percent of the farming population was illiterate.[184] One reads the history of Communists with skepticism, but perhaps one-third of factory workers were illiterate prior to the Revolution.[185] In 1868 of 100 military recruits from the Russian peasantry, only 8 could read or write. By 1882, the figure had improved to 20 percent.[186]

The Controls up Close

Learning theory provides the lens. The generalization Kolchin applies to Russia's serfs applies across the sweep of the classic peasantry: Rural life meant village life. Inside the village, the family is a burden no one will escape. The margins are thin enough, particularly in that dramatic year, to enforce a kind of solidarity.

The first villages must have been largely familial creations. The ancient political pattern in China was for the central authority to recognize families as organizing entities.[187] Until modern times, the Chinese were apathetic toward the needs and demands of the central state, and not noted for their patriotism.[188] In more than one small village, the claim was made that virtually all the members were somehow related to a founding family.[189] The tension between familial and village loyalties, and the very real biological need for non-consanguineous marriages is a constant theme of peasant history.[190]

The peasant village is a place where scarcity and morality intersect, a place of controls. Isolation is a basic characteristic of village civilization. The Chinese experience is typical: Peasants spend their entire working life in one small village.[191] What follows from that is vital to a sociobiological interpretation of the peasantry, and mostly at odds with traditional political high history.

In 1982 China still had villages which were a half days walk from the nearest road, and where women did not attend school. The sheer distance between the peasant and the modern world can best be measured through anecdote. In one village the central government had introduced a mechanical hand controlled agricultural tractor. The inhabitants were very pleased with its work until it stopped running, whereupon they began beating it with sticks.[192]

During the extensive television coverage of the Tiananmen Square demonstration I heard one academic recite which occupational groups were represented. After she completed the list she noted that the peasants were not represented and expressed the hope that they would soon show up. Well, they did. At the very end.

In a country where, prior to the 20th century, over 90 percent of the population was engaged in the behavioral monotone of a peasant agriculture, it would have been absurd not to expect that the peasants interpretation of events would be very different from that of the reporter. From the perspective of biobehaviorism, the fit between the man, the controls, and the environment created the Chinese polity. It is telling that at least one reporter who actually visited a peasant village came away with the impression that the village approved of the crackdown.[193] There are good reasons why the political split between the peasant and the intellectual looks like the difference between the blond and the peasant generally.

India as recently as 1961 had one-half of its population in villages of less than 1000, and 80% in villages of less than 5000.[194] At the time of the Serfs Emancipation, Russia had only about 1000 miles of railroad track.[195] This isolation fits with the maxim that the Russian peasantry adopted serfdom through custom, rather than force.[196] It is also another window into the stated Communist goal to change not simply production equations, but very fundamental, long established living habits of the peasantry, within the rural village.[197] Yet as isolated as the villages were, within an endless steppe, an observer remarked on the remarkable behavioral uniformity of the Russian peasantry.[198]

A distinctly sociobiological argument could be crafted around the functions of the village. The reproduction requirement would obviously put some limits on how isolated the villages could be. Beyond the obvious physical requirements, there are issues of specific agricultural practices that may appear once someone closely mines the data on the ground.

When one considers how and where the peasant has put his gardens, one sees that while the environment shapes the man, the reverse is also true in very dramatic ways. The sheer effort is remarkable. Chinese peasants may walk three hours before they can start to work;[199] Mediterranean peasants walk ten miles to look for greens.[200] As late as the 1950's and 60's, peasant women in Southern Italy, walked several hours to and from fields carrying a lunch bag, a hoe, and a water container: the peasant reality around most of the globe for millennia.[201]

The village as an extended family entity, its distance and isolation from the central authority and from other villages, and the nature of a very intensive, localized agriculture, all operated to reinforce the already dominant authority of the family. The threshold for a sociobiological account, however, is higher than it is for a historical analysis. Sociobiology's task is to establish a space where it's main competitor, mentalism, is uneasy.

No Left-Handed Women

Biobehavioristic analysis is a tool for pulling the ghost out of the machine. Ethnic differences are real, and they are important. But just as there are anecdotes that Freudians, or ethnologists, or Marxists relish, so there are anecdotes that biobehaviorists relish. Probably no item in the entire traditional punch list separating the blonds and the peasantry appears as often, or as predictably, as the very different status of women. Compared to the blonds, the peasant women seem to occupy a smaller, restricted, "closed" area of life experiences.

It is interesting to see how often the blond observer spots the authoritarian father as the characteristic mark of the peasant. The Chinese father is labeled a "supreme autocrat", both before and after the Revolution.[202] Ancient records suggest that some Chinese believed a disrespectful son was the greatest civil sin.[203] The authority of the Russian father has been described as almost absolute.[204] The differences between the Mediterranean family, whether Catholic or Muslim, and the blond family, are visible to everyone.

Now, I think that the peasant experience makes an authoritarian family structure rational, although no one engaged in the behavior sees the rationality. There is no way of knowing, before really big innovative behavioral changes take place, whether the behavior will change in a given direction. Before the peasant women moved to the slum, she had 5 to 7 children for a thousand years. The outside observer could have very well assumed that there were genetic influences in this behavior. It is only after the dramatic change that one begins to look for environmental constraints.

While ethnicity undeniably plays a role, one could hold ethnicity constant and pick up a replicable pattern of differences between the peasantry and the slum dweller. It is the place where one world ends and another begins. Urban populations were always different from the peasant populations that surrounded them.

The authoritarian family structure and the restricted area of women are surely related throughout the peasant universe. Do men enforce it, or do women? All men have mothers.

The necessity of marriage was a constant in the peasantry. Rural life meant village life, and within the village, to be was to be part of a family unit. The real enemy of a free and independent woman is a certain kind of familism, which may be enforced by women, as much as by men.

The peasant boy faces a mandate, chiseled in stone: Get married, have children. There is no toleration for eccentricities on the matter. An Italian interviewee in Canada in the early 20th century put the matter in perspective:

He had never heard of a man who did not marry in the old country.[205] In Russia, marriage for the serfs was described as nearly universal.[206]

Economic realities in rural China mandated marriage as a familial security system. It was understood that the young married couple would provide support for the aged. Consequently there was a real need for the young to start their family before the old became too much of a burden. One observer noted that the poorest families in the village appeared to be those who were relatively old before they started their families. As a result a middle-aged father was required to provide both for his own small children and his now aged parents.[207]

The nature of the Japanese village is revealed when one learns that there is no word for privacy in the Japanese language.[208] One reads these sorts of observations often enough, but an educated Westerner does not have any way to grasp the magnitude of the distance between his life and the peasant's life. It would be desirable to develop some sort of "objective" data, removed from ethnic, or ideological influence, to establish some quantitative demarcation line between the industrial worker and the peasant.

The control of women in the hydraulic world is objectively revealed by the absence of left-handed women. Not enough has been made of the differences in handedness between the peasantry, and their neighbors. Apparently handedness is a trait which is biological in origin, but one that can be overridden by an intense application of effort at an early enough age.

Among hunting populations there are no significant differences in handedness between men (12.5 percent) and women (10.3 percent). At the other end of the scale, a study which included 330 females, by combining the samples from a number of peasant groups, including African peasants, Hong Kong Chinese from Canton, and some others; found no left-handed women. [209]

Probably a definitive account of how people learned and disseminated agriculture will be out of reach for many generations. But it is interesting that an analysis of European cave drawings made 8000 years ago, well before the widespread adoption of agriculture, suggests that left-handedness was more prevalent then, than it is in Europe today.[210]

Three points: It is very difficult to explain why the peasantry makes an effort to extinguish left-handedness. Second, the parents must be the ones who pursue the orthodoxy. Third, one wonders if it would be possible to scale the behavior within the peasant world. Does the preference for the right increase as other traditional behavioral markers of the peasant life increase? Can the preference be related to the availability of water?

While the difference in handedness may represent an actual evolutionary change, it may also suggest a tightening of controls that developed with a settled agriculture, a tightening that is perfectly compatible with behaviorism. Moreover, the fact that the same move away from left-handedness follows the hydraulic peasantry today suggests an adaptive advantage that could have been mediated through behaviors the peasantry was not consciously applying.

Control of women probably assured that the village was not faced with large numbers of fatherless children during the famine year. The controls are also consistent with the male's need to know that the child he supports is his. The expectation of the wedding night bloody bed sheet is a common theme in Orthodox Russia,[211] in the Islamic world,[212] and the Catholic Mediterranean.

Extinguishing left-handedness fits with the bloody bed sheet. But it also has a more general, simple, and direct function.

The penalties delivered to females for violations of sexual norms within the peasant societies are undeniably horrific. One thinks of the destruction of the home of the pregnant woman in Maxine Hong Kingston[213] or the familial revenge in Southern Italy,[214] or the punishment handed out in Muslim societies for a range of infractions by females.

Urbanized young people in China are reported as being "stunned" by the division between the sexes in the rural villages. Girls reaching puberty in rural China are educated about the realities of life by certain older peasant women.[215] The division, like the controls may be a general devaluation, it is difficult to speak of infanticide of baby girls in any other way, but the consistencies are so striking, they invite a second look.[216] The connection between bound feet, infanticide, and no left-handed women, all of which operate at a very low social level, may ultimately help to preserve a certain balance between the village and its environment.

Do women, mothers-in-law, establish and perpetuate the orthodoxy? My guess is that older women are the main carriers of the control of women orthodoxy. Arguments that would connect it to religious traditions do not seem to me to be particularly convincing. The "repression," exists within a sea of illiterates. The scaling of the repression does not seem to follow the roads where religion and literacy meet. In Italy, the repression of women, whether by men or by women, increases as poverty, illiteracy, a kind of anticlericalism, and a lack of regard for both religious and secular authority increases.[217]

Familism is the common thread that keeps outside influence, democratic or authoritarian, at bay. It is when one considers family structure that one sees how different the blonds are from their neighbors.

Mood, Mind and Morality

When one regards the blonds, on either side of the Channel, certain consistent patterns of informality, trust, social awareness, and "mood" can not be missed. The Germans and the British look too much alike, believe too much alike, enjoy a lot of things in the same ways, dislike a lot of things in the same ways, and share a basic attractive optimism. The enormity of World War One and Two can be measured by the overwhelming distance that they created between blue-eyed Englishmen and Americans, on the one hand, and blue-eyed Germans on the other.

The general cheeriness, self-sufficiency, intelligence, great physical appearance, and high public morality comprise a package. American blond academicians, with those traits forming a kind of norm, look around the globe, particularly in Asia, and see something very different: apathy, crummy looks, dishonesty, backwardness, a familistic amorality, and a kind of resigned hopelessness.[218]

The emotional differences between the blonds and the peasants are as real as the concrete physical ones. Some peasants apparently express depression through less abstract terms, and more direct recitations of physical ailments.[219]

More than nature/nurture is involved. Do "economic" activities, which is to say in peasant societies, living activities, reward moods differentially than tribal, or industrial, or fighting societies.

One observer accounting for the difference in response to depression, labels the Chinese response "sociocentric", and contrasts it with the American "egocentric" norm. The Chinese approach of somatization of the pain does not threaten the kind of rupture with the group, which the American response of "felt alienation" might provoke. Further, a physical illness is a perfectly acceptable occasion to appeal to the group for help. Depression expressed as body upset may help establish social glue that peasant societies need more than fighting societies. One wonders. How do Chinese in the United States handle depression? Does education make a difference?

Probably there is no one general answer as to why the blond seems to be a different emotional package than the peasantry, generally. Substantial arguments could be crafted around any of the usual candidates. But it would be a mistake to assume that the less buoyant, more cynical familistic peasant package is a mistake.

A prohibition against something as spontaneous and natural as left-handedness suggests a certain density in human relations. It is impossible to see the characteristic being extinguished outside the confines of the family. Here one sees the advantages of a sociobiological approach over traditional "cultural" explanations. "How" questions begin to push out "why" questions. The analyst begins to lose interest in the grand account.

Perhaps it is true that the peasant experiences depression in a less individualistic and less solitary mode; one might expand the generalization to other aspects of life. Part of it may be the setting, but part of it may be the people. The data that has been developed around depression is useful because it helps to make real styles and directions that would otherwise be anecdotes. The shift in perspective that is required for behaviorism to play a role, accompanies a realization that the expression of the mood may be either biological or environmental, just as the mood itself may be.

In determining the fit between nature and nurture, biobehaviorism would break down the distinction between "core" and "residue." It is tempting here to resort to "culture" as a kind of organizing force creating pathways, along which people in specific ethnic groups do specific things.[220] There may be an organizing track to explain the consistency, but calling it cultural rather than either biological or environmental is not likely to be much help.

The degree of westernization a society has experienced may be more predictive of individualistic types of expressions for guilt, hopelessness, self-accusation, and suicide; and less of ideas of persecution, anxiety, and somatic upset.[221] However, what if, after industrialization, there are still vital differences in the characteristic way different populations see the world? The Japanese may be more like the English after industrialization than before, but one expects that at very deep emotional levels they would be more familiar to a 14th century Japanese than a 20th century Englishman.

Skinner's comment that men are not born with a readiness to heed warnings may just be wrong.[222] Populations may differ on this scale. Lumsden and Wilson develop a theory of interdependence among organizational traits, which has some similarities with traditional top-down analyses of social controls. As they see it, the increasing size of human societies mandates the development of new human traits to maintain orderly conduct.[223]

For example, the political hierarchy in the Plains Indians changed according to the task and behavior of the participants. In the summer months ten or more bands would coalesce to exploit the buffalo, and the loose internal controls which operated most of the year gave way to a hierarchy composed of a council which elected a premier chief, and organizations with very specialized functions.

It is tempting to see the summer months as the critical months. But perhaps the greater truth is that the really effective way for hunters to organize is small bands with loose controls: democrats.

Wilson offers a glimpse of his thinking on the source of an authoritarian politic. He claims the evolution of "indoctrinability" is essentially biological. Human beings seek indoctrination.[224]

Wilson discusses the advantages of indoctrination to both the individual and the group. The member who conforms enjoys the benefits of membership. The conformist may risk his life for the whole, because the group benefits from the conformist genetic package selected at the level of group behavior. What I found most arresting about the argument is that his imagery features a backdrop of violent struggle.

But what one notices about the societies which would readily be identified as conformist, or authoritarian, is that the populations just do not look like good fighters; certainly not compared to the blonds. And, while it can not be quantified, it is telling that, for centuries if not millennia, the blond story about what is out there has not featured a peasant as fighter with a tribal loyalty. Their

reports from the Mediterranean basin to the Asian mainland have featured bad
fighters exhibiting a more or less corrupting familism. A weakness that proved
fatal time and time again when they were forced into combat with the blonds.
The fact that the blonds took over three continents in fifteen hundred years has
to count for something. A population that features a combination of an intense
racial identity and a limitless and democratic idealism is very difficult to turn
around.

Work does play a role in determining the nature of the society. I had discussions with a former German soldier who was captured, transported to the
United States, and imprisoned in work camps in the American Southwest. The
German prisoners were supposed to weed and maintain agricultural crops, to,
in effect, simply join with Mexican workers in doing work that had to be done,
and which many many Mexicans do every day, all day, for an entire working
life.

The Germans simply refused. The work was too tedious, too hot, too demeaning. This was not the work the blonds do. Day after day stooped over, in
a continuing dull ache, was too different. The Germans filled their sacks with
rocks, and sat down waiting to see what the American guards, men who looked
like them, would do.

Well, as things turned out, blood was thicker than water. The guards understood. They did not force the Germans to do what the Mexicans did.

However, if one transports the Germans prisoners to a Slavic farm, a Russian
farm, it turns out different. For one thing, the people playing the role of
Mexicans were Slavs. The next step would have been the awareness by the
Slav guards that the Germans did not just mean the peasant was demeaned;
the Germans also meant that the guards were demeaned. The Germans are
shot. Ethnicity makes a difference.

Thomas Sowell cites various authorities to demonstrate the proposition that
Southern whites worked less hard, less constant than others. They felt long
hard detailed agricultural work was beneath them. It was particularly galling
if the work was at the direction of another.[225] Virginians were described as
terrific fighters, who scorned boring, hard, demeaning agricultural work.[226] In
his history of the peoples from the British borderlands, Fischer posits a severe
dichotomy: The work ethic in an agricultural society is weak where the warrior
ethic is strong.[227]

The most dramatic demonstration of the point must be in Asia. Any European
flying into Asia must have a sense of wonder about those miles of terraced
landscapes. The boring detailed strain of it, generation after generation. The
blonds scoff at, or hate, or attack the social structure that produced that terrace,
but it made possible a density that looks like an incredible biological success.

How different would the landscape of Asia looked had the blonds been there?
Surely, either the landscape would have changed the blonds, or the blonds
would have changed the landscape. Behaviorism favors the observation that a

somewhat dampened mood, a certain familial piety, and a very different woman fit the terraced landscape.

The mood of the peasant, his generally smaller size, no left-handed women, and familistic control generally, contribute direction to a polity which, inevitably, would serve biological ends. Behaviorism brings plasticity to a sociobiological account of peasant agriculture; an account which otherwise would be hard wired, or excessively mentalistic.

Another fairly consistent highlight of the blond report on the peasantry has to do with that social glue "trust." Trust is the muscle of the beating heart of a great fighting force. It is unlikely to develop where populations intersect, where there are large and intense differences in religion, ethnicity, and genetics.

Effective armies are armies that fight on their own, armies that look alike, and can handle most challenges informally and democratically. The lighter controls of the blond world have traveled hand in hand with the blond ability to make that space, their space. The trust the blonds feel for each other was the other side of the coin of a consistent and powerful distrust and dislike of the racial outsider.

The blonds' boisterousness, their ability to drink in groups, to work in democratic structures, to fight well, all outside familial ties, point to a confidence in themselves and each other. Loss of control is "high jinks", rather than a threat.

The peasantry is very different. Ancient China required everyone to keep a tight control on alcohol; drinking spirits in groups was discouraged.[228] The Mediterranean, Catholic and Islamic, condemns public drunkenness.

There are exceptions. The Russian peasant, who is also the peasant who is a great fighter, has had a reputation as a drinker of epic proportions. Three hundred and fifty years ago a secretary to a German ambassador reported that drunkenness was the common vice, claiming both sexes, all classes and professions, ecclesiastic and secular.[229] Perhaps it is no accident that the Slav looks most like the blonds, and has the physique of a fighter. One wonders how often Russian women were left-handed.

The greater intensity of familial controls in the peasantry travels with a much higher level of political corruption. Northern New England with its town meeting, its low level of crime, its tradition of voluntarism and public involvement, really is different from most of the planet.

Different on the corruption issue; different on the racism issue. Is there a kind of trade-off there? Is there a general theme that people in very large numbers have to make that trade off? Or is it a matter of specifics in an intensely ethnic world? Could the blonds be different? Could the Portuguese or Chinese, or Indians be different?

One of the serious differences between the blonds and that mixed stew of peasantry is the regard the blonds have for themselves, and their society. The British Empire was as big as it was partly because the Chinese, the Indians, the Arabs, the Africans etc. could not duplicate that impressive social morality. It was not just a matter of economic advantage. From Italy to East Asia, there are a number of populations that in the 20th century have gone from less than a third to a rough parity of the per capita wealth of England, without matching that spectacular public commitment and honesty of Englishmen.

Familism is the enemy of the great package: high public morality and racism. Democracy flourishes where racial identity is strong.

Traditional peasant populations may have created a more effective tax system for themselves than the more honest and "efficient" systems of the blonds. British imperialist administrators applied an honest, rigid and efficient tax system that did not allow for traditional factors of corruption, play or tolerance. Those procedures wrought havoc to large sectors of the Indian peasantry.[230] The manner and thoroughness of the collection process for head taxes in Burma put a greater strain on the peasant than traditional systems that allowed for some maneuverability in really bad times.[231] A strong central state, even though not democratic, could be an ally of the poor peasant in his struggle with the local landlord.[232]

The differences between the blonds and the peasantry are alive and well today, and are measurable. There is no doubt that England, Germany, The United States, Australia, Austria and New Zealand have higher rates of tax collection than Egypt, China, Italy, Korea, Russia and Argentina. Moreover, there is a consensus that just much more of the national economies in France and Italy is "off the books" than in the U.S.[233] In Italy in 1981, factory workers, whose taxes are withheld by payroll deductions, declared higher earnings than self-employed businessmen.[234] A political party was formed in Japan on the single issue of income tax fairness. In 1984 it was estimated that Japanese businessmen only reported about 60 percent of their actual income.[235] Over 90 percent of the Buddhist Temples gave their priests off-the-book money in addition to their salary. An American executive was reported as being surprised over a written request by his landlady that he participate in a scheme to underreport her income to the government.

Karol van Wolferen's report about Japanese social mores is as interesting for what it says about the author and the blond assumptions generally, as its insights about the Japanese. The blond intellectual insists that the peasant societies become like England in every particular except the racism. Evidence that the Japanese were much less changed by World War II and the Occupation than Americans once thought, should not be a surprise.[236]

In a way Japan presents an interesting problem to main stream blond thinking on modernization. Van Wolferen sees a number of indelibly ethnic characteristic traits which should be obstacles to development: an insufficient commitment to abstract organizational goals, and indifference among the people to the clear fact that the elite is manipulating the system for their personal gain.[237] What Van Wolferen and the blond critics generally would like to see as abstract and transcendent remains intensely social, familistic and vaguely sordid.

A national magazine cover story on Japan in the early 1990's featured a shadowy feature accepting cash under the heading, Hidden Japan.[238] The article reviews a number of business practices and economic policies that the authors clearly disapprove of: securities companies making paybacks to customers, payoffs to gangsters, and governmental payola. Bribes to political parties from government contractors, rampant collusion and illegal favoritism are part of the accepted methodologies.

Why do the authors think that it is so different from New Hampshire and Vermont? They find the difference in a system that rewards personal relationships, rather than efficiency enforced through adherence to abstract rules. At the personal level, however, the Japanese display a real sensitivity and honesty to foreigners. The lost-and-found center of Tokyo's Metropolitan Police Department collected over a million items in 1990, about three-fourths of which were returned to their owners.[239]

Van Wolferen endorses the common criticism that Japan does not play the international role which one would expect, given Japan's wealth. It is an argument that has become familiar in the American press. He and the American elite never address the alternative story; that it is the blonds who are so different, not only from the Japanese but everyone else on the issue whether the world needs a secular worldwide messiah.

Given their common peasant past one imagines that a socialist China would bear some resemblance to a capitalistic Japan. A 1981 newspaper article reported that clerks in China often withheld the best produce unless customers paid bribes.[240] Another report claimed that production improved after the breakup of the communes, but corruption became worse.[241] The payoff for the family which has a member appointed to a high post in the Communist party is extraordinary.

One sees the same pattern in Latin America. A Peruvian think tank demonstrated that a person establishing a small clothing enterprise would have to pay 8 unavoidable bribes and work over 40 hours to complete the registration process. An equivalent process in Florida can be completed in a few hours.[242] An estimated 60% of the Peruvian economy is "informal;" the company can ignore labor laws not to mention taxes. Similarly a researcher in Argentina concluded that 3 out of 5 workers produced goods and services for the unregistered economy.[243] It fits with the observation that of an estimated three million people who should have paid taxes, only about 130,000 actually did.[244]

One is accustomed to hear that post Communist Eastern European societies share two characteristics which have exasperated the blonds for a long time: sensitivity to ethnic differences, and a low public morality. Western reporters claim that the most dramatic result of democracy and privatization has been a spectacular increase in corruption.[245]

The communism which was practiced in Russia was, by the 1990's so discredited, even within the left, that no one thought communism had produced a better man, much less a new one. Astute observers doubted that the collapse of communism would be as bad as some predicted because so much economic activity had been unreported that a large part of the system was capitalistic anyway.[246] In the cities almost half of apartment repairs, and over a third of tailoring, auto maintenance and shoe repairs took place off the books.

The blond report on what is out there has a large truth. Out there, they are familists. An observer in 1989 drew parallels between Russia and Southern Italy and concluded that there were common behavioral patterns that worked against economic advancement.[247] I believe that there is some truth to the claim, but that the larger truth is that once the peasantry leaves the village for the slum, economic advance can accommodate a lot of corruption.

How dramatic the blond economic advantage will be once virtually every population has put its 15-year-olds in school remains to be seen. If one plots the economic advance of Japan against the United States, or that of Italy compared to England, one might conclude that social morality carries much less economic freight than once thought.

Fernand Braudel emphasizes the role of Mediterranean elite in amassing wealth. I think that he misses the larger point. Peasant familial controls played that role. They operated to keep the birthrate high, child labor in place, dissent and play at bay, and behavior focused on simple repetitive hard work that was biologically successful: maybe the most biologically advantageous behavior for populations which could not fight.

Populations that are not good fighters have to make do with the assets that they have. The tedious difficult labors, the terror waiting for the bad year, the need to handle human excrement, the intensive effort to trap and store vast supplies of water, are universals throughout the peasant world. How harsh do the controls have to be? The answers are in the societies one sees.

———————————— 2 ————————————

Morality as Strategy by Control

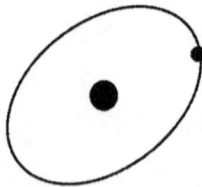

Legend, and the story of the journey of the blonds across half the planet in about two millennia, is evidence that they celebrate a risky approach to life. They look like they would be good fighters. The evidence is that they are.

In the course of their journey, they have bumped into an infinite variety of peoples that they have measured against their strengths and their values. The first insightful anthropologist strolled behind a great fighter.

The difficult thing is not fairness. There is no such animal. The difficult thing is to try to understand how what one sees fits with things one can not see.

A kind of establishment debate about what is going on in the peasant's world is delineated in two really excellent books: James C. Scott's *The Moral Economy of the Peasant: Rebellion and Subsistence in Southeast Asia* [248]and Samuel L. Popkin's *The Rational Peasant: The Political Economy of Rural Society in Vietnam.*[249]

There are serious differences between the authors on the "character" of the peasant and his setting, the village; but both would have to be classified as mentalists. This would distinguish them from either sociobiology, or biobehaviorism. Wilson and Skinner differ on the size and strength of environmental and genetic influences, but both would be skeptical about claims that either altruism or a continuous economic calculus inside the peasant's head defines the reality. Their analyses are just not much involved with the hidden calculations of the peasant. This is the divide that would put the Scott/Popkin debate in one forum, and the Skinner/Wilson sociobiological debate in another.

Scott's book is largely about its subheading: rebellion and subsistence survival in Southeast Asia. To treat the argument fairly, one has to remember this.

But some of his insights are more general and provocative than an account of the rebellion. The central thrust of the argument has to do with the rural village and the level of drama between the normal poverty stricken ho-hum years when everybody is parasite ridden, ignorant, sick, fearful, and hungry all the time; and that very exciting year when there really isn't enough food. Scott's great insight is that the brutal reality of that year is central to what goes on in that village all the time.

The peasant is involved in an intense struggle to survive in that horrific year when the crops fail. Survival for people in the village that year depends on how people behave in the years leading up to that year.

The bad times in the peasant's world are not like times of depression in an industrial society. Class analysis misses the behavioral point. Any industrial worker in any urbanized society has more in common with the man who owns the factory and visits the South of France with his yacht on holidays, than he does with the peasant the year the crops fail.

A secondary result of recognizing the threat of that year is accepting the possibility that a classical economics that assumes a continuing drive for more might miss the main story. The key to understanding economic behavior in the village is to see that the behavior has been shaped over centuries to try to keep the population and resources in a balance.

The first sociobiological dictum must be that no animal designed for lethargy or lassitude could survive. That includes people.

The entry into Scott's theory is through apparent peasant preferences for irrational activity:

- The peasant plants a series of small separated plots even though they are far removed from each other and much time and energy is spent moving from one to the other.[250]

- The peasant resists innovation (20).

- The peasant refers a tax system which varies with his income, even where the take over several years is greater than a flat, more honest, more efficient system. He is willing to pay a considerable premium to avoid a flat tax, good year and bad (11). Arrangements which create a subsistence level for the workers become normative expectations (6).

- Loans in bad times help with housing and with medical needs, and sufferance after bad harvests were attributes of the "good landlord." Dependence is not morally objectionable, and the system is fair (51).

- The actual "take" of many Southeastern Asian pre-colonial governments might have been 5 percent of the harvest, or less (53).

- In Vietnam, at least, there seems to be no doubt that the fiscal claims of European colonial states far exceeded the traditional norms (106). Compare this with the Wittfogel's description of the claims of the hydraulic political establishment on the issues of severity and economic confiscation.[251]

- The critical questions in industrial societies deal with productivity, or "mobility," change. The critical issues in traditional societies deal with the performance of obligations.[252]

- Scott's comments on land tenure systems are of particular interest, because they may be subject to quantitative analysis. He places land tenure systems along a spectrum with "A" representing systems in which the landlord bears the risk of a bad year, and provides the peasant with subsistence; and the "C" end representing systems where the landlord is entitled to a fixed income from the peasant come what may. Poorer agricultural societies, characterized by small plots, variable yields, and few opportunities for outside employment should cluster toward the "A" end, while wealthier villages should be more likely to be found toward the "C" distribution. Wealth creates a long-term rational, bargaining, relationship in place of a patron and his dependent (44–45).

- The peasant showed a consistent preference for reliable subsistence crops such as corn, over more profitable alternatives, cotton or cocoa, even though there were real financial advantages for cash crops in good years (21).

- The peasant insists on using traditional, less profitable but hardier seed stock over newer more profitable seeds that were more sensitive to variation in water supply (20).

- Most studies of Southeast Asian villages report that the minimal needs of the peasants are met by an informal set of controls, and moral imperatives (41).

- A large percentage of arable land was classified as communal land. In some areas of Vietnam over 50 percent of the paddy land was so classified, and a substantial percentage of the output was used to support orphans and widows (43).

- Of special importance for the baseline argument: Where weather conditions made for variable crop yields, resistance to fixed rather than variable rent was most intense (97).

The above examples are not exhaustive, but do represent a reasonable representation of Scott's store of data and impressions about the social structure that he labels as "moral." There are four indicia to support the thesis that the peasant trades profit for safety: stratification, norms of reciprocity, patterns of land tenancy, and taxation (35).

It is not clear to me if Scott thinks the peasant is "exploited" by land ownership arrangements. There are times when the landlord is a patron. But there are times when the peasants discuss the landlord in very critical terms. Whether or not the peasant is skeptical about the nature of the landlord/tenant relationship, however, much of the violence that the peasant instigates is not directed toward revolution, but with the aim of forcing the owner to follow established economic norms (189–190).

Scott acknowledges fault lines within the little tradition, but asserts that the tradition does appear to recognize and enforce moral arrangements. It does hold that the poorer members of the community are entitled to help during times of stress (182–183). In really bad times, most of the village would be hungry all the time before anyone actually starved (43).

When one really understands that, one understands the threat that an open female sexuality would represent in the village. Kingston's pregnant woman in the well suffers monstrously, but it is clear that she represents a dagger aimed at everyone in the village.[253] The blond human rights activist sees the well, not the bad year.

The certitude of being able to have enough to eat during the bad year gives everyone, including untouchables, a life and death stake in the system.[254] A corollary of the settled nature of agricultural activity within the village is that the central moral issue has to do with obligation, not mobility (185). The village ethos promises a certain minimum income, rather than equality (40).

There may be an opportunity for sociobiology here. Would it be possible to compare the amount of communal land in villages of comparable size and wealth, but greater or lesser amounts of consanguinity?

Now, to be fair to Scott's critics, there are times when he seems to idealize the village. He suggests that perhaps the hostility and "amoral familism" that characterize reports on peasant societies in Mexico, Italy and Ireland may be the result of the increasing village dependence on an expanding urban civilization (212–213). He seems to think that the mutuality of the corporate village gives ground, as agriculture becomes a niche in the process of industrialization. But amoral familism really is not at odds with what Scott reports. There is no need

to posit a spirit of generosity to explain a process of sharing risk: Enough time
and behavioral controls are adequate.

Which leads to the final point: Does it make sense to call the peasant, or
the collective, either moral or rational, if life rather than people chooses the
arrangement?

Rationality and Order

The assumptions that Popkin makes are the assumptions that we all make a
few years out of high school. His peasant is a very recognizable figure. He could
be a cabbie in New York. The fundamental assumption is that one can not be
cynical enough.

Popkin's avowed strategy of emphasizing the role of individual decision, may
demonstrate simple common sense, a common sense which is also compatible
with sociobiology. After all, sociobiology is what Wilson says it is, and he says
that the mind works on meaning.

A central presumption of sociobiology must be that evolution produces,
everywhere, creatures that pursue advantage for themselves and their progeny,
in a world where someone else wants what they have. Wilson also tells us that
from a biological perspective social altruism is "soft." "Hard" elements exist only
within the province of the individual, his progeny, and close kin.[255] This could
suggest that the "moral economy" would scale with consanguinity.

Popkin ties to work out the calculus for a pre-industrial capitalist, by positing
a kind of inner directed peasant inside the peasant one sees. He follows the
peasant around, and reports behaviors as decisions which make economic
sense. These are the decisions that show that this peasant is not burdened by
any more social conscience than? Rockefeller? Gates? You? Me?

He cites numerous authorities who very explicitly underline what must be the
most common blond observation about the peasantry after "They look funny."
They do not have the same open, social, pleasant, honest, selfless relationships
among themselves that the blonds do. There is a lack of idealism for the
realization of non-familial social aims generally. What cooperation does exist
tends to be task specific and is directed toward minimal standards.[256]

Some of Popkin's specific objections to the notion of the moral economy are:

■ Stratification and exploitation developed in Annan, an area not subject
to French colonial power. Europeans did not have to teach the Vietnamese
how to treat each other badly. The French created new behavioral possibilities,
but the villagers themselves were responsible for shaping the actual exploitive
structure.[257]

■ The accuracy of the French tax lists were a tribute to the willingness of
the Vietnamese to inform on each other.[258]

- Christian missionaries thought that Vietnamese mandarins bullied and tormented the weak.[259]

- The individual striving to better his economic status fashions the village, and puts borders around the degree of cooperation that can be achieved in a fundamental competitive setting. Popkin explicitly rejects the notion inherent in the moral economy that the village shapes individual behavior. Popkin has developed dichotomies: village/altruism versus individual/selfish.[260]

- In parts of Vietnam, the French simply continued a fairly rigid procedure for collecting taxes. Still, Popkin does make a concession of sorts when he states that the authoritarian but weak governments that preceded the colonial experience had some sensitivity to the peasant's economic realities. The colonial powers were more democratic, but also more powerful. They could enforce the demand that taxes be paid in currency, not crops. He cites one local instance where imperial France forced the peasantry to sell more than 15 percent of the land at one-tenth of its normal value to meet tax payments in coin. The British in India enforced similar actions.[261]

- The fact that four of the most successful organizing forces in rural Vietnam: The Catholic Church, the Hao and Hao, the Cao Dai, and the Communist party were all radically at odds with traditional feudal arrangements suggests that the established order was not all that moral. Vietnamese Catholics and Communists began to vigorously assert themselves once they were free of the threat of force. They began to see their lives in a new context.[262]

- Actual experience seems to support reports, which describe the peasant as an amoral familist. They are typically not represented in anyone's literature as committed to their class or ethnicity. Actual experience seems to support the view that they tend to favor individualistic or familial solutions to problems that have a social dimension.[263]

- It is curious however, that Popkin seems to minimize the role of the family in the creation of the village, and emphasizes political institutions. He thinks that governmental demands for funds were a major factor in the creation of the corporate village.[264] The corporate village had its origin in the inexorable growth of the militaristic, rationalizing, aggressive, bureaucratic, and ambitious central state. The familist remained a familist, but the need for taxes, as isolated villages were transformed into the modern state, grew layers of bureaucracies to maintain records, to lease communal land, and to obtain cannon fodder for next year.

- The moral economy implies a collective rationality. Actual behavior reflects a determination to enjoy consumption at the expense of others.[265]

- The traditional bureaucracy fosters clientism and stratification, not egalitarianism.[266]

- The scattered fields system supports the economic rationalist theory. The peasantry as a collective is losing about 10 percent of its output because each family is willing to sacrifice output to ensure that they will not be dependent on the collective. Had the peasant really been part of a moral economy, family units would have consolidated the plots so that they could be efficiently farmed by individual families, and the collective would have had an additional 10 per cent to give to those families which experienced crop loss because of insect infestation or some other localized disaster.[267]

- Agricultural communal land was less productive than privately held property.[268]
- The villages appeared to prefer a system which gave them permanent holdings, even if mediocre, to a system which periodically rotated ownership, of bad, mediocre and good land.
- Village political procedures tended to harden class distinction and status, rather than soften them.[269]
- Peasants do engage in investments and apply investment logic to their behavior. Whether or not to procreate is one such investment decision.[270]
- The relationship between peasant and lord is fundamental to understanding the village. Unvarnished, the relationship is about power, and is exploitive.[271]
- Popkin rejects the notion of a simple, fixed minimum subsistence. Peasants continuously strive to improve their level of consumption, and the "minimum" which runs like a red line through the moral economy literature is actually a social construct and reflects what is required to fulfill social obligations. The line is pink instead of red, wavy instead of straight, and economic rather than biological.[272]
- The local landlord leaned against those changes that, Popkin assumes, would make the peasant a more efficient peasant. The lord uses his influence to keep the peasant ignorant and illiterate. The lord was against changes that would make the peasant more efficient, but also more astute and skeptical. Popkin appears to believe that the fundamental characteristics the peasant exhibited over millennia have been wrong ones. He thinks that educating the peasant would make the peasant a more effective, as opposed to a less effective, peasant. But if one accepts a very weak technology as a given, it is just as likely that educating a peasant makes him less able to endure the limiting, boring, harsh, physically exhausting work that must be done. However, Popkin makes a valid argument that the actual behavior of the landlord casts doubt upon the morality of his relationship with the peasant. The lord is also, as sociobiology would predict, a familist.[273]
- Peasants typically hide wealth to avoid paying a fair fraction of village taxes. Popkin believes that this is at odds with what he sees as the heart of the moral economy argument.[274]

When one steps back and reviews all of Popkin's arguments, one might conclude that Popkin's version would be more compatible with sociobiology than Scott's account. I think that would be a mistake.

Taken individually Popkin's observations may be true. But they do not really answer Scott's questions.

The hydraulic systems that are the basis for the great rice civilizations of Asia reflect the efforts of unrelated families occupying small plots for generations. How did those civilizations get put together? How much time separates the first scrapings for the first irrigation ditch and the moment someone saw the need to "rationalize" family ditches into a system? This is the intersection where the profit maximizer can not help much. Silent calculation inside the head of the peasant thousands of years ago would not predict the explosion in security and wealth the system, as a system, produced.

Moreover, the concessions that Popkin makes are more damaging to his thesis than he seems to realize. Popkin would argue that the village should be seen as just another factory. But he admits that on certain issues there was a collective. Tenants did sometimes bond together to prevent outsiders from gaining a foothold.[275] The poor, widowed and aged did receive plots of land for their support.[276] Periodically the village did experience a land redistribution that tended to even out levels of wealth.[277] Finally one figure cited by Popkin is so dramatic that one wonders why it does not seem more remarkable to him. In Tonkin and Annan approximately one-quarter of the productive land was owned and managed by the corporate village.[278]

There is a space where the moral economy and the incipient capitalist can be reconciled. However, one first has to give up both the morality and the mentalism of the moral economy.

Popkin misses the real kernel of Scott's challenge. The peasant is different than the industrial worker. The difference does not have to do with morality, exploitation or poverty. It has to do with the particular fit between what the peasant does, as a social creature, and the village environment.

How the Moral Economy Might Look to Skinner

In most of the non-blond world, up to the very recent past, for the overwhelming majority of peasants the political, social and cultural worlds were one. An agricultural order in which 85 plus percent of the labor force did the same thing, and lived the same way, has to be like that.

From a perch within the blond world, the intellectuals tend to see the same things over and over. The characteristic hallmarks of the village are scarcity, familism, corruption and controls.

Scott sees a common peasant ethos that was shared by a wide variety of populations including Russians, Asians, and Mediterranean peoples as a result of living so close to the margin.[279] The narrow margin amplified the effect of even a small ripple. The narrow margin and the inherently cyclical nature of agriculture operated to develop a certain type of morality. The village in this historic sea became an arrangement to insure a very basic minimum in the horrific year.

Scott does see a bond of mutuality and protection defining the peasant-landlord relationship (75), but it would be a mistake to push it too far. He also sees evidence that there is exploitation by the landlord class which relies on force, not mystification (228, 240).

Now, a fundamental assumption of this book is that the blonds were never peasants; rather they defined the "non-peasants." Scott sees it very, very different; he has a completely deracinated analysis. In his search for the generic peasant, Scott goes to England itself.

He claims that the peasantry will take the same road to the modern state that England took. But the transformation will be complete within decades, much less than the three centuries the process took in England (9).

Scott sees parallels between laborer and landlord relationships in pre-industrial England and in the peasant societies that he has studied. As long as the English landlord conformed to expected behavioral norms, the English farmer like the classical peasant accepted the patron-client relationship, no matter very disparate income and status levels (181-182). He would join English rural laborers who rebelled to protect their ancient rights against the landholder, and the Mediterranean and Asian peasantry (190). Bitter and sarcastic expressions of hostility on the part of 18th century English peasants find an echo in 20th century Vietnam (234-235). The level of violence, which accompanied the political change from an agricultural to an industrial England, had some parallels with the transition to modern agriculture in India's Punjab (208).

Popkin takes a very different historical view. He makes a sharp break between the process that transformed an agricultural England, and the experiences of the modern Third World peasantry, not in ethnic or racial terms, but on historical and economic grounds.[280] Their varied analysis of the English experience, illuminates the differences between Scott and Popkin on the issues of the origin and fundamental nature of the peasantry as a social type. Scott uses the English experience as a sort of precursor for the changes which would be forced upon the non-European peasantry centuries later.[281]

Popkin thinks that the general pattern of the Third World peasant village must have been established for political reasons by force. As time passed the peasantry by and large accepted the arrangement forced on it because it did confer certain benefits. Membership gave them some minimal physical security, as well as certain political benefits. Members of the village, no matter how poor, were probably better off than lone families. Indeed, one of Popkin's criticisms of the moral economists is their avoidance of the moral issue of the non-member.

It is not clear if Scott is committed to a particular fit between the peasant and the ruling polity on the issue of the creation of the village. I think one could conclude that he does think political forces played a major role in the creation of the village. For example, he tells us that a subsistence income was a requirement for the landowners to attract a pool of workers (6-8). The peasant also needed the protection of an army to keep other ethnic groups from his produce. The starting point is a fairly brutal question: Who can force the other off the land?

But Scott also sees the familistic nature of the village in the natural preference of the villager to go to his kinsman in times of crises (28). There is a kind of implicit scale to this: Ties to the village are strongest when times are bad, and weakest when times are good.

Now, Popkin and Scott have serious areas of disagreement, but they also have certain areas where they make common assumptions about what is, and is not, important. While they parse the reality differently, power and morality are the lead actors for both Scott and Popkin.

One doubts that this would be true for either Wilson or Skinner. The reality of the peasant on the ground is just different, and more interesting.

It should be clear that my analysis on the ethnic issue is very different from both Popkin's and Scott's. There are populations that were never peasants, and one could not imagine those populations becoming peasants.

In the beginning there was no elite, moral or not, to create the village. Primitive agricultural villages came into existence with the first agricultural settlements ten thousand years ago, or more. That is more than enough time to establish a system with its own integrity, a system that works.

Initially the village was the creation of the family, or the tribe. The trans-village elite could not have preceded the arrival of the source of its income, and life.

If the elites are set off into the distance, the question becomes more basic. What are the peasants doing, and why are they doing it? Even better, How are they doing it?

Where does one begin? With parsimony as a guide, one begins with a search for a believable theory of learning.

The further one can move the outside elite away from the early village, the more space becomes available for behaviorism. While Scott and Popkin each acknowledge the role of culture in shaping the village, they do not spend much time with knowledge issues. How do the peasant and the village get to know what they know?

Both ignore the role of the village as a tutor that shaped the first peasant's behavior. Density is undervalued by both. A familiar blond morality, one that celebrates the dignity of the individual, shines through both.

The discipline of agriculture must, at first, have been a very different path from what preceded it. And here, right at the beginning, the world probably witnessed the division that persisted through thousands of years of the agricultural monotone: the populations that pulled weeds, versus the populations that could really fight.

Scott cites the fact that the Russian village periodically distributed land to village members, depending on family size, as an example of an ethic of "fairness" (177). He draws some parallels with this behavior and the urban proletariat demand for a "fair" price for bread, and other staples. But I believe that this is an example of how much space exists between the peasant and any modern industrial worker.

The actual act of land redistribution is as foreign to the experience of the industrial proletariat, as it would be to the plutocrat. What does one make of it? Where to begin? In a comparison of consanguinity where it takes place and where it does not? In different religious traditions? In studies of comparative wealth? How would the behavior have become established in the teeth of familial demands?

Presumably the rational peasant's answer would be that it is an insurance scheme that one day would benefit him or his immediate family. One wonders whether the relative size of the village might offer a clue whether this could be the case. Where the populations were small, and related, perhaps the felt need for redistribution would be muted.

Redistribution might also make sense as an agricultural scheme. Different families may have used certain different agricultural methods. Perhaps diversity over the years would be beneficial for the soil. Redistribution may have been another way to avoid excessive risk from concentrating too many resources in one locale. While the blond take on the village has been an unrelieved sense of poverty and oppression, the interesting kernel is the behavioral correspondence between so many different ethnic groups, developed in so many different crucibles, separated by thousands of miles and very different cultural histories.

Now it is my responsibility to try and develop some data or information that would prove my account wrong. The details of Columbus' trip as recounted in the PBS special were both fresh and fascinating. Two features were especially riveting: the isolation he experienced from his own crew, on ethnic grounds, and the revolutionary changes the voyages forced into agricultural practices on three continents.

Those changes present a problem to the account pressed here. Certainly they point away from the village, more or less autonomous behavioral units, as the real creator of peasant agriculture. The speed with which Columbian changes were adopted suggests that biobehaviorism and what it implies; local tradition, dense familism and low-level authoritarian controls, was not the only story.

The rapidity of the changes following Columbus' voyage suggests that the landlord did more than collect the rents. The experience points toward a capitalist mentality overseeing elements of the experience, and more than a little risk taking.[282] One assumes that when the crop changed, a host of economic and behavioral changes from the planting to the processing, to the marketing, changed as well.

However, if the irrigation system were not changed, the control system for the peasant would not have to change. He could still function in small isolated villages consisting of fairly closely related families.

Popkin spends some time trying to see into the peasant's character. He thinks that social stratification was a very early phenomenon, and preceded the production of agricultural crops for the market. That was the sequence, he assumes, because the peasant valued individual security first, and thus chose the village. He then saw opportunity and chose the market.[283] It is an interesting viewpoint, and is familiar. Societies are presumed to reflect decisions.

The blond intellectuals begin with what is most visible to them at the top, and work their way down. Political concerns drive the process.

Biobehaviorism starts at the family, then the village, and finally the elite, who, one expects were the descendants of fighters, and always behaviorily less orthodox than the village.

The difficulty of maintaining controls once one leaves the village is crucial here. The strength of dialects is revealing. Can one imagine a blond population unable to converse across village borders separated by only a few miles? The fighters are populations on the move. They can not be defined within a series of isolated villages.

Mobility and a fairly democratic structure, along racial lines would advantage the great fighters. One assumes that a certain built in racial antagonism would be helpful. Morality travels in ethnic costume.

Popkin appears to charge that the moral economists claim that traditional economies are more moral than industrial economies. Well, perhaps. But the claim is not intrinsic to their argument. Popkin objects to what he sees as the undue credit to the peasantry for its morality on the grounds the peasant may simply have been forced into a certain role. There were no alternatives.[284] Of course.

From the perspective of biobehaviorism, Popkin misses the main point. No doubt the peasant is interested in economic gain. That has to be a basic quality of every human society. A population on the brink of starvation that was not interested in economic gain would soon be dead.

In the beginning, there must have been peasant who reverted, who became nomads, or hunters. But inexorably agriculture and the village took up more and more space. Because they were successful.

The number of children the new behavior could support was critical in this struggle. Popkin's classification of children as investments does not exhaust the possibilities. Can he be right when he traces this to the individual man or woman? Biobehaviorism would suggest an alternative; that the number of children people produced in the village, initially, would have been the same that they produced as hunters.

Assume that there was a limitative force at work, and that the peasant was not aware of it. What does that make of the notion, that there was a calculus operating, either in the service of a morality, or the pursuit of economic gain?

Scott's analysis, that the peasantry did provide a collective insurance for its members against starvation, points to a differently sized universe. He presents a few people in a small, intensely crowded space. Starvation is a real possibility and that explains much. The agricultural nature of the village demands reciprocity; it would be unlivable without it.[285] Reciprocity operates "largely" within the geography of the village.[286]

Popkin takes a more narrow "political" approach. He stresses the role and opportunity of the skilled leader in negotiating the resolution of conflict among the villagers, thereby enhancing his own prestige, power, and opportunity for economic gain.[287] Moreover, in the pre-colonial village, reciprocity and welfare were not village wide concepts, but were limited to small groups that enforced strict rules. The ability of a given individual to navigate sophisticated and selfish relationships helped to develop and maintain a reasonably consistent and selfish morality, throughout the village. The Vietnamese villagers of the 19th century drew sharp distinctions between natives, and outsiders, and discriminated against the latter, including those who had married village women.[288]

Popkin states that moral economists would predict that wealthier villagers would help their poorer neighbors in bad times. The actual evidence shows that the powerful developed and enforced regulations that placed resources in the hands of the wealthy.[289] He quotes an anthropologist who found an Indian family that had left the village, contacted a sickness in the new town or city, and had returned to the village. Instead of helping, their former neighbors abandoned them to die.[290]

But reciprocity is not suicide. Scott may be on to something.

I suggest that the real operational alternative to the peasant's familistic rule of reciprocity is the kind of racial identity the great fighters, particularly the blonds, demonstrate again and again. The difference is demonstrated in the difference between a public spirited, honest, heroic defender of a racially aggressive Alabama; and a corrupt, familistic, but more racially tolerant Brazil.

To a behaviorist, the premise of the moral economy, whether one views it as an individualistic exercise, or as a socially maintained set of controls, does not require abdication of self-interest. But it does require a very specific kind of place which was very foreign to the blonds: the isolated stable familistic village. The place the blonds went to attack.

One sees the traditional pattern: some common land, everyone on the verge of starvation before anyone actually starves, periodic redistribution of land, separated family plots, and a patron based agriculture, and one sees the need for a different type of analysis. How do these behaviors fit with the stability and balance one tracks in different continents over centuries. Popkin's observation that small bounded communities develop high coefficients of suspicion, distrust, and envy sounds right.[291] They are not an effective fighting force, or very likely to develop a worldwide empire based on racial aggression.

What if the blond anthropologists filled out the same checklist in Seoul, Tokyo, Manila, Moscow and Peking at the end of an urbanized 20th century, that they filled out in an agricultural 18th century? I suspect that they would, although the characteristics would be muted.

Reciprocity is the statute that applies particularly well to the distrust and familism of the peasant's village. Given the very high level of suspicion among the laborers, and the critical need to develop and maintain an irrigation system, reciprocity was indispensable. Except for the great fighters, it seems doubtful that any pre-modern farmers had a morality other than reciprocity.

The 20th century more or less destroyed the peasantry as a behavioral system. Universal education for boys, the size and reach of the enormous slum cities, roads everywhere, unbelievably cheap and unbelievably sophisticated communication systems, all operate to make the world less dense, more abstract, and more a matter of choice. I suspect that it really is not possible now to test whether Scott or Popkin were more right about the village in that desperate year. The key probe is gone. Outside of Africa, no one starves any more.

If one wishes to fairly understand the argument, one should not require that the "moral" peasant exhibit a complete selflessness. Sociobiology would not be surprised by a corporate arrangement that ran on reciprocity, and discriminated against outsiders.

Scott's claim that the study of the moral economy must start with economics, but end in culture and religion is wrong. [292] The village was in place before risk aversion became an idea. The moral economy begins with learning theory, and a willingness to observe behaviorism at work.

A basic familistic focus and a restricted role for women are two of the greatest boundaries between the peasantry and the blonds. Both contribute to what countless observers have noted about the differences between the blonds and their neighbors. In a sense the wogs did begin at Calais, but when one tracks the racial morality of the British throughout the world, they did not end at Calais. Given the burden of blond idealism in the 18th and 19th century, a peasant China with nuclear weapons aimed at Queen Victoria in the 21st century, was probably a lock.

Today, modernization has a known behavioral shape. No one could have guessed at that shape when England and Germany began one of the most creative processes in human history. Whatever wealth and power were historically, it became clear that, in the new age, they were not an endless series of isolated villages, populated by laborers all engaged in the same behavior.

Until the Fascists and Communists actually did it, no one could have predicted that political forces; dictatorial governments and educational bureaucrats could recapitulate the process the blonds inaugurated, albeit with a different political tune. Free markets may have been economically preferable, but they were not necessary to the destruction of the peasantry, and the commencement of the modernization game.

It was inevitable that the modernization process would not only not be of the village, but opposed to the village. The behavioral system, the familism and the close control of women had been a spectacular biological success; but the behaviors that the village generated were incompatible with the loose controls a differentiated work force requires. Scott sides with the peasant and sees the state as a "claimant" (91). From inside the village, the dream was a village without outside interference, and outside taxation. The resentment against the colonial powers was, except for the issue of racism, merely a continuation of the resentment the villager had always had for the landlord. The pre-colonial state may have been preferable inside the village on two issues: It prevented the export of food crops, and it did soften market forces at certain times (116, n).

Finally however, the peasant's world would be forced to adapt to the new economic order featuring industrialization, urbanization and universal education for males. Scott sees that the integrated world economy decisively weakened the peasant's status (156). And that is right. But what is missed is that it is precisely that peasant's labor, in a non-peasant uniform that has to create the expanding economy. In the real world the peasant is not simply a consumer; outside the blond continents, he has to produce the new economy.

Where the old poor village and the new poor city coexist, Scott never sees new skills, just scavenging. For him, overall the new slum is an economic negative. It breaks down the moral integrity and social awareness of the villagers. He thinks that the migration of the most enterprising and intelligent members of the village siphons off the talent that could be used in the village. He would have the state create infrastructure or provide welfare to the peasantry; which is seen as a gigantic and stable class. Scott mentions road building and menial jobs in the public sector as attempts to marginally improve or stabilize the peasant's income.

Land distribution, limits on land rents, affordable credits, are "more lasting remedies" (215). Land reform seems to be a major structural priority. He tells us that the peasant is faced with a subsistence problem produced by demographics and exploitation (225). There is no understanding that a low level of simple repetitive hard work by the majority of the work force has to lead to a low level of consumption.

Popkin also sees the state playing a role in the village, but he emphasizes different features. There were places and times where the Absolutist State and the peasantry operated as allies against the local landowner.[293] Moreover the central power could help establish linguistic and religious standards.[294] Popkin highlights the rational, beneficial strands in the connective web between the village and the central authority.[295] He sees that the sheer physical distance between the central authority and the village as a major impediment in the ability of the central power to enforce detailed mandates.

While laws, courts and land registers are very visible political tools or weapons they operate to regulate an agricultural order that must have come into place without them. And the village has powers of its own to hide both income and draft age people.

I believe that the most telling commentary on how active a role the central government actually played in the village was given by the 19th century traveler who was amazed how little trade existed within Vietnam.[296] Neither Popkin nor Scott sees the possibility for the central authority to kill the village orthodoxy by forcing the villagers to educate their sons. Neither sees the power of the central government to finally kill the village itself by encouraging industrialization, and the accompanying urban slum that has marked every transformation to modernization, since the development of Manchester.

Neither deal with the opportunity an early industrialization, coupled with an historic and aggressive racism, gave to the blonds. Neither sees what Third World industrialization coupled with a determination to keep the blonds at bay produces. Aggression by the English and the Japanese helped force the development of a bureaucracy in China which would force a new behavior into the guts of a population that had learned things that had been right, but became wrong.

Skinner rightly tells us that there are advantages to being a social animal. Millennia transformed a tribe into a village. Before risk aversion could become an idea, a population had to learn what no one could put into words. But everyone did not have to endure that 7th or 10th or 45th year to learn how to prepare for it.

It is not surprising that so many of the taboos revolve around sex and the threat children without male providers presented to the collective. It is not surprising that the great fighters had less of the taboo than the peasantry. Scott has a powerful message, but sociobiology can not accept his dictum that the study begins in the domain of economics, and ends in the domain of culture. The more one can track a predictable behavioral order to the village, across ethnic and religious lines, the more interesting the simple behavior becomes.

For Scott, as for so many American observers, economic development is a matter of getting the agricultural question right. He has some impressive company here. One nationally known economist tells us that an efficient agriculture is the first step in economic development, partly because the agricultural sector in the undeveloped world is so large.[297]

The view here is different. Peasant societies are something in themselves. They are very, very old and practice a very, very weak technology. The odds are high that, given the constraints of a weak technology and a stable population, the food development the peasantry practices is more efficient than either the peasant or the economist knows.

Scott briefly touches on, but does not develop the theme that outside powers such as the central state could create the slum city that would replace the familistic village. The giant slum cities that dot the Third World are the behavioral foundation for a new world.

To consume more the peasant has to produce more. He has to stop being a peasant. There are two places where that can happen for large numbers of people. The first is the classroom. The second is the city. There is no road to a more efficient agriculture that does not lead through the urban slum.

————— 3 —————

Urbanization and the 11th Grade

There are at the present time two quite different modes of approaching the behavior of organisms which are hard to distinguish theoretically but which are clearly different in practice. The statistical approach is characterized by relatively unrefined methods of measurement and a general neglect of the problem of direct description.

B. F. Skinner[298]

As a rule, traits as complex as human behavior are influenced by many genes, each of which shares only a small fraction of the total control. These "polygenes" cannot ordinarily be identified by directing and tracing the mutations that alter them. They must be evaluated indirectly by statistical means.

E. O. Wilson[299]

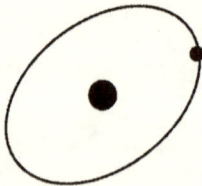

A behavioral answer to a behavioral problem. Skinner's admonition that the natural environment in which most animal behavior is studied is generally only one of the environments in which that species has lived, may be seen as a caution to those who would draft a human behavioral inventory.[300] The constants in peasant societies, so visible in the blond literature, may be informative, but details which suggest authority, rather than adaptation, point away from biology.

Compliance in a village of 1500 souls, and compliance in the slums of Sao Paulo, or Seoul, or Palermo, or Hong Kong, are wildly different things. A central fact about human populations in the 20th century, perhaps the central fact, was the process of urbanization that took place across the planet.

The outlines are commonplace, but the details can still shock. Cairo, during one man's long life, has grown ten fold.[301] Mexico City took over 400 years to reach one million, and then, in roughly one half century grew 16-fold.[302] During the 1970's over 15 million Russian workers moved from the farms to the cities.[203] Stalin's daughter, after a 20 year absence, stated that she could hardly recognize Moscow because of the tremendous numbers of large, monotonous apartment buildings.[304] In 1960 only about one quarter of Turkey's population lived in cities. By 1981 that percentage had roughly doubled.[305]

One observer, in the 1970's, after stating that China's classic problem had been how the cities might govern the village, projected that by the year 2000 the countryside would contain over a billion people, and the city 300 million, the latter figure being an increase of about one-third in 20 years.[306] The UN predicted a higher percentage would live in China's cities by the year 2000: two in five.[307] By 1993 some observers, based partly on the fact that in the prior 10 years China had experienced some of the world's fastest economic growth rates, were suggesting a more dramatic change: By 2003 one-half of the working population could be employed in the non-peasant sector.[308] A 2003 almanac estimated that in a work force of about 700 million, 50 percent were in agriculture, 24 percent were in industry and the rest were in services.[309]

I do not think that it would be unfair to observe that most of the blond literature on the tide toward urbanization treats it as unfortunate. The option the northern intelligentsia seems to favor is "land reform." One might conclude that if the Third World land owner would simply burn his deed, and leave, economic deliverance would be at hand. Part of the accepted wisdom about the role of Communist governments in Russia and China is that they derailed other political and economic movements, which would have gone on to salvage the village civilization. That is what many Russian observers believed. It is an up to date version of what many agricultural reformers believed. In the 1660's I. Urii Kriziianich wrote that the Russian ruler could create abundance through more intelligent policies.[310] In 1888 a Russian intellectual termed the taxation system of the serfs as "monstrous," but claimed that as bad as the system was, the more destructive influence evolved from the legislation that emancipated the peasants, and introduced a new and foreign land tenure system.[311]

The sermons remain constant: The village could be attractive, prosperous, rational, and democratic. There is another way of seeing this, however.

For the blond to be right, the people in the village have to be wrong. And wrong for hundreds, even thousands of years; generation after generation. No twenty-first century social scientist would approach the behavior of any other species with that assumption.

The economist in the blond tradition sees agricultural behavior, as the agricultural "sector." Often, the first assumed priority is the need to improve the productivity of the small producer.[312] India's economic development is said to require a more efficient village peasantry.[313] There is a literature on the optimum relationship between urbanization rates, and the rate of economic development.[314] Many people thought that their national economic future was bound up with the efficiency of the agricultural work force. Some American political leaders once thought that immigration policies should favor agriculture.[315] At one time Brazil required at least 80 percent of the immigrant labor force from each country of origin, to be made up of agricultural workers.[316] There is a Latin American "Jeffersonian" tradition of viewing the cityscape as too big, too new, and too parasitic in form and function.[317] A distinguished physicist deplores the growth of the mega-city. It is aesthetically ugly, it depopulates the village, it results in a limitation of genetic diversity in plants, and it destroys the beauty of a primitive agriculture.[318]

That there are limits to urban growth may very well be true both theoretically and practically. Whether one can say that one has identified those limits however, is a very different matter. In practice, the imposition of limits means that the peasantry has to remain a peasantry. One celebrated assertion of the reality of limits opined in 1972 that the urban unemployed would not be able to buy or grow enough food.[319] In the 1960's a writer satirized the economic development, and accompanying urbanization of Korea as a matter of bars and billiard halls.[320] The blond audience is familiar with the description of the Slum City whether in Korea, Vietnam, where Scott describes the locale as a place for scavenging,[321] or Mexico,[322] or dozens of other places.

One observer noted in 1984 that throughout Asia east of Pakistan, human fertility was dropping, while food production was increasing. He suggested that a reverse migration from the slum back to the village was likely.[323] The writer's preference for the village was evident in a 1982 article, which pointed to Taiwan's experience in developing villages that have small-scale factories and are electrified and educated.[324] The author expressed the hope that a free market and 10,000 small factories manufacturing consumer goods, would keep the peasant prosperous and at home.

What is missed in much of the blond op-ed type punditry is the message that if a country that is 70 to 80 percent peasantry is going to develop; the peasantry has to do it. There are no levers a government, an army or private elite can directly manipulate which can give that country electricity, factories, or a 70-year life span. What governments, democratic, authoritarian, and dictatorial can do, is to force the peasant father to keep the peasant son in school until the son is 15. And, essentially, that is what happened in the first half of the twentieth century.

I suspect that at the beginning of the twentieth century virtually no European or American intellectuals would have predicted the high percentage of Chinese, Indian, Arab, or Latin American 15-year-old boys who would be in school at the end of the century. Whatever the deficiencies, crimes and mistakes of the totalitarian governments of the twentieth century, they billed themselves as agents of modernization, and they were.

There is no mystery why investment dollars go to the burgeoning cities and not to the hand to mouth village. I suspect that most studies would find a positive correlation between the wage rate, and the transfer of populations to the new slums.

There is a curious and counter intuitive aspect about this argument. The human race did not evolve in the 2000 member agricultural village, but neither did it evolve in the technological city. How curious then, that the fit between some people and modern technology is as good as it is. One sees the post World War II development of Japan and wonders what the foundry of the really gifted electrical engineer was.

The transformation of the peasant is unidirectional. Having become literate and urbanized no population disavows behavioral diversity for the monotone of the village. The blond intellectual does have a good eye, and is able to track consistencies as the Slav, Latin, Asian, Arab villager moves to the city. But the city does not equal the village reconstituted with a different geography.

The village is not about poverty. It is about an order created to keep poverty at a distance. Given the tools available to pre-industrial governments; central states could have affected consumption in the village only at the margin.

Reports that track economic results to attitudes about work or effort miss the larger point. It may be that a survey of Russian folk tales will reveal that cunning and deceit promise more reward than hard work.[325] The deeper truth is that the overwhelming majority of peasants everywhere would work many more hours if they had the choice. That is one of the charms of the great slums.

Italian Immigration to the United States: A Statistical Solution

Probably no large European national immigrant group has experienced a more diverse academic literature about their economic adaptation to North

America than Italians. The reports range from "poor" to "affluent." How the academician regards the history depends, I think, on how smart the writer thinks Italians are. Here too, the reports are diverse.

H. J. Eysenck cited Italians as an example of an immigrant population where circumstances forced the less intelligent to emigrate, and where they achieved significantly lower IQ scores than a random sample of the original population would have demonstrated.[326] It is clear that there is a broad consensus among educational experts that the IQ test is an effective predictor of academic success.[327] There is also a substantial consensus about the correlation of IQ scores with financial, social, and business success, and the experts who favor biology make extremely broad claims.[328]

Arthur Jensen is the name most readers will probably associate with the claim that IQ scores reflect capacities that are, to some degree, determined at conception. He makes the claim that the class divisions that characterize America, and every other industrial society, are explained in part by differences in native abilities. These observations about genetics, IQ and educational performance did not start with Professor Jensen. They have been part of the IQ discussion for much of the 20th century.

The heart of the theory presented here is precisely the claim that the blond intellectuals were right about the predictive power of IQ tests. And that because the blond political leadership ignored or misinterpreted what the IQ data reflected they have made their own children vulnerable to nuclear weapons for countless future generations.

While intermarriage finally will break down the singularity of most European ethnic groups, ethnic differences are still big enough and visible enough to warrant study. Some of the better known reports on Italians have not simply documented differences between them and the majority; they have traced the differences to cultural and biological deficiencies.

The Stanford-Binet test, the first major American IQ test was introduced to the public as part of the effort to screen draftees for World War I. The results indicated that immigrants from Southern and Eastern Europe had not done well, and that information caused concern.[329]

Now, in fact, the if one reads the blond literature on racial and ethnic issues prior to the early 20th century, IQ data was nothing new. It simply underscored what the blonds had known for generations: I would argue that there was not a day in two millennia when the blonds were not convinced that they were superior to Latins, Slavs, Asians, Africans and a whole stew pot of other populations. Aesthetics mean something.

If one simply toted up all the places where the blonds, at one time or other, had established prohibitions, formal or informal against different groups intermarrying with blonds, the conclusion would be inescapable. Professor Terman's warning that the continuation of existing reproductive rates for 200 years would mean that 1000 Harvard graduates would have 50 descendants, while 1000 Italians would have 100,000 reflected the sensibility of a man who was committed to his society, and a sensitivity about what his society was all about.[330]

If aesthetics was the central actor in shaping blond racial attitudes, religion played a supporting role. The two are related in the most basic biological sense. Almost 30 percent of the genes in "black" people can be traced to white males having sex with black women during the period of slavery. The protestant religion in a blond country, being democratic, was bound to accommodate the blond aesthetic. There could be two Protestant churches, one black, one white, in a way there could not have been two Catholic churches. Brazil represents a threat to the blonds that Alabama just does not. Alabama represents a threat to blacks that Brazil does not.

The threat that the blond intellectuals saw in the Catholic Church on the intelligence issue however, was not expressed in terms of miscegenation. It was rather the threat that a celibate clergy represented. A Harvard dean suggested that the reason for the low IQ scores in Catholic countries was that the monastic orders and the priesthood had prevented the more intelligent from reproducing.[331]

College texts as recently as the 1940's presented data which showed the median IQ scores of Greeks, Italians and Portuguese at 87.8, 85.8 and 82.7, respectively.[332] Given a white American median IQ of 100, one sees that the difference is about 15 points.

Two Stanford professors state that a 1923 scientific paper included IQ data that established that Italian-Americans have a median IQ of 84, 16 points below the national average. They ask, rhetorically, whether the National Academy should be petitioned to institute a national research project on the intellectual inferiority of Italian-Americans, and whether the hereditarians believe that Italian-Americans have improved genetically in just a couple of generations.[333]

Now, Arthur Jensen has addressed the implications of a 15-point difference in IQ scores at various points in the distribution. Add 15 points to someone with an IQ of 70, and one moves from dependency, and possible institutionalization, to someone who is self-sufficient. Add the 15 points to someone who is average, and one sees someone who can succeed in college.[334]

A difference of 15 points in the IQ scores of two different groups would make some dramatic differences. Jensen focuses on the lower end of the distribution as the most important area of concern. In any population with a mean score of 85, between one-sixth and one-fourth of its members would score below 70, which is about seven times the percentage for the American majority. The American Association on Mental Deficiency has changed part of its definition for mental retardation from two standard deviations to one standard deviation below the mean (which would mean about 85), because of the increased demands modern societies place on the work force.[335]

The Mobility of Italian-Americans

The Other Bostonians: Poverty and Progress in the American Metropolis, 1880-1970[336] is a study of various immigrant groups, including Italians, into the City of Boston during the period 1880 to 1970. The book tracks the progress of original migrants and their children, and then makes comparisons between the different groups. Although the data is restricted to the Boston area, Professor Thernstrom appears to claim that he has identified characteristics which operate in a much larger social universe, and many reviewers appear to accept his claims. The cover carries a quote from the *American Historical Review* that labels the study as the best analysis of social mobility in America. The *New York Times* went beyond that, and called it the best quantitative historical study to be published.

Professor Thernstrom offers an explanation for what he believes he found, which would have national, perhaps international, implications. He stresses that Italians and Irishmen moved ahead economically in a sluggish and erratic fashion. He cites factors that they appear to have brought from Europe for the poor social mobility of Irishmen and Italians. More than readily available measurable European background handicaps were involved; certain features of the cultures the people brought with them were also responsible.[337] Religious affiliation appears to be one, perhaps the major, factor responsible. The parochial school system is an institution that he believes may have contributed toward the creation of a certain alienation from the host society, and dampened ambitions for conventional success.[338]

There are two major mistakes in Thernstrom's work. The first concerns his use of immigrant groups to locate those cultural factors that he clearly associates with success in a modern economy. The second has to do with his use of the term, "mobility."

Thernstrom follows a well-worn path in using data from Northern European immigrant groups to reveal certain features of American society. Further, he has not compared Protestants and Catholics, but immigrant groups representing both religious traditions.

Although he does not pursue it, Thernstrom tells the reader that he is aware of an anomaly. The data clearly indicate that the American migrant into the city of Boston has done better than the native for one hundred years. His samples for 1880, 1910, 1930, and 1960 all show that American migrants into the city were more likely to achieve upper white collar status than the native born. An incredible 32 percent of American migrants into Boston were professionals in 1960, more than double the percentage for non-migrants.[339] There is evidence, then, that the American migrant into the city of Boston, has not been a random sample of the American population, since, if anything, Boston was relatively more white collar, professional and educated than the American population, as a whole.

The process would have been just the reverse for the Catholic immigrant populations. It is a truism that the more able left the city and the ethnic neighborhoods first, for suburbia.

The evidence supports the position that the English immigrant to Boston was like the American migrant, an unusual representative of his culture. The evidence does not support the view that, compared with the majority American Protestant population, Italian Catholic immigrants were at an economic disadvantage.

To pursue the point I will limit the review to two groups: Englishmen and Italians. There are enough similarities between England and Italy in the size and sophistication of the their economies for the comparisons to be useful. Second, their different travel times to their present economies help reveal what the process is all about.

Industrialization involves a number of changes, and the most critical change concerns behavior. The change from an agricultural peasant economy requires that increasing numbers of people develop skills to handle more complicated tasks. There is no doubt that industrial economies develop larger professional and managerial classes as they mature.[340]

Thernstrom data indicates that in 1910 35 percent of the male labor force of Boston was classified as white-collar. Of this group, 5 percent were professionals and 30 percent were other white-collar workers. By 1970, the white-collar category had increased to 51 percent with 21 percent working as professionals, and 30 percent as other white-collar.[341] Thernstrom's data also shows that 53 percent of second generation British men born in the period 1860-1879 were in white collar occupations: 13 percent high white collar and 40 percent low white collar.[342] Now, one can assume that the 1910 data would reflect the occupational status of the native Bostonian born in the period 1860-1879 since they would have been between 30 and 50 years old at the time of the census, long enough to have established themselves as white-collar. We can then draw the following conclusions:

- The sons of British immigrants were over 50 percent more likely to be white-collar workers than Bostonians as a group in 1910.

- Indeed, the British immigrant's son born about 100 years ago and entering the work force before or around the turn of the century was more likely to have achieved white-collar status than the average Bostonian in 1970.[343]

While Thernstrom says that the data used for the norm of the Boston work force in 1910 and 1970 is different in some respects to his other data, the disparity is so large, it simply has to call attention to the British sample. What can explain the totally disparate level of achievement of British immigrants, compared with native white Americans? National per capita income figures show that England has a lower per capita income than America for most of the century. This should suggest a proportionally smaller technical and professional class.

While the two economies may have been more equal in 1900 than they are now, certainly 53 percent of Englishmen born in the period 1860-1879 did not become white-collar workers in England. It is clear that Boston has continued to attract a very unusual English immigrant throughout the 20th century.

Thernstrom presents an "Index of Representation" to show the proportion of different immigrant groups in various occupational categories compared to the proportion of the entire labor force of the City of Boston in the same category. Male British immigrants, 45 or older in 1950, were only 43 percent as likely to be unskilled workers, as chance would indicate.[344] The score for Italian immigrants of the same age was 273 percent. Second generation British men in the 25-44 age category were somewhat more likely than their fathers to be unskilled laborers, but their score of 61 percent was still far below the norm,[345] What Thernstrom found for British immigrants, is true nationally. The lifetime earnings of British immigrants to the United States are about 20 percent higher than natives.[346]

Data from Canada support this analysis. Canada has a per capita advantage over England. But the same anomaly that characterized the record of English immigrants in Boston followed them in Canada. The post-war Canadian immigrants from the United Kingdom represented the immigrants with the smallest proportion with a below average educational background.[347] Approximately half of post war British immigrants enjoyed white-collar status, and the group as a whole was remarkably different from other immigrant groups in that they contained very few unskilled workers, and they were unlikely to come from families where the father had a low status job.[348] One researcher concludes that lower working class Englishmen did not immigrate to Canada.[349]

White-collar positions are quite often filled through informal contacts. Certainly an immigrant group which can equal or surpass the host populations in cities like Boston, Vancouver or Toronto must be gifted. However, English immigrants simply do not constitute a reasonable sample to form the basis for generalizations about religious or cultural factors within an American setting.

Thernstrom's use of the term "mobility" consistently favors arguments that reinforce his perception that Catholics are low achievers. The children of British immigrants, like their parents, were only about half as likely to be in the unskilled group as the Boston native. By contrast the Italian participation which had been almost three times the norm for the immigrants had been reduced to 131 percent for their children, not much different than the city norm. And the city of Boston, without unskilled agricultural labor, is certainly more skilled than the U.S. average. Certainly this means that Italian unskilled workers were much more mobile than the national sample of unskilled laborers of native descent, who would have been Protestant. No national economy reduces its unskilled work force by over half in a single generation.

It is interesting that Thernstrom deals with Lipset's and Bendix' study which found no difference in the occupational mobility of Catholics and Protestants with the observation that since more Catholics have been raised in big cities where there were more professional positions, they should have been much more mobile than Protestants.[350] If the issue is mobility, however, and not simply percentages, there are clearly powerful economic forces which should favor Protestant mobility. By all accounts the South and West are growing more rapidly than the Northeast and should be developing their professional and managerial sectors faster than the heavily Catholic cities. Moreover, to the extent Thernstrom is right when he notes that the development of truly large cities of over three million is associated with a higher percentage in the professional and managerial categories, the rate of development of such cities should work to the advantage of the Protestants.[351] To be sure, there may still be more professional positions in the North as a percentage of the total work force. However, in order for this to benefit Catholic mobility the Catholics would have to take the positions, from Protestants, since the total professional pool is not growing as fast as in the Protestant sectors of the country.

Given a large enough city, one can see the dynamism of the adjustment to industrialization within Italian populations in the same city. In Bensonhurst, a traditional little Italy in New York, one-fifth of the population is 65 or over and more than 10 percent of women workers are blue collar. In South Richmond, on Staten Island, where over one-half the population is Italian, less than 8 percent of the population is 65 or over, and less than 2 percent are blue collar.[352]

Thernstrom's data indicates that there was a much higher degree of mobility by Italians in Boston than his comments suggest. Italians were the most overrepresented to the non-English speaking immigrants in the very lowest occupational category, unskilled labor. Yet we have seen that in a single generation they nearly reduced their participation in that category to the city-wide norm. While it may represent a dramatic change in some particulars, it occurs at a social level which is really not of interest to most academicians. Their underlying assumption is that white Protestant America is upper-middle class. Accordingly, Thernstrom merely notes that Italians moved up a notch without attempting to analyze what really happened.

Someone who attempts to account for what happened within the confines of the IQ theory, however, sees a puzzling problem. In order for Italians to have lowered their representation in the very lowest unskilled labor cohort so dramatically, they greatly outperformed the native white population in the same labor category.

Now, IQ psychologists maintain that the argument for the genetic basis of the IQ score is inextricably tied to the bell curve. "Intelligence" follows a certain distribution. Why did Thernstrom not find that Italians made fairly rapid advance into white-collar occupations? He did but his terminology blurred the reality.

Thernstrom's use of words like "rate" and "trajectory" is as misleading as his use of "mobility." For example, he notes that only 10 percent of Italian men employed in Boston in 1910 held white-collar jobs, approximately the same as the Irish 20 years earlier (12 percent). In 1910 65 percent of the Italians were unskilled or semiskilled workers, again, the same percentage as the Irish in 1890.[353] Thernstrom then notes that Italian immigrants increased their representation in the middle class from 12 to 35 percent during a generation, while British immigrants of an earlier period, had enlarged their representation in the white-collar world from an already large 26 percent, to 53 percent. The text suggests that the mobility of the Italians was less than that of the British, but the figures indicate the reverse. The British doubled their representation in white collars while the Italians tripled their membership. The success of the Italians in putting about a third of its members in white-collars within a single generation suggest a very rapid acculturation when one realizes that in 1940, when practically everyone in the 1910 sample would have achieved his final occupational level, only 39 percent of the male labor force of Boston wore white collars.[354]

Thernstrom's confusion on mobility is even more obvious when he applies the concept to the achievements of the sons of the original immigrants. Only 18 percent of first generation Italian men 45 or older were white-collar workers in 1950, compared with 52 percent of first generation British immigrants. Second generation Italian men in the 25 – 44 age bracket (the "sons" of the older group) had increased their representation in the white-collar category to 31 percent, while the second generation British figure remained roughly the same at 49 percent.[355] Yet Thernstrom suggests that Italians made slow progress between generations compared to Englishmen.

Thernstrom mistakenly assumes that he found that Catholics had a low oc-cupational mobility because he began his research with preconceived notions about Catholics. While he is skeptical about Greeley's findings, he enthusias-tically embraces Herbert J. Gans' *The Urban Villagers: Group and Class in the Life of Italian Americans,*[356] which contains very little data. Gans' report on Ital-ians' attitude toward work could not be clearer. They do not like the stuff: It leads to ulcers, heart trouble, and early death.[357] They would find tough sled-ding in the future as automation decreases employment opportunities in sim-pler jobs. However, they will be able to sustain tough times because their ethnic and cultural background allows them to accept job loss and unemployment as inevitable.[358] This sounds something like Jensen's prediction that the most se-rious problems associated with an IQ deficiency will be found at the lower end of the distribution. As work becomes more demanding, there will be increasing numbers who will be able to find any employment.

One should find then that the unemployment rate among Italians is higher than that of the majority. What if one does not find that? How one locates an "attitude" toward work by different ethnic groups is a very difficult matter. The blonds have, for a very long time, had an appreciable advantage in per capita wealth over most of the planet. But did that reflect an attitude about work or something different?

In English speaking Australia, the host population found a very different attitude about work among Italian immigrants than Gans found. A Committee of Enquiry established in 1931 by the Australian government caused some alarm precisely because the Italians worked hard. In spite of government sanctioned preferences in favor of blond Australians, farms were passing to Italian owners. The problem appeared to be that the Italians would put in longer hours than the host population. "We found impartial northern Queenslanders genuinely alarmed at the steady Italian penetration, which is still in progress. The Italian works harder and for longer hours than the British Australian."[359]

As I noted, there is a literature that finds that Italians made a rapid economic acculturation. A European sociologist writing about Italians in Montreal found a high commitment to work. Almost half of his sample had been small farmers or agricultural laborers in Italy. But through extremely hard work they were able to dramatically improve their position. "Thus, while only 14 per cent of the immigrant generation work in white-collar occupations, 57 per cent of the second and third generation Italians do. This is a striking commentary on the social mobility of persons of Italian descent."[360]

College age Italian Americans should probably read some of the literature about them with a certain amount of skepticism. It has only been in recent years that scholars of Italian American background, and other turn of the century Catholic immigrant groups, have begun to describe themselves in the academic press.

I have a kind of litmus test to determine whether the anthropologist or sociologist was actually looking for information about Italians, or was "reporting back" to the host culture what the blonds thought they knew anyway. The test is how the report deals with savings.

If there is one hard, objective, numerical economic generalization one can make about Italians, it is that they can save money. At every level of income, Italians can be characterized as savers; often saving much more than their neighbors, whether at home in Italy,[361] in Protestant Australia,[362] Catholic French Canada,[363] the United States,[364] Argentina,[365] and Brazil.[366] While I disagree with some of Samuel L. Bailey conclusions, his data confirm the ability of Italian immigrants to save money.

The most telling evidence in the blond Protestant academic canon that the anthropologist had pre-judged Italian immigrants is in William Foote Whyte's classic Street Corner Society[367] discussion of savings. He finds an enthusiasm for gambling that periodically allows for display and popularity, but finally must prove harmful.[368] He thinks that he has evidence that Italians share an inability to appreciate money and the centrality of its importance in the modern world, and a willingness to sacrifice the steady day by day discipline of savings for a momentary increase in status on the corner.[369]

Gans' description of Italians attitude toward savings is predictably similar: The Italians' need for display destroyed their ability to save and eventually purchase their own homes.[370]

Even though Italians had one of the lowest family incomes in New York City in the early 20th century, of the groups studied they had the lowest percentage of households with a budget deficit, and the one with the highest budget surplus. The director of the 1909 study concluded that while Americans, Germans and Irish did not save until they had yearly incomes in the $900 or $1,000 range, Italians and some other southern and eastern European groups began saving at $700 or $800 levels.[371] After spending some time on this issue I am convinced that there are no objective studies that suggest Italian Catholics save less money at various income levels than blond Protestants.

Perhaps locating "attitudes" about work and savings make a simple story unduly complex. Assume that one finds that Italians go from having a per capita income of about a fourth of England's, to roughly the same as England's; or the Japanese from one-half of the U.S. norm to about the same as the U.S., in just two generations. Have attitudes changed? Or did something very simple, and very easy to measure, occur?

The Mobility of Italian-Americans: A Sociobiological Analysis

Apart from the issue of comparisons between Italian and English immigrants, the curious close similarities between the Italian experience and the history of the Irish in Boston demonstrate the hard biological ledge beneath the reality the sociologists see and report. On virtually every social and educational measure: Appearance, linguistic background, family structure, size, familiarity with the host Protestant population, independence of women; there was simply no comparison between the two groups. Italians were "foreigners" in a way the Irish never were. The fact that second generation Italians were reflecting roughly the same occupational and income experience as the Irish, about 20 years earlier, when they were second generation, points to something about the shift from an agricultural to an industrial society which has its own integrity, its own potency, operates across ethnic boundaries, ignores class, and is not much affected by the collection of qualities usually bundled under the label "cultural." Something is moving people around the chessboard.

I know of no study that claims to have reliably compared the intellectual potential of whole nations. Such a study may be impossible since language and behavioral experiences are so different across ethnic boundaries. Nevertheless there is some evidence that suggests that the IQ distribution for Italians is not much different than for the white American majority.

There is a close correlation between the IQ test and several other types of examinations that have been used to predict occupational and educational achievement. Practically everyone in America takes one or more such exam during his or her educational and working lives. Because the tests are often administered to groups under less than optimal conditions by non-psychologists, a score for any particular child may not be as good an indicator for that child's ability as a score on an individually administered test. Nevertheless, when one compares the performance of very large groups, one might assume that imperfections would creep in randomly and that mean scores of the groups would be more or less accurate.

In the 1960's the International Association for the Evaluation of Educational Achievement began a study of reading comprehension which included England, the United States, Italy and twelve other countries.[372] It would not be possible to make fine comparisons of national intelligence from the survey. Some countries have wealthier, and superior school systems. Some languages may allow for more precise and more difficult distinctions, in different areas. Also, different percentages of the total age cohort were in school systems. Still, the report itself suggests that large differences in ability would have been found, had they existed. The differences among the industrialized countries were small and somewhat inconsistent from age level to age level.[373] There was a report in the academic press which does not address the issue of Italian intelligence directly, but does present data which indicates that the IQ of Italian children in the study did not differ significantly from the U.S. or English average.[374]

Recent economic history shows a more decisive break with the 18th 19th and early 20th century experience than most intellectuals realize. It is interesting that both Greeley and Thernstrom make respectful nods to Weber's thesis of the Protestant ethic. Greeley notes that Weber himself was dubious whether the differences in economic wealth between Catholics and Protestants would survive a lengthy period of industrialization.[375] Thernstrom states that while the attacks on the thesis in America have been heavy, he does not find them persuasive.[376]

The place to examine the theory is not America, however, but where it was promulgated: Europe. While it may seem strange today, there was a voluminous literature in the nineteenth and early twentieth centuries that assumed that the British were the highest representatives of capitalists as financiers, engineers, organizers, and merchants. An American geography text in 1933 reported that the British had a higher per-capita wealth than any population in the world outside of North America.[377] A careful analysis might have revealed some problems in the productivity trends of the British economy; certainly the impression that the English enjoyed some innate superiority in dealing with an industrialized order was understandable enough. They had enjoyed a sizeable advantage in consumption since they gave birth to industrialization. Catholic Southern and Eastern Europe remained backward and poor for a very long time. Weber's thesis must have simply put an academic stamp on what most people already knew.

In fact, however, Europeans had known something about the English and the blonds generally, for a long, long time prior to industrialization. It may be anyone's guess when a really substantial advantage in living standards was established, but there is anecdotal non-quantitative literature that would locate the advantage generations, centuries even, and prior to industrialization.[378] Adam Smith, writing around the time of the American Revolution, in the last quarter of the 18th century, favored a tariff for England to protect her work force from imports made by cheap foreign labor.[379]

There can be no doubt that by 1900, after approximately a century and a half of industrialization, England had an overwhelming economic advantage over Italy. One estimate placed the United Kingdom's share of world manufacturing output at 18.5 percent, while Italy's share was 2.5 percent; and the Italian per capita level of industrialization was about one-eighth of the U.K.[380] By 1914 per capita income in Italy was only 45 percent of Britain's.[381]

But by the 1950's a change was becoming visible which would make a dramatic difference in the long-standing ratio between the living standards of the average Englishman, and the average Italian. A study of over 100 industries in different nations estimated that real per capita compound annual growth in Italy's GDP from 1950 to 1987 was 3.9 percent in Italy, and 2.2 percent in the United Kingdom.[382] By 1968 the Italian per capita GNP was about two thirds of the U.K. figure.[383] Wages and benefits in Italy were approximately equal to Britain's in the late 1980's,[384] and the CIA reported that by 1988 the Italian and British GNP were virtually identical.[385] One commentator opined that Italy had a higher standard of living than Britain,[386] which may or may not be the case. While there continues to be a division in consumption between the Italian north and south, it would be a mistake to exaggerate the matter. The two sections have traveled in tandem. The ratio of the South to the North in yearly per-capita income was about 60 to 70 percent in the 1980's.[387] While large, the difference is not much different than the ratio between the northern Atlantic states in the United States, and many Southern states; a ratio which has also remained reasonably stable across generations.

It is clear that a tremendous advantage that Britain had enjoyed for centuries essentially ended in the last half of the twentieth century. Certainly there were institutional political "environmental" forces which played a role in the change. The most obvious and dramatic difference between the economic policies of the Italian and British governments dealt with the Common Market.

The difference in the way the two populations received the Common Market surely reflected the difference in the ways the respective populations felt about Roman Catholicism and Catholic Europe at a very basic visceral level. The city which was chosen to identify the initial treaty in the evolution that led to an economically integrated Europe, Rome, was probably indispensable in bringing together the two peoples which would be responsible for the market succeeding or failing: French and German. Rome may not have been able to play this role if a heavily Protestant East Germany had been part of the equation at the time.

England, predictably, was not enthusiastic about the market, and tried, over a number of years to find alternative trading structures to join. But, in retrospect, one sees that the alternatives the U.K. tried just could not have worked. On the continent, a few miles away, an enormous economic reality was coming into existence.

However, basically, the change that allowed Italians for all practical purposes to catch up with England was not a trading arrangement. The change that enabled Italians to consume as much as Englishmen in Europe was the same change that enabled the children of Italian immigrants to earn as much as the white average in America.

When one compares the economic history of Italian immigrants and their offspring in America with the census population that most closely represents the IQ distribution for the American white norm, one sees the same behavioral change that occurred in Europe. The reason for the disparity between Greeley and Thernstrom becomes immediately visible. The population category that reflects the white American IQ distribution is "native white of native parent."

The Bureau of the Census has published data on various groups indicating occupational distribution, education, unemployment rate, entrepreneurial activity, rate of institutionalization, income and percentage living in poverty. Table 1 and Table 2 at the end of this chapter compare first and second generation Italians with native born white Americans for 1970, roughly the time of Thernstrom's study. Table 1 assumes that the native whites of native parents in the 25 to 44 year old cohort are children of people included in the 45 to 64 year old cohort. Similarly, Table 2 assumes that foreign born Italians in the 45 to 64 year old cohort are parents of the population listed as American born ethnic Italians of foreign or mixed parentage in the 25 to 44 age cohort. While these assumptions are obviously not true in each instance, the 20-year difference should enable us to spot major changes between the generations. Thernstrom uses a very similar procedure to buttress his findings, although he restricts his sample to immigrant groups in the Boston area.[388]

Behaviorism plays a large role in explaining the activities of populations in centuries old agricultural villages of a few thousand souls, but when it is time to explain what happens to populations that encounter industrialization, behaviorism must be wrong. If one looks at the tables with the background noise turned off, what is really striking is the "orderliness" of it all.

The key is the change in the locus of the experiments. If the experiment is conducted in the modern city, instead of the pre-modern agricultural village, one sees a curious fit between people, and school. On the narrow issue of economics, it is virtually certain that by the second generation transfer payments move funds from ethnic Italians to native born whites of native born parents.

There are probes in the domestic U.S. that are analogues for international reading scores: They can substitute as kind of IQ tests for certain large populations. The Armed Forces Qualification Test (AFQT) was given nationally to over a million potential white servicemen. While the AFQT is not precisely an IQ test, its correlation with standard IQ test is about as high as the correlation among the various tests.[389] Rhode Island is emphatically a state with a non-British, non-Protestant stock. A majority of the state was either foreign born, or the children of immigrants as recently as 1910.[390] It is the most Catholic State in the union, has a majority Catholic population, and Italians may be as much as one fifth of the total population.[391] In 1968, the last year for which data is available, Rhode Island had the highest pass rate of any state in the continental United States. Jensen suggests that the sample is good enough to indicate that the mean IQ of white Rhode Islanders is somewhat above the national white average.[392]

By 1968 the overwhelming majority of Italian, Irish and French Canadian (a Catholic population heavily represented in Rhode Island) youngsters registering for military service, had grown up speaking English. It was very different from the situation that had prevailed in the first third of the century.

I sent an earlier version of this paper to Dr. Eysenck, and he was gracious enough to respond. A copy of his letter is attached as an appendix at the end of this book.

For some reason the two Stanford professors cited did not pursue Pintner's writing on Italian-Americans. They clearly left the impression that Pintner was comfortable with the conclusion that there was about a 16 point difference between the white average and Italian Americans. When one actually looks at what Pintner wrote, one has a very different impression. He pointed out that Italians scored much better on non-verbal IQ tests, and discounted the notion that there could be a 16 point difference between them and the majority.[393] Indeed, some of the test results he presents seem to indicate that Italians were performing at national norms. In a 1923 paper he characterizes the difference between the Italians and the national average on non verbal tests as "not very great."[394] One wonders whether the place where the sample was taken would have made a bigger difference than Pintner suggests. He notes that, for native-born Americans, IQ scores from urban groups were higher than for rural ones, and scores of children from the largest cities were about 10 points above scores of children from the smallest.[395]

Psychologists have attempted a finer grained analysis of the country versus city deficit, by dividing the country children into two groups: those living in a district where the land was hilly and the soil inferior, and those in districts with good soil. In the poorer areas only about 20 percent scored above the median for the city pupils, versus 36 percent for the children from the superior farm areas.[396] The authors interpreted the results to show that the more intelligent farmer would find the greater opportunity. Whatever the merits of the conclusion, the data reveals striking difference between the rural and urban child, among native born whites. Again, this demonstrates that test results that compared Italian youngsters with urban white Americans students, rather than the native born whites as a whole, dramatically overstate the American norm. The states that performed the worst on the AFQT were states that are heavily white rural and protestant.

Certain psychologists recognized this at a very early stage in the development of IQ tests. As early as 1926, some psychologists used Armed Force data as indicia that the blonds did not have the dramatic IQ advantage that the majority apparently believed. They pointed out that states with heavy representation of Southern Europeans were scoring higher than many states of the Old Confederacy.[397]

Mexican-American youngsters in the American Southwest may represent a parallel to Italian children in the Northeast three of four generations ago. The children do poorly in verbal tests, but their scores on IQ tests utilizing drawings or designs were not much different from the white American norm. The fact that Spanish as well as English was spoken in over 80 percent of the Mexican-American homes was largely responsible for low scores on the language tests.[398] In Toronto very similar results were obtained from tests of children of Italian immigrants. They did poorly on tests that relied on language skills, but their mean score fit within parameters established by Canadians of other European ancestry on the more culture free tests.[399] While language tests may be the preferred type of IQ test for certain purposes, they present an obvious problem to children from households that do not speak the test language well.

There is a parsimonious explanation consistent with IQ theory which can account for the fact that second generation unskilled Italians left the unskilled work force much faster than their age cohort among native born whites, for the advantages that English born immigrants maintained over their American born cousins, and for the fact that Italy has basically reached parity with the British economy. Greeley is more right than Thernstrom, but he is not convincing when he attempts to use economic statistics to locate psychological types, albeit somewhat at odds with Weber's analysis.

The great economic advantage that the blonds, particularly Englishmen, enjoyed for centuries was primarily due to behavioral differences. A very wealthy agricultural society from the beginning, it became differentiated along educational dimensions very early.

Until the very recent past Englishmen and Italians lived within very different behavioral/economic systems. In 1904 one observer claimed that 85 percent of

Italian immigrants to America had been peasants in Italy.[400] A source from 1911 stated that 67 percent had engaged in agricultural labor in Italy.[401] Immigration records of the United States Government indicate that the occupational distribution of Italian immigrants who gave Louisiana as their ultimate destination during the period 1899-1903 was as follows: 33.7 percent were farmers or farm laborers, 12.5 percent were laborers, and 36.4 percent (including women and children) had no occupation.[402] Those listed as having no occupation probably spent at least part of the time doing unskilled agricultural labor. The figures not only indicate that Italian emigrants were agricultural workers; they suggest the nature of the society the emigrant left behind.

Danilo Dolci states that in 1953 47.7 percent of Sicilian breadwinners were agricultural workers.[403] A Danish sociologist writing in 1965 reported that about 29 percent of the Italian labor force were engaged in agriculture versus only about 5 percent for Great Britain.[404] Indeed one text states that only about 7 percent of the British labor force were engaged in agriculture as far back as the 1930's.[405]

An Italian publication reported that in 1963 about 38 percent of employed workers in the Italian South were engaged in agriculture. Over the next 20 years the percentage of the Southern workforce engaged in agriculture was cut in half to about 20 percent. This was about the percentage that had been engaged in agriculture in the Center/North in the early 1960's. Between 1950 and 1985 the average per capita productivity tripled in the South.[406]

By 1983 the percentage of the Italian work force in agriculture had been reduced to 15 percent.[407] The change was accompanied by a dramatic improvement in living standards. By the late 1980's economically Italy had roughly caught up with Great Britain. While the history, in certain particulars, is a specifically Italian story, the theme is general. Removing agricultural labor from the national work force, via a school system is an economic improvement, always.

Weber's analysis is pre-IQ. That is its great handicap. I believe that emigrants from backward agricultural villages probably do carry a mindset into the industrialized world that is a handicap. The overwhelming thrust of the data, however, is that if the IQ scores are roughly comparable with the host population, it does not much matter.

Peasants from agricultural villages moving into the great urban slums that inevitably accompany industrialization are forced to perform at that seam between the behavioral monotone of the agricultural village, and the relentlessly differentiating city. What happened within the population of Italian immigrants to the U.S. has to happen within every large, newly industrialized work force. In a nutshell, the kid that can do more does more, and he gets paid for it There is no way to subject this hypothesis to an experimental analysis, but if economic figures continue to show that certain national economies, particularly in Asia, gain ground on Britain or the U.S., it is inevitable that it will attract attention.

Baily posits a kind of continuum representing Italian adjustment with Buenos Aires at one end, New York and Toronto at the other, and San Francisco and Sao Paulo in intermediate positions. In a sense five different stories.[408] Certainly one thinks that on the social level there is something to it. Like most minorities, Italians probably live in a somewhat limited social universe in Toronto, exhibiting a more or less defensive style. But on economic issues, my position is that there is only one big story, a story that is at the heart of economic development generally, and, in an intense and dangerous way, at the heart of nuclear weapons.

That is, even if Toronto is more different than Italy than Argentina or San Francisco the larger economic reality should not be much different if the playing field is more or less fair. I sent an earlier version of the paper to Professor A. H. Richmond, one of Canada's most recognized authorities on European immigration, and he too graciously replied. His response is included as an appendix.

What one has then is a dispute among academicians concerning Italian economic advance. Thernstrom and Gans report slow advance; Boissevain, Greeley and Richmond find an impressive ability to play the economic game; and Baily suggests that "it depends."

I am proposing a model of economic development that utilizes the data that indicates IQ scores follow a more or less normal distribution. A schematic representation of the difference would show agricultural societies by a behavioral curve that is skewed to the left against a normal distribution. The tasks are simple and do not tap the mental abilities of most of the work force. Industrialization tests the intelligence of the population in a new way. It pushes the behavioral reality to a closer fit with the IQ distribution.

No one else is saying this. Everyone else is wrong.

Besides being original the concept has some advantages over traditional accounts which make use of "class" or "culture." It is consistent with a great deal of IQ data and it can be disproved. Agricultural workers are moving into industrializing urban centers around the globe. If the theory is right, the children of the newly arrived peasantry should be more mobile than the host population, everywhere. Differentiation is the behavioral spine of the modernization process.

The theory could also account for the fact that British immigrants were more successful than native white Americans. Workers in industrialized countries have had an opportunity to realistically assess their abilities. After nine or ten years of education, most people probably have a sense of the kind of work they could do. People who are factory workers in England, and do not think that they could do much more in the U.S., stay home. They are aware of their strengths and weaknesses, and have a certain degree of affluence. Peasants in backward agricultural villages are faced with a very different option. Anyone who can leave does.

Now, to be fair to Thernstrom, his method of identifying economic performance is the accepted norm of labor economics. One identifies various ethnic groups, makes comparisons across these groups within middle age cohorts, and identifies more and less productive groups.

Professor George Borjas of Harvard University, identified as America's leading economist on immigration issues[409] presents data showing that between 1940 and 1979, the typical immigrant went from having more education than the typical native, to having less.[410] Similar trends are found with labor force participation, unemployment rates, and earnings. He abstracts various economic data such as income inequality and skill levels in source country to provide a functional explanation for the lower economic performance in the U.S. But income inequality is not a variable that can be separated from behavioral issues. Tremendous inequality is inherent in a country compressed into three classes: peasants, administrators and owners. The only possible avenue of change leads through the 11th grade, which is to say the peasantry disappears into the urban slum. There will still be income inequality, but there will also be the beginning stirrings of an educated middle class.

For some, that trip to the city takes place across an ethnic seam. They emigrate. It is bound to cause some problems for the relatively unskilled native. Intuition and data point to the same conclusion. The immigration pattern of the 1980's, which saw the foreign born share of the U.S. work force move from 6.9 percent to 9.3 percent in 1988, created disproportional competitive burdens for Americans who were already struggling to hold their own.[411]

Borjas presents a model that identifies the quality of immigrant as a function of how certain data of the host country match up with data of the U.S. The "quality" issue is a matter of positioning the immigrant in the upper or lower tail of his native country. He says that the U.S. insures a poor result in its immigration policies because it insures the poorly paid and low skilled worker against disasters, while it taxes highly skilled professionals.[412]

The argument may be more misleading than helpful. The fundamental issue is not income inequality, political freedom or ethnicity, but behavior. Income distribution in a peasant society is not related to political equality: It is an unbundled feature of the behavioral monotone. My response to Borjas is that the income distribution of a source area can not perform the discriminatory function he assumes it performs, if the population has not been in the 11th grade, or in the 11th grade long enough. The conclusion that the immigrants will remain a permanent disproportional burden is not warranted. The children of that immigration cohort may become as productive, which is to say as differentiated, as the native population.

Parsimony is the test arena. Does the theory handle the data with a simpler theoretical structure?

The U.S. share of world production is a place to test the theory. There is no doubt that the American/Great Britain share of the world economy shrunk in the second half of the 20th century, while the share of newer industrialized states, particularly East Asian states, increased. According to one estimate, between 1950 and 1992 the Japanese share of world gross economic product went from slightly over 3 percent to 8 percent. In 1950 the West created about 64 percent of the world's economic product; in the 1980's the percentage had shrunk to 49 percent. By 2013 the share will have decreased to 30 percent.[413]

Lester Thurow sees the wage pressure on that portion of the American work force with low skills as an inevitable result of "factor price equalization." Very large international trade flows have forced the American worker to compete with the foreign worker.[414] Unskilled American workers began the 1980's with wages far above the unskilled foreign worker. Competition forced wages for unskilled Americans toward a more appropriate alignment. Practically all of the U.S. improvement in GNP in the 1980's went to the top one-third of the work force.

Thurow does not treat IQ data, but clearly it is germane to the discussion. As more foreign workers leave peasant villages, and join the industrial work force, the pressure on wages for the low skilled work that that former peasant can do must increase.

The American unskilled laborer was receiving wages above what he "deserved" in a competitive market place, because the skilled American engineer was giving the American worker an opportunity to be the first low skill participant in an activity which was far more productive than agricultural labor. That protected status can not continue, once foreign peasants, with more or less equal IQ levels, are brought into an industrialized economy.

Thurow suggests that recent trends in technological development and test data reflect that Americans are not smarter than other populations. He tells us that when the rest of the globe puts in more effort, it receives higher returns.[415] But effort is really a peripheral issue. The important question is the locus of the effort. Effort expended in maintaining a peasant-based agriculture can not measurably alter wages, consumption or technology. It can only hide a potential. While traditional economics accounts for development changes through "sectors," learning operates throughout every economy, all the time.

It is not helpful to approach agriculture as just another sector for economies that have 60 or 70 percent of the work force in the direct production of food. A true peasantry behaves as a member of a system within separate villages, outside the reach of the national government. The central governments of most peasant-based societies played a much smaller role inside the village than the blond critics thought. The central government can create a new economy only where it can force the village to support a school.

The school and the slum are not enemies of agriculture: They are the places where the village is converted and rationalized: The man with a shovel, writ large, has to consume like a man with a shovel. A handful of intellectuals and idealists can not deliver a modern living standard to millions of men armed with only shovels.

Economists who call the peasant condition "poverty" miss the reality of the system: The controls at the heart of that condition maintain the balance, and keep true poverty, that murderous year, at bay. The industrial worker or intellectual, experiencing a recession, or even a depression, has experience and abstraction available to him. He knows something is going wrong. The peasant, faced with the bad year, has no such awareness. He has been through these before. The verities got them through before, they will work again. And, often enough, they do.

I suspect most intellectuals would be surprised how many European nations have experienced the same development changes as Italy. Between 1965 and 1993 the European farm population was halved.[416] Between 1950 and 1972 the proportion of the Soviet population classified as urban, went from 39 to 59 percent.[417]

The migration of agricultural workers to the major cities of South America has been well publicized in the past few years, but the movement has a long history. Japanese immigrants told their children to leave the farm and the agricultural life, for life in the city and opportunity, decades ago.[418] In Canada, the fact that the French province has more or less reached economic parity with the mid-point of English speaking Canada reflects a very large, and mostly unexamined change. An industrialized Quebec is a very different part of the mix than it was when it was overwhelmingly rural and agricultural.[419]

I argue that the move from the peasantry to the urban slum must always involve the differentiating effect that the IQ distribution demands, but that the move also vastly improves the material lives of everyone involved. Consumption issues for very large populations must involve productivity issues for the same population.

One wonders when it was that people first thought that a society could consume what it could not produce. One wonders when it was that people first made the assumptions that because people have some power to manipulate the environment, they have all the power they need to manipulate their society.

Theodore Parker's celebrated sermon in 1846, A Sermon on the Perishing Classes in Boston,[420] concerned the Irish and may have been the earliest attempt by an intellectual to grapple with the problems posed by the entry of a non-Protestant peasantry into an industrializing America. His observations would fit comfortably on the op-ed page of the Boston Globe today. Among the points: Any society that can engineer a canal system to harness the power of the mighty Merrimack River could certainly prevent poverty and delinquent behavior. A nation that could expand across a continent could abolish crime, intemperance, and pauperism.

Between June 9, 1845, and June 2, 1846, over 1200 people were committed to the house of correction: one of every fifty-six residents of Boston over the age of 10. Education would be the answer. If Catholics would not attend public schools, perhaps it would be possible to for them to have separate schools, as was done for the Africans.

Now, Parker was addressing the problems presented by the first great wave of foreign agricultural workers to enter America. And he was fairly sympathetic. Still, he did not see what no one could have seen without IQ data. If some of the Irish had problems, some of the Irish were very, very smart, and were going to do very, very well. And there would be a population in the middle.

TABLE 1		
Native White Males of Native Parents		
Age in Years	45–64	25–44
% Classified as Professional, Technical Managerial & Administrative	27.1	31.0
Median School years completed	11.4	12.5
% Unemployed	2.6	2.7
%Self employed workers	15.2	8.8
% Institutionalized	1.1	.93
Family Income of Native White Population of Native Parents		
Median income	$11,149	$10,559
% Below Poverty Level	6.8	7.3

Source: U.S. Bureau of the Census, 1970, *National Origin and Language.*

TABLE 2		
Italian Males		
Origin	**Foreign born**	**Native, foreign or mixed parents**
Age in Years	45–64	25–44
% Classified as Professional, Technical Managerial & Administrative	15.1	31.8
Median School years completed	8.4	12.4
% Unemployed	3.3	2.4
%Self employed workers	13.6	9.7
% Institutionalized	.45	.51
Family Income of Italian-Americans		
Median income	$11,360	$11,832
% Below Poverty Level	4.6	4.6

Source: U.S. Bureau of the Census, 1970, *National Origin and Language.*

Appendix A

University of London
British Postgraduate Medical Federation   INSTITUTE OF PSYCHIATRY
The Bethlehem Royal Hoapital   De Crespigny Park
          and   Denmark Hill
The Maudsley Hospital   LONDON SE5 8AF
                                                              01-703-5411

DEPARTMENT OF PSYCHOLOGY
Professor H.J. Eysenck Ph.D, D.Sc.

Mr. R. Peppe
5 Ray Street
Manchester, NH   5th May 1975

Dear Mr. Peppe,

Thank you for your interesting letter of April and the enclosed data. I think the problems you have are not problems for the theory at all, and the findings could have been predicted from genetic theory. The phenomenon of regression to the mean ensures that even if you start out with a specially selected low scoring sub-population, future generations resulting from an inter-breeding of this sub-population will regress more and more to the mean of the total population which one imagines would be 100 for Italians, Greeks, etc. *

I discuss the problem of regression in my book The Measurement of Intelligence in some detail; I think it is a most fascinating and intriguing aspect of the theory and one that is not widely known or well understood. If this explanation does not satisfy you perhaps you could write to me again.

With best wishes,

Yours sincerely,

H.J. Eysenck

---

* Author's Note: Sentence not pertaining to Italians deleted.

Appendix B

INSTITUTE FOR BEHAVIOURAL RESEARCH
SURVEY RESEARCH CENTRE
667-3022 Area Code 416

YORK
University
4700 Keele Street,
Downsview, Ontario M3J 1P3

December 4, 1980

Mr. Richard R. Peppe 25 Birch Street Derry, New Hampshire U.S.A.
03038

Dear Mr. Peppe:

Thank you for sending me a copy of your article on "Italian Emigration and Economic Productivity". I find your conclusions interesting and in no way incompatible with the Canadian experience of immigration from Italy and other southern European countries.

I enclose a reprint of a recent article which may be of interest to you.* You would find further relevant materials in the following publications:

A. H. Richmond and W. E. Kalbach, <u>Factors in the Adjustment of Immigrants and their Descendants</u> (Ottawa Statistics Canada 1980).

A. H. Richmond, <u>Ethnic Variation in Family Income and Poverty in Canada</u> (Toronto: York University, Ethnic Research Program, 1978).

I hope you will find these materials useful.

A.H. Richmond
Director
York-IBR

---

* Anthony H. Richmond and Ravi P. Verma, "Income Inequality in Canada: Ethnic and Generational Aspects," *Canadian Studies in Population* 5, 1978.

—— 4 ——

The Blond Invasion of Asia

> The Queen did not respond, while Palmerston
> was not one to hear sermons from a China-
> man.
>
> Walter A. McDougall[421]

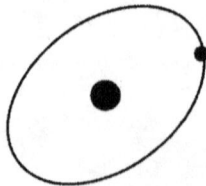

The first interesting issue is to see how the blonds fit with the development of the communist bureaucracy. Was it a creation of an elite from an undifferentiated peasantry that had been educated by the blonds, and then turned on the blonds? Or was it the evolution of a class that had long predated the blond assault, and had, bureaucrat by bureaucrat, indignity by indignity, formed a coherent political movement to do many things, among them, keep the blonds out?

How important a role will the blonds play in future histories of Japan and China? Assume that I am right about the centrality of the 11th grade and that the 11th grade would never have been introduced into the traditional peasant village without a central authority with enough force to shove a school system down the peasant's throat. Given the reality that bureaucrats, democratic or not, are educated people, it was inevitable that a modernizing central bureaucracy would introduce education into the wider population.

Were nuclear weapons inevitable in China? I believe that the informal racism that Englishmen inevitably practiced against the Chinese did insure the development and maintenance of a nuclear weapons program. The Chinese, democratic or not, will not forget the insults and slurs that accompanied the blue-eyed soldier in Asia.

It was inevitable that any modernizing bureaucracy would take on a specifically anti-Western posture. The histories of most of the former colonies of the U.S., France or England reveal a fair measure of racial resentment against Europeans. Nuclear weapons carry the promise of "never again."

Nuclear weapons do not reflect the immense economic effort and stress that American periodicals have suggested for half a century. If you have a growing economy, if you can save money, and if you have a large talent pool of young men who are really good in 11th grade algebra, you can force the blond three-year-old into the betting pool.

However well or poorly the blonds and Third World modernizing bureaucracies fit together in the future, the die for nuclear weapons was cast in the 20th century. The fundamental truth about nuclear weapons in Asia has a central core: China will never give them up.

Insofar as industrialization means that productivity comes from a differentiated work force, we are not in a "post industrial" age, and none is in sight. The behavioral changes that one identifies with industrialization snap the age-old connection between a resource base, and consumption.

The book on the behavioral change from a peasantry to an industrialized work force is told in a number of chapters: the move to the city, the education of the boys, the limits on family size, the differentiation of the work force. But the chapter, which really makes a long-term difference on nuclear weapons, is the one on the East Asian boy in algebra class.

Japan from 1956 to 1987, changed the inside of the blond's head more than anyone would have thought possible in 1956. The movie Back to the Future has a marvelous scene where the 1950's American is scornful of Japanese products, and the 80's version is surprised to hear it.

An economic corollary of the rule that peasant populations moving into urbanized industrialized cities should typically be economically more mobile than the host population is the rule that the country with a larger share of its population undergoing urbanization should show a faster rate of economic growth than countries with more stable populations. Macroeconomics has abstracted and reified national experience. What is convenient to measure within national systems: tariffs, monetary policy, government spending, tax issues, become operational categories. Dissonance mandates the second look. Parsimony favors behaviors that occur everywhere.

Japan is exhibit 1, China exhibit 2, and Korea exhibit 3 for the claim that the introduction of a school system into a peasant society overwhelms every-thing else. Success in enjoying much higher living standards amidst political repression is not much of a riddle.[422] Indeed the repression was the first step in the process of higher living standards. Both communists and fascists forced the peasants to keep the 15-year-old boy in school. The repression brought by the central government into the village, when one regards the 15-year-old as the important variable, was trivial compared to the truncated lives of 100 previous generations of 15-year-olds who spent their lives pulling weeds.

The movement of the peasant away from the fields has not escaped notice. In 1993 the Chinese government apparently became concerned that the increas-ing consumption gap between the 200 million involved in the industrializing economy and the 900 million who remained peasants, was a problem.[423]

The conventional western orthodoxy is to celebrate the free market, rather than the man in motion. There has been concern about the future of un-employed Chinese agricultural laborers, possibly 100 million, out of work and "afloat," drifting around China, causing crime, instability, and ever more Chinese.[424] But without Chinese workers in motion, China has to remain an agricultural peasant country, and must consume what the peasantry can pro-duce. Sometimes that production can not even keep people alive.

That tremendous mass of people is not a horde. Given what we know about IQ data and China, some, among that 100 million, have immense talent.

Whether in fascist Brazil, Communist China, or democratic England, the behavioral change always has to look a certain way. There will never be a better economic historian than Charles Dickens. There is no easy way to make illiterate peasants into an industrial workforce.

Virtually any activity the peasant attempts will be more productive than the seasonal agricultural work he left behind. The behavior of a handful of powerful men hundreds of miles removed from the village is, in truth, not of much moment, and can not cancel out the gains of millions of young people learning how to read.

Economic development inevitably involves migration out of the village. One thinks principally of the migration of men. But there are examples in Southeast and East Asian countries where young women play a key role in the shift from agriculture to industry. It is not new. A marvelous statue honoring the Mill Girls is an outdoor display in Manchester, New Hampshire, the site of the Amoskeag Mills, one of the earliest really large industrial sites in the country. An exhibit in a nearby museum shows living arrangements for the young women in the new city, away from home and the farm. Samuelson celebrates a China without cities full of filth, cursing in the streets, and beggars.[425] But the city is the site of education, differentiation, and capital accumulation. The village and its controls were not wrong, but they must be replaced.

The new city is a peculiar mix of the village and the present everywhere. Businessmen in Hong Kong maintain a water tank with 5 black fish to absorb the office bad luck.[426] Whether the Germans are racists or not, it is not possible to read of their anguish at having Mediterranean families slaughter lambs in the apartment downstairs, without some measure of sympathy.

The slum forces the peasantry to give up habits and preferences. Certain behaviors will remain constant, but much will change. The standard blond punch list of familism, corruption, parsimony, low public morality and control of women will remain; but they will not be as intense as in the village.

Moreover some of the list will be helpful in developing an industrialized economy. Virtually every peasantry, at every income level, will save more than the blonds. I suspect this is particularly true of East Asians.

Just as the peasant moved into, and helped shape the behavior of the new city, so the city begins to form the new village. The modern rice farms that engineers and technicians from the urban areas are creating in Southern Brazil are going to destroy the market for innumerable small inefficient rice farmers throughout South America. Sao Paulo helps insure a continuing march of peasants to its slums.

Inflation may be another phenomenon that is inherently part of the path to development. Designing a currency for a stable sea of peasant villages is one thing. Hitting the right mark once the sea of peasants starts to move, and the product mix explodes, is very different.

The Japanese experience of jumping the gorge between a peasant society and an industrialized society will be very difficult for another population to emulate, because Japanese scores on quantitative tests will remain out of reach for most. Japan forced the world-class Sony engineer, the most important member of the developing middle class, to pay higher prices for food by keeping out competition which would have crushed the inefficient 5-acre citrus farmer.

There is a downside if the subsidy which the industrial sector pays to the agricultural sector goes on too long. One is not surprised to read that Japan in the 1990's still had more people in agriculture than in manufacturing steel, cars, auto parts and metalworks totaled together.[427] This has to affect the overall productivity of the Japanese economy. On the other hand, when one considers what the productivity of the Japanese economy was at mid-century when the Japanese were considering sending their surplus agricultural labor to compete with Mexicans in the California sun bowl, the overall judgment has to be that they handled a tremendous behavioral transformation very well. The policies did carry the seeds of certain inefficiencies that would become visible, but they also offered some protection to the workers who were actually planting seeds.

There is an economic risk that American pressures to force the Japanese to open its markets to agricultural goods will backfire. The trend toward fewer farmers is inevitable everywhere. By accelerating that process, America may find that it has simply increased the efficiency of an intellectually superior work force; a work force that has cost America good jobs.

Japanese may resent American advice, and bullying on the issue,[428] but, to be fair, it appears that there are a fair amount of Americans, both conservatives and liberals who resent Japanese success.[429] Even scholars, such as John K. Fairbank, cite "motivation" as the quality which is responsible for Japan's successful drive to reach technological parity with the U.S.[430] That is, he imputes a kind of social minded animus to the familistic Japanese.

The view presented here is that as the Japanese agricultural population began to shrink, it was inevitable that Japanese would begin to overtake the West. The workforce was simply too smart for it not to happen.

Europeans and Americans have longed viewed the future as a contest among white people. Alexis de Tocqueville, writing 150 years ago, observed that America and Russia each seemed destined to hold the destinies of half the world.[431] A century and a half later, Americans assert their duty to demonstrate "Global Leadership."

A developing East Asia disrupts the blond agenda, changes the focus, destroys the simple dichotomy, and deflates the imperial sail. The heroic example and political tutelage that Anglo-Americans have felt destined to bring to the world for three centuries or more begins to give way to algebra, long hours, putting money in the bank, and head down engineering. When an Asian minister predicts that by 2020 East Asia will have a GNP larger than that of Europe, and twice that of the U.S., one sees that blond cohesiveness has helped develop Asia cohesiveness.[432] Polls seem to suggest that the Japanese are quite confident of their abilities to compete with Americans.[433] Is it reasonable to suppose that where Japanese and American policies diverge, the Japanese think that America is exerting "leadership?"

As rapidly expanding school systems in Asia and Eastern Europe identify the academically gifted, it was predictable that they would put pressure on the blond economies. Factor equalization is a fact of life for labor too. The product is not the only item in motion.

Education of any type makes a very dramatic difference to the first generation of peasants to experience the process in a disciplined way. The difference between no school and the very poorest school is behaviorally a much bigger jump than the difference between the poorest school; a dilapidated, unheated, poorly furnished shack at the edge of a cow field, and the most modern building at Philips Exeter.

Authoritarian governments do create military structures, and do inflate the currency; but they also can do something else that will be of longer duration. They can force the peasant father, in the village and in the slum, to keep the boys in school until they are fifteen. The skill that the first generation of peasants learns, reading, is more important than any skill that any generation learns after them. For all their mistakes, that is the skill that the fascists and communists brought to millions of boys and girls in the twentieth century.

As time goes on, and economies develop, reading is taken for granted. Sharp demarcations develop between subject matter, and disciplines, for a number of reasons, one being narrowly financial. People bid for the services of an outstanding student in the computer sciences all over the world. The fact that roughly one fifth of college graduates take jobs that do not usually require a degree indicates that specific technical expertise makes a difference.[434]

The scores that East Asian students reach on quantitative tests are indicia of how their economies will do as they become more complex, more computerized, more engineered. Hopes (?) that with increasing wealth the Japanese will become inefficient compared with Americans, will be disappointed.

America did build on a tremendous base of talent and resources: Machinery, iron and steel, cars and trucks, and petroleum accounted for over half of American manufacturing exports in 1929.[435] The tie between that product list and America's natural resources can not be missed. But it would be simplistic to connect the asset base with the export success. Without researching the matter, it looks like the same list which, except for petroleum products, would be very well represented in Japan's post war success. The list represents a lot of money. Everyone wants the list. The key to holding on to the list is a work force than can improve the list faster, and at less cost, than the competition.

None of this is new, of course. Many economists have tried to locate economic development in discrete variables, and there have been studies that find that education has been a very large contributor to development.[436]

The Japanese and Chinese are not going to fade as economies become more technologically driven. They will have problems, as all economies have problems. But over time, year after year, decade after decade, the advantage they have on quantitative tests just has to become more visible as economic life becomes more technological, more abstract.

What is missing in conventional economics is the understanding that a peasant society is not an absence of education, nor an absence of wealth, nor an absence of learning. Skinner would have guessed that. It is learning within a system, a system that worked, but a system that can not survive the building of the schoolhouse.

Peasant learning kept millions alive for millennia. Writ large, on the issue of mentalism, there is more than one economics. There is an economics where Skinner is more right than anyone else; and then there is an economics where IQ data trumps everything else.

Physical capital is important; intelligence can not do the job unaided. In the early 1990's Poles, Czechs and Romanians went to France to pick grapes for $40.00 a day.[437] The wages exceeded those that even skilled workers, such as computer programmers, could earn at home. Literacy rates in Poland, Czechoslovakia, Hungary and some other Eastern European countries are 98%; as high or higher than they are in parts of the European Community; and the production of scientists and engineers in Poland Hungary and Czechoslovakia compares favorably with the EC.[438] However one sees how recently this work force was transformed from a peasantry when one reads that the road density is only about 40 percent of the EC figure.[439] Urbanization, education and capital accumulation all ride the skin of an expanding behavioral balloon.

It is a great curiosity that an agricultural population can turn into an industrialized work force so quickly. As the forced fit of the village turns into the free form of the slum, one sees a very rapid adaptation. The prediction that the slum will have a deleterious effect on intelligence is questionable. The alternative to the slum for the great majority of the world is not suburbia; it is the village. At the most basic biological level, increased mobility of both men and women diminishes marriages between related people, and dramatically expands the potential pool of mates. Moreover, it would be a great curiosity if intelligence began to decline just as the environmental payoff for intelligence dramatically increased.

East Asians have to be the most dramatic example of the underlying truths about mental measurement tests. In a sense one could make the same observations about peasant societies that one could make about low status jobs in industrialized societies: They include a much wider distribution of IQ scores than high status positions. The well-known affinity East Asians have for quantitative subject is a special problem for a strictly environmental analysis of the data.

How one should account for Japan's quite dramatic and quite sudden improvement in IQ scores has been the topic of a fair amount of discussion. A 1975 test given to over a thousand Japanese youngsters in 1975 revealed that the average was 111, a full 11 points above the U.S. average.[440] Apparently Japanese scores have always been a few points higher than western scores, but the great advantage appeared with the generation born after World Way II. Schooling was one variable that might be responsible. One forgets how rural and agricultural Japan was as late as the 1950's, and how that inevitably hindered education. In the fifties only about half of junior high graduates continued to high school; by 1980 that figure had improved to 94 percent.[441]

Perhaps isolation of young people is the kind of social deprivation which compresses IQ scores in a way that other familiar negative phenomena; low income, poor schools, inferior housing, bad diets, do not. In which case the sociologists evaluation of the urban slum really understates the advantages the new environment offers.

Certainly no blue-eyed country changed so dramatically and so recently as Japan did. The fundamental high distribution of the Japanese may always have been present, but education, and social contacts beyond the village, permitted the Japanese people to demonstrate their capabilities.

A telling detail about the Japanese is their history in Brazil, a country where, surprisingly, they number in the hundreds of thousands. They began as agricultural workers, replacing black slaves. While they did not face the kind of discrimination black people faced in the U.S., they were still perceived as different, and certainly they faced handicaps both as Asians and non-Christians.

Three generations after their arrival in Brazil, the Japanese have helped transform Brazil. At one of the best known universities about 12% of the student body is Japanese, a figure much higher than their share of the Brazilian population, and they have done very well there.[442] One wonders how a purely environmentalist explanation would handle the same phenomena in Japan, Hawaii, California, and Brazil. And the key is to remember that the Japanese in each setting began the journey as agricultural labor, the least favored employment classification.

China and Japan are ancient civilizations. Tinbergen speculated that, because more able and enterprising people will leave, one might expect to find the poorest people at the site of the most ancient civilizations.[443] By the end of the next century no one will offer that speculation. The Japanese and the Chinese have demonstrated that a population can be very intelligent, but have their intelligence hidden by the behavioral monotone that is the peasant village.

The central theme for economic development is the fit between IQ data and the modern economy. Other issues are important but the economic issues can not be changed until the population changes its behavior and begins attending school. The process once begun is irreversible.

Plans to maintain the kind of lead the blonds, particularly Americans and Englishmen, had in economics and technology could never have been realized once the rest of the world began educating its boys. How should the English-speaking blonds handle the challenge?

No one is certain, but I believe that the plans one hears to subsidize high tech operations by squeezing low-tech service jobs may carry a risk. The Asians will be very tough long-term competition. Maybe it would be better to have relatively fewer assets in high tech, international trade, and more in concededly lower paying less productive domestic operations, where they will not be as vulnerable to a smart but poorly paid work force.

Assume that a graph could be constructed showing the world's awareness of the Japanese as engineers overlaid on the movement of Japanese peasants to the cities. The articles extolling the Toyota would follow the transfer of populations from the country to the city.

None of this is meant to deny the long term advantages of free market industrial economies. North and South Korea may be as good a real time, real world test as one will ever see.

Throughout his writings, and over a long career, Skinner maintains an impressive consistency of focus, as well as an awareness of his preferences, on epistemological issues. He liked analysis; the problem with statistical solutions is that they open the gates to the invented cause.

Wilson is less clear on the issue. Sometimes he seems content with the statistical solution; one assumes a biologist would have to feel that way if he thought that he has insights which students of human behavior could use. I confess that I become uneasy when Wilson uses an analysis that refers to the familiar "edifice" of knowledge, with a broad base presumably consisting of physics supporting a kind of pyramid topping out with either human behavior or knowledge about human behavior at the commanding height.[444]

There is simply no way to determine if the fundamental unit is biology, or the behavior you just performed, until you know what it is you want to explain. Human intelligence picks and chooses between history and statistics as it tries to predict within a discipline. The discipline, like the man, comes with preferences that it may not be able to lose.

Ethnicity seems to be downplayed in much American sociobiological writing. Of course the same issue is missing in Skinner too, but since he thought that he was locating lawfulness, science, in environmental history, it is less curious. Perhaps sociobiology really has not addressed the blond's behavior because the blonds are writing it, and their behavior seems to them to be the universal behavior.

The assumptions the blonds make are the same every large dominant ethnic population make. Their behavior is the universal behavior. Consider Lester Thurow's observation that if a fifteenth-century observer had been asked to predict that one part of the globe was about to conquer the rest of the planet, he probably would have chosen China as the conquering party.[445] It had the familiar requisites: technology, population, and organization.

An outsider however might have noticed something else. The Chinese behavior was just different from the blonds' behavior. The English noticed it. One supposes that others had they seen as far, would have noticed it. Perhaps, if one researches German literature, one would notice very similar patterns in what Germans noticed. The Chinese were like many other populations: in closed villages, familists, very poor, and more likely to be tied to specific regions than the English or the Germans.

And I doubt that the astute 15th century observer, when he tried to predict the future, would have overlooked a much more important variable. The successful army is the army that carries its aggression informally, inside the head of its soldiers. The great army is the army that carries its idealism within the same cutout as its racism. Nobody doubts that the British inside China just look both more impressive, and more racially aggressive, than the Chinese look inside Britain.

A TV documentary on Caucasoid mummies found inside China indicated that some of the Caucasian graves included Chinese. The conclusion was that the Caucasians and the Chinese had learned to live in harmony and intermarried. I doubt it. It does not sound like the blonds anywhere else.

Peppe's First Sociobiological Rule is that The Size of the Behavior Indicates its Age. If, in the 21st century, we see the blonds everywhere exhibit a consistent pattern as far back as we can see we have a good idea of what they were doing in small isolated tribes thousands of years ago, where we can not see.

A TV news story featured 11 American women who had adopted Chinese babies; all baby girls; 11 to zip. It is not possible to see that statistic and realize that something is going on, something that is not random. The only rational conclusion is that American women think that something is wrong with Chinese males; in a way that they do not think that something is wrong with Chinese females.

Now, this is innocent enough; China and the U.S. are separated by thousands of miles. But what if China and the U.S. were next to each other; think Germany and Poland?

What would the conclusion be if the sex ratio of the Chinese bodies in the graves of the mummies favored women by a very large amount? It would mean the blonds were able to kill the men and appropriate the women. Is this a basic biological thread that ties the pre-Christian blonds together with the 21st century blonds, through four thousand years?

Is the discovery of the mummies an opportunity to see something real about ethnic relations? Suppose the researchers found virtually no male Chinese skeletons? Could it help move English speaking blond history from a political theory featuring a principal thinker, John Locke, and supporting characters on three different continents to a different deeper reality? Could it do something deeper? Could it really present, as nothing else could, the story of history as ethnicity? Could it help everyone accept the presence of nuclear weaponry as a specific answer to a specific blond characteristic?

The graves could establish the historic integrity of ethnic types. If the final nuclear conflagration features Chinese and American engineering, "History" could be reduced to three Major Events: The Caucasoid graves, the 11th grade, and nuclear weapons.

Sociobiology and Nuclear Weapons

On July 21, as Truman presided over the fourth day of plenary sessions, we noticed a decided change in the President's manner. He seemed much more sure of himself...to challenge some of Stalin's statements...

It was not until four days later that an Army courier arrived with vivid detailed accounts which showed how greatly the power of the bomb exceeded expectations. It was this exhilarating report which so changed the manner of Truman and Churchill.

Robert Murphy[446]

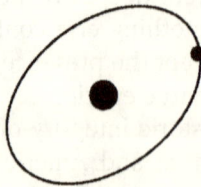

The twentieth century was a curious century for blond democratic English-men and Americans—the most curious. They began the century as they began many, many earlier centuries: with the ability to go everywhere and to do every-thing. They ended it, after numberless celebrations of triumphalism; 40 minutes from nuclear annihilation.

At least two of the classic peasantry, the Russians and the Chinese (the model for the brand?) could, at the price of mutual annihilation, destroy England and America. This more or less equivalency in the murder category represents an enormous historical elevation for the Russians and the Chinese. Once Englishmen were on Slavic dirt, killing Slavs in the name of progress, and calling it the Great Game. Once, Americans were all over Asia, having sex with Asian women, and threatening Asians with jail for racial intermarriage. Nuclear weapons are a basic threshold ethnic issue. At the beginning of the 21st century they mean that the blonds will not invade Russia and China again.

The change favors the dictator. The Chinese were always willing not to invade New Hampshire to protect the Abenaki; the Russians never considered invading England to protect the Irish.

There has been a decline in Anglo-American power, but it has not been long, slow or gradual. It has been sudden and dramatic, taking less than three generations; and totally related to how nuclear weapons are behaviorally different from other weapon systems. Those differences can be conveniently grouped under three behavioral headings: the Game, the Product Line, and the Kid.

The Game

Nuclear weapons were developed by poor peasant societies like Russia and China through an inside, small, sophisticated, private, destructive, hidden game; which was an intense high-octane, focused, concentrated version of the big, visible, and creative outside game, called economic development. As the shift from an agricultural to an industrialized, which is to say educated, society proceeded in Russia and China; there was a desperate search for the resource that could help in the overwhelming need to keep the blonds at home.

What the world sees in nuclear weapons pointed at the blonds is that the search was successful. The peasants located the most important resource in the weapon system: the 15-year-old boy in a run down shack in an incredibly poor agricultural village, amidst 40 other boys who look at the blackboard in math class with distaste, fear and confusion; the boy who looks at the blackboard and thinks, "What is the matter with these guys?"

Everything became different for the blonds in an historical blink. The Vikings, for all their advantages, had become targets, and targets at home.

The nuclear game, contrary to 40 years of blond wise men punditry, is not an expensive game. North Korea demonstrates the future. A country with a very excellent cohort of 15-year-old math students, but a poor economic base, can put fear in the soul of the aspiring world-policeman. For Russia, after millennia of staring at the blonds in Germany with some apprehension, the single most surprising thing about the nuclear threat is how cheap it turned out to be. China could not hold the United States at bay and Russia could not hold Germany at bay if they had to match the blond physical plant. It is because the game is about the engineer, not the resource base; that mutual assured destruction is a reality; and from the Chinese and Slavic perspective, a sensible, and affordable reality.

The nuclear weapons game is an intense and concentrated reflection of ethnic realities. Certainly the blonds, being wealthier, can afford more impressive weaponry. But a key difference between what the American establishment has been telling Americans for half a century, and the position urged here, is that the relative weight of stuff and talent in nuclear weapons is dramatically tipped toward the talent side of the equation. Economic success is not irrelevant, but it is no surprise that, where the IQ scores are not dramatically different from the blonds' scores, the natives will be able to force the blonds into MAD.

Product Line

Nuclear weapons represent the ultimate meritocracy. Either you can do the engineering or you can not. It is ironic that the discussion of IQ and meritocracy in the U.S. has tracked, predictably, the orthodoxy about political democracy. The meritocracy is assumed to be dependent upon democracy. But in the real world, the most dramatic feature of the nuclear meritocracy is that it protects the autocrat.

Extrapolating even a two-percent growth rate over a period of a couple generations makes it clear that Russia and China will have the ability to make enormous improvements in their nuclear arsenals. Of course the same is true of the U.S., but a continuing advance in the destructiveness and accuracy of the system does not imply the futility of it all. It is an enormous achievement for the population that has an ambition to kill its Indians; but, no ambition to fight wars to stop Indian killing anywhere else.

Vietnam demonstrates that the basic, bottom of the line, a no frills hydrogen bomb strapped to a missile that goes 10,000 miles an hour, is enough to keep out the most determined, idealistic blond. There is no world policeman for China.

The American ambition is a continuation of the English ambition to police the planet. And the English, being terrific fighters, whether in Europe, or Latin

America, or India, or in China, were undoubtedly successful in many battles to help worthy struggles.

Well, what was it, is it? Racism or doing good? In a relentlessly ethnic world, there is no way to give an answer to satisfy everyone. But a nuclear armed Russia and China obviously will not be the staging areas for wars to do good anytime soon. However upset Queen Victoria or George Bush may be about Chinese in Tibet, the blonds stay home. The ability to just kill everyone makes a difference.

If one compares a 1994 article about Russians,[447] and compares it with Iurii Krizhanich's Politika,[448] written in 1663, one can not avoid the similarities. The Russians are the same, and the Germans are the same. After the inevitable observation on aesthetics, the report addresses the differences in intra-group morality. The blonds have an open, easy, informal way with each other; they are not backstabbing schemers. As pronounced as the blond aesthetic advantage is, the advantage in public morality is even more impressive.

From the perspective of the peasant societies protecting themselves from the blond morality, nuclear weapons are an engineered, artificial, focused, and political response to a set of advantages which are aesthetic, physical, organizational, social, and ubiquitous. It is the Slavs, living next to, but never among, the Germans, who know the value of nuclear weapons. It is the Chinese who know what they have to be able to bring to the table to keep the sign equating dogs and Chinese off of their sidewalk.

Nuclear weapons systems may be considered in three constituent parts: the blast, the delivery system, and the instrumentation. All other weapon systems, from clubs to carrier fleets, are very different at the seam where they intersect with ethnicity. The key is not sophistication; a carrier fleet represents incredibly sophisticated engineering. The key is how that technology fits with an ethnic world. The Rand study that found that North Korea could profoundly affect the strategic regional balance of power with as few as 10 bombs sounds right.[449] I suspect two, might be enough, if they could be delivered to the North American continent. The issue is what the blonds have to bet.

It is remarkable how little notice has been taken of the change in the blonds' attitude toward nuclear weapons between, say, 1950, and 1995. The change has been in one direction: more and more fearful. Intellectuals became fearful earlier, but, over time, the fear level increased throughout the society. It was something like rock and roll. It wasn't there, and then, it was. The informality, the refusal to dress up and smile, the first snicker at the big band as posture; a few dead end kids at first, then everyone. A few Americans are still enthusiastic about nuclear weapons, but unlike August 1945, most are not.

If one reads the national press of the 1950's one sees the earlier enthusiasm in the democratic blond delight in threatening nuclear weapons. But over 30 years the music changed. Swing became a dirge. People who became teenagers in the 1950's can remember the breathless reports of American technology carried in the Bomb. People who were in ROTC classes at the end of the decade can remember military debates about whether China should be bombed to teach her not to fool with nuclear technology. They also remember the impressive technology buried inside a mountain where American leaders could direct the world after a nuclear exchange.

If the blond intellectuals were honest with themselves, they would see how profoundly the Cuban Missile Crises changed American swing-time. It was so necessary to claim victory, to insist that it was the Russians who blinked, that the fundamental ethnic realities were ignored.

For most of the world, the real lesson of the confrontation was not that Russia did not make Cuba, but that the U.S. did not invade a small Latin neighbor. Without Russian nuclear weapons an American invasion of Cuba would have been inevitable. How many times had the blonds invaded Latin America in the 20th century?

Given a hundred years of history between the United States and its Catholic Latin neighbors, no one could doubt that in any previous decade the U.S. would just have invoked the Monroe Doctrine, and started killing Cubans. See under "the Philippines." But I suspect that the first, most intense, most important reaction to the stand off was not in Latin America, it was in Asia. Literate Asian revolutionaries saw something that they never thought that they would see. Americans stayed home.

Anyone in Washington, D.C., at the time, will remember the overwhelming electricity in the city. Lyndon Johnson remembered the experience when he calibrated force levels in Vietnam, and so did President Nixon. They remembered nuclear weapons taking center stage for a brief moment, over Cuba. That memory saved Communist Vietnam.

The blond intellectual failed to see how profoundly the Cuba crises changed America's reach and ambition. Moreover, the establishment has never honestly dealt with one singularly defining mark of nuclear weapons: How few it takes to keep the world's sheriff at home. In 1962 Russia may have had as few as four nuclear weapons which could have struck the U.S.[450] Four turned out to be enough.

Churchill, F.D.R. and Truman would have been surprised by 1962. They would have been more surprised by 1975. America absorbed 57,000 dead men and went home, rather than "go nuclear."

The issue of the likely longevity of nuclear weapons can also be addressed in the three categories: the game, the product line, and the kid. Because the development of nuclear weapons is simply an intense reflection of the economic development game, there is no reason to expect the game to have to end because of economic pressures. Because the product is cheap, because of what it promises to the Slavs, who live next to the Germans, and the Chinese listening to Anglo-America about universal rights, and remembering the blond racist when he was on their sidewalk; the cost/benefit ratio is unbelievably favorable to the poor country that can match the blond engineer.

The rationale inside the blond establishment for instituting, developing and accelerating the manufacture of nuclear weapons is, of course, that nuclear weapons are a very different type of product than argued here. One of the best arguments briefing the American establishment view appeared in a column by George Gilder in 1985.[451] He recites several failures of the U. S. to embargo technology which would be useful to Russia's nuclear program. Inevitably leaks, theft and reverse engineering wash away American advantage. What to do?

Now, by 1985, the number four of 1962 had clearly grown into thousands. Gilder's answer, notwithstanding what his generation had clearly witnessed, is that technology is beyond the reach of command economies. Therefore, he asserts that America should accelerate the death business, present the communists with such a dazzling array of devices, ideas, and systems that they will never catch up. Appropriately, he paraphrases Kipling. The Communists will be forever sweating, a year and a half behind.

What is wrong with the logic is that, for nuclear weapons, if you are poor, have an inferior technology, but you want to prevent Kipling from coming on your dirt to stop you from killing your Cherokee, a year and a half inferiority is just fine. Not excellent, but good enough. Kipling and the British, Teddy Roosevelt and the Americans, had great strengths and great courage. But they will not send their soldiers to kill people to do good, if they have to risk their 3-year-old inside Buckingham Palace and the White House. Prior to the nuclear age, all of the British games with the wogs were away games. Nuclear weapons change that. Last year's model is plenty good enough to be able to deliver the oven to Kipling's home.

The term "proliferation" is a window into the blond establishment thinking on what nuclear weapons are. Essentially, it invites an inquiry into property: stuff that people have. The word has become a kind of trap for the blond imagination. First, the term focuses the discussion on nuclear weapons as an assemblage of more and less sophisticated items and processes. Second, it tends to force the debate into a discussion about what the western powers, which have a lot of the stuff, are doing to keep them out of enemy hands.

But the blond intellectuals have largely ignored what they themselves witnessed in the first half century of the nuclear age. Espionage has not played a really major role in Russia's ability to produce thousands of the things, or in China's ability to drop a few on Los Angeles.

Besides being different on the balance of talent and stuff that they represent, nuclear weapons are unique on the issue of threshold utility. A mere handful changes everything. Cuba demonstrated that. North Korea may demonstrate it again.

The evolution is inexorable: more bombs, more powerful, more accurate, faster, more deaths. The Greenpeace protester, who screams that the proposed

UK submarine program will result in a weapon that equates to 2700 Hiroshimas, imagines that he is underlining a monstrous, and dramatic, change.[452] In fact, to the blond everyman, it is about as exciting as watching a fishing tournament. The American public has heard so many doomsday stories for so many years about the effects of nuclear weapons "over there," that it would not really matter if the number became 800,000 Hiroshimas.

What is new and provocative about the 21st century is that there is no guarantee Hiroshima will remain over there. In fact, there can be a fair amount of confidence that if the blonds invade as many places in the 21st century as they invaded in the 17th 18th and 19th, Hiroshima will come home. Far from being the end of history, the advent of nuclear weapons meant history would become more interesting than ever before, precisely because it has become more interesting for the Viking three year old.

Now, this does not mean that the kind of technological advantage that a really big economy gives the United States can not have important consequences. In certain places, and at the right time, as with Iraq; the setting, the mass, and the identity of the players meant that technology could disarm an entire army with practically no casualties. But if one focuses on nuclear issues, one sees how different the result would have been if Iraq had been protected by a nuclear armed patron.

With nuclear weapons in hand, Roosevelt, Truman, Churchill and a couple hundred years of blond imperialism said that the secret page of the universe held a single word, "Force." If that is correct a thousand years of teaching from very different traditions are wrong. Catholic philosophers were wrong, and so were religious thinkers from a host of other traditions. So were Machiavelli, and other skeptics from a secular perspective. If the blonds who spoke English could make the world behave because they had nuclear weapons, everyone except the blonds who spoke English, were wrong. What we see with nuclear weapons in Russia, in China and maybe in North Korea, is that the blonds who spoke English were wrong.

The American establishment is right in its estimate about the kind of differences a few nuclear weapons will make. It is wrong in its analysis of what nuclear weapons are, and whether reasonable predictions can be made about their production, from economic data or technological reports.

The blond intellectual; curious, dispassionate, and secular, has failed to ask one very basic question about the changes he personally witnessed in the last half of the 20th century. In 1950 the United States could destroy everyone, and no could destroy the U.S. Then Russia could destroy the U.S. Then China could destroy big gobs of the U.S. Then, possibly, it was not inconceivable that North Korea could destroy parts of the U.S. The question the blond intellectual, Harvard University, the CIA, the Congress, the President, failed to ask is, "Is there a certain orderliness about this story?"

Yes, there is. It is inherent in the fit between the game, the product and the kid.

First, the game has to do with 15-year-old boys in school. Once that change is made in an agricultural society, it swamps everything else. No society "regresses" economically once that behavioral change begins. The material conditions never revert to those that prevailed prior to the change.

For example, studies which find that Southern Italy has less "social capital" than northern Italy, and remains poorer than Northern Italy may be correct. They may be correct that southern Italians are more familistic, more authoritarian, and less trusting than their northern cousins.[453] Much the same observation could be made about any of the peasantry compared to the non-peasantry. But the studies do not, and will not, find that any population becomes poorer as they abandon a peasant way of life, and begin attending school. And, for nuclear weapons, that is the detail that matters.

The fabulous morality and the enduring racism of the blonds travel together. America demonstrated that sense of social commitment and public morality, us against them in a struggle for a country, right from the beginning. One is impressed when one reads in reports from the town of Hampton in the province in New Hampshire in 1689 about a vote to combine forces with other colonies, including Plymouth Colony, for the prosecution of war against the common enemy, the native, in defense of "our" country.[454]

The year 1689 is separated from the landing at Plymouth that established America's hometown by roughly one lifetime. The blonds had already identified where they were as their country, had identified the racial enemy, had instinctively realized one with another that they were not going to move into the teepee, and had developed an effective fighting force against the "intruder." They would retain that image of the intruder in a 200-year sweep across a continent.

The series of forts that founded America was done without a central authority, without the necessity of central controls; an advantage that made the aggression as effective as it was. One sees the same in Australia, Canada, indeed England itself. Had the Slavs been less competitive one would have seen it in Europe. What one takes for granted in a blond society, is largely out of reach to a peasantry that is willing to become the racial "other," and move into the teepee. The bravery, the self-awareness, the aggression, the racism, and the democracy of the blue-eyed people, fit together.

If on the East Coast the clear racial enemy was the Indian and the black, on the West Coast, it was the Indian, the black, the Mexican and the Asian. Chinese were only permitted to work mines abandoned by whites.[455] Simple intimidation was enough to marginalize the Mexicans and the older Hispanic families.[456] In 1848 the number of Indians in California was approximately 150,000; just 20 years later the number was cut to thirty thousand.[457] While disease played a role, the size of the number and the speed of the change suggest that when they needed a man who could shoot a 3 year old, he was available. From a biological perspective, one sees how much more effectively an informal racial consensus operated than any authoritarian central authority could have. Any of the colonial subjects who actually saw the British would have guessed the same.

The reasonable response, a shrug, has become a danger to the blonds. The point, from the colored perspective, has to do with how effectively nuclear weapons answer a social question.

A high degree of social morality is one of the reasons why the blonds fight so well, as well as why black women were sperm receptacles in North America, and not in Brazil. Lincoln was wrong: The races in America did amalgamate. There is no other way to develop the statistic that American blacks are over 25% white. The amalgamation was hidden because the child's father was so good at covering a genetic reality with a social abhorrence.

As understandable as that is from an aesthetic viewpoint, that is one of the reasons that Slavs looking at Germans, and Chinese looking at Anglo-Americans, will never put down the nuclear hatchet.

The Kid

The blond 3-year-old has become a target, at home, in America, in England, in Buckingham Palace, even. That happened, because a certain 15-year-old showed up in Russia and China.

Shacks called schools were developed in an endless series of isolated small villages. No population once it moves from 2 or 5 or 17 or 20 percent of the boys in school, in favor of 60, or 70, or 80 percent; climbs back down the ladder. That is the real key to understanding the future of nuclear weapons; not failed attempts by the blonds to rein in the technology that they created. The peasants under fascism and communism went through a tremendous behavioral change. They began to go to school.

To adopt a Russian or Chinese perspective, one sees that the heart of the struggle to keep the blonds out was a search shack after shack, for a very specific kid; one who could contribute to a very specific engineering team. While nuclear weapons are an expensive, nation driven, massively dangerous product; their main ingredient required a search for an unbelievably small number of young, extraordinary students. The IQ distribution was a guarantee that the kid would show up.

The kid will continue to show up every September. No society having educated 70 or 80 percent of its 15-year-old boys reverts to its peasant past. Nuclear weapons, the great equalizer, track that change.

The three fit together: the game, the product, and the kid, and the greatest of these is the kid. The planet including, now, London and Washington, is 40 minutes away from a manmade oven. The engineering the kid can do puts pressure, seen and unseen, on everyone, everywhere, for generations, as far as the eye can see. The kid shoves everyone, including American intellectuals, into one of two betting lines: One window receives bets that nuclear weapons are about stuff. The other window takes bets that they are about talent. Everyone on the globe is intimately affected by that bet. And, there is a post time.

I doubt that there has ever been a more momentous decision, outside perhaps of very fundamental religious decisions, which will affect as many people for so long as this fundamental bet about the identity of nuclear weapons. If the socio-biological approach is a better fit with reality than the engineering/economic approach, American nuclear policy has been wrong. There is no other word for it.

American intellectuals see the problem just as 16th century English intellectuals would have seen the problem, as England began its vast racist aggression. The central problem with the world, outside of the obvious one of the way other people look, is unreasoned, arbitrary, despotic political and religious power. Racism for the blonds then, just as for the blonds now, occupies a different moral ground than despotism. The problem with nuclear weapons is that the constancy of blond purpose has become a problem to the next generation of blonds.

One can see that the racist impulse must have played a great role in the blond biological success from earliest times. The real trick isn't to have an effective army; the real trick is to be an army: To have everyone carry the enemy around in his head.

The blonds have sent a consistent message. The view here would suggest that the Mediterranean peasant always had more in common with the Asian, or Arab peasant than he did with the German or the Englishman. Estimates that the Roman army never reached 1 million, out of a population pool of 55 to 70 million, while placing the German fighting force at a fifth or even a quarter of the total population, sound right.[458] The citizen soldier, particularly if a spirit of racial dislike can animate him, is the effective soldier. Would racial feelings among the fighting populations, be kind of an analogy to no left-handed women among the peasantry?

Think of the British soldier among a hundred different populations, all of which, to some degree, disgusted or amused him. What made him fight so long and so hard? The power of the blonds in war was never really dependent upon a prop as flexible as a moral certitude in the rightness of loose social controls. One sees the sweep of the blonds across the Temperate Zone, marching, unified with their distaste for the natives.

Teddy Roosevelt is an American hero to both conservatives and liberals. The informality, the physical strength, the commitment to his society, the honesty, the democracy, the impatience and even contempt for formality and authority, are all central to the American character, and no less to British, or Australian, or white South African, or German national character. Teddy Roosevelt's racism sounds dated today, but on an informal level, how different is it? When he asserted that the only alternative to the white race using force to annex Hawaii was to leave it for low caste yellow people, was he saying anything that the Pilgrims, Boers, Australians, Germans, New Zealanders, had not said?[459]

The ability of the blonds to "take over" really large populations over very large land areas, with surprisingly few troops, indicates the overwhelming peasant nature of the "target societies." Peasants in isolated villages, speaking different dialects, not able to understand each other, and not really aware of the central authorities, do not make an effective fighting force. The experience of the blonds in ancient Europe had an echo not just in the British Empire in Asia, but also in 20th century America. Intellectuals who have been both apologists and critics have treated America's Banana Wars of the early 20th century as economic events. I suggest that they should be treated as another point on the blond ethnic continuum. The Marines lost just 79 men in forcing an occupation on Haiti, the Dominican Republic and Nicaragua for a combined period of 35 years.[460]

Now, undeniably, what the blonds created: in the British Isles, in Australia, In the United States, and in Canada is impressive. If it consistently required some version of cowboys and Indians, well, the world is violent anyway. But that does not exhaust the story or even the most important part of the story as it concerns nuclear weapons.

The really critical part of the story is that the blond intellectual will not call it cowboys and Indians anywhere else. Everywhere else it is called evil. That is why the blonds have to be able to cook the planet. It is when one sees what the blonds object to, and how intense and sincere their objections are, that one sees the real revolutionary nature of the kid, now that he has been to the 11th grade. No one else could keep the blue-eyed people at home.

Ideology probably never played the role in international affairs ascribed to it by Anglo-American intellectuals post 1920. Europeans must have always been intensely aware of a line with Germans on one side of it, and Slavs on the other. There is a good reason for 20 million dead Russians. There is a good reason for Cherokees living in Oklahoma, instead of Tennessee. The dramatic defeat of National Socialism and the collapse of communism have not brought History to a close.

With nuclear weapons alive and well in a world which presents itself as unabashedly ethnic, history becomes interesting as never before. Now everyone can watch an honest drama.

Serbia was the first honest major play on the stage in half a century. In a pre-nuclear age, the blonds, German and Anglo-Americans, would have intervened with armies on the ground. The leadership class would have required it. The reasons: altruism, political stability, balance of power, human rights, economic progress, would have sounded like the reasons given today. But a nuclear armed

Russia, no matter how poor, disorganized, and dispirited, plays a revolutionary role. It plays a frankly ethnic role. It helps one side and hurts another. It keeps the blonds out.

The bomb means that no one will invade Russia. It is the same reason the US left Vietnam. There is no long-term successor to the British Empire.

The kid's ability to handle numbers: a point on a bell curve looks extremely abstract. But in the working out, the effect is very specific and tangible. He has to represent an ethnic community. That is how the world is organized. Sakharov, an opponent of Communism, consistently, self-consciously, and continually protected his knowledge of the Russian nuclear program. He knew the Germans. The same must be true among Chinese nuclear engineers, as they consider Anglo-America. How could it be otherwise?

In 1992 Jean Mayer, a sophisticated and talented member of the academic establishment, predicted that the breakup of the Soviet Union would mean that one-third of America's mathematicians, physicists and research engineers would be laid off.[461] The fear was that these laid off workers would become a technical lost generation. Nothing of the sort happened. Similarly, while Russia went through an economic depression and a dramatic downsizing in certain military functions, it has found the funds that were required to continue research on nuclear weapons. The fact that nuclear weapon spending was so resilient demonstrates the fundamental truth that the world is an ethnic world.

The issue of employment for the Russian nuclear engineer has been the subject of numerous columns and editorials. One reads the threat that Russian nuclear engineers were receiving lucrative offers to relocate to anti-American Third World countries. After pointing out that the nuclear brain trust was about 3,000 people, one editorial suggests a revival of "Operation Paper Clip," a post World War II program whereby Britain and the U.S. cooperated to relocate German scientists, presumably to get them away from Russians.[462]

Now, one assumes that the author of that editorial was at least 40 in 1992. When that writer was born, Russia had no hydrogen bomb, no missile, no instrumentation to really guide the missile, and would have needed incredible luck to deliver any kind of weapon to American soil. Today, after what the author apparently thinks was a vast success, MAD, mutual assured destruction is a certainty. America has become immeasurably more vulnerable than it was in 1950. How successful was the attempt to stop Russian nuclear progress by buying up German talent?

The ambition of a Harvard faculty member to cement ties between Los Alamos and Arzamas-16, its Russian counterpart, reflects an attractive idealism.[463] But the sense that the problem is people who know something, trivializes the real problem. The real problem arrives every September, year after year, in algebra class.

Expectations that Russian governments would no longer be interested in nuclear weapons once the Soviet Union disappeared looked hopelessly naive just a few years later. It is impossible to imagine that Russia will relinquish the choke hold on Germany that nuclear weapons represent.

I believe that proposals to put money into the pockets of Russian nuclear engineers are bad ones. If there is a general economic truism that applies here; it is that you get more of what you invest in.

Imagine how the leaders of the non-nuclear powers must have regarded the things from about 1950. You have scant wealth, but you have the beginnings of a school system. By the 1960's you sense that there are young men in that system that can engineer anything the Vikings can engineer. You recognize the significance of Hiroshima and Nagasaki. The lesson is that these things work, that they make a difference, and that the blonds have no compunction about using them. Dispersion of stuff has never been the problem. And the dispersion of a few thousand very specific people has not, and will not be, the problem. The problem has been and will remain the dispersion of talent.

The American fat yellow school bus will remain 40 minutes away from a nuclear fireball for as long as the eye can see. It is time for the American triumphalists to recognize that.

When the Air Force general who is the head of the US Space Command calls for the end of nuclear weapons on the grounds that their total elimination would vastly increase the power of the U.S. the soft, slow, steady disquiet that has been building for half century becomes visible.[464] Very different from the optimism of Churchill and Truman. Of course their elimination would increase American power. In fact, the US could then be the world's policeman.

One wonders how the role and that ambition began for the blonds. The British Empire was the idealistic attempt to take on the policeman's role, albeit at a profit. One wonders whether it would be possible to analyze the early British imperial impulse by ethnicity within England itself. Fischer points out how certain features of British founding groups developed very characteristic patterns in America. Was that true of the developing empire? Were there populations inside England that really supported aggression, and others that did not?

Whatever the fundamental ethnic reality might have been, nuclear weapons have brought it to a close. At least as far as Russia and China are concerned. The kid who is dynamite in algebra class blows up the blond idealism.

The Migration of Nuclear Weapons

I do not know which generation will finally kill the nuclear weapons assumptions of the World War II generation; but I know the murder instrument. The migration of nuclear weapons across category boundaries has become one of the weapon's distinguishing features. They break old forms and aggrandize new territory. Sooner or later they will require a new policy, and a vocabulary dramatically at odds with the vocabulary of the World War II orthodoxy.

In the beginning, the 1950's, they were an instrument to use in a war; a form of activity to further a policy. Consider the buoyant optimism from an ad in a popular magazine from the mid-50's: "At any moment, day or night, SAC's training operations can be changed into combat operations, unleashing mighty retaliatory nuclear strikes against the war making power of any aggressor, anywhere."[465] Thirty years later, after everyone had seen the kind of difference nuclear weapons made once the other side had them, the blond buoyant enthusiasm had largely dissipated.

From about 1955, after the Russians exploded their first hydrogen bomb, it should have been clear that the nuclear game would be played on a much longer field than Churchill and Truman would have guessed.[466] The weapons system began to take up more space, to force a crack in the category wall, and shift from an instrumentality to an end. In the 21st century no policy issues are more important than the issues surrounding nuclear weapons. There is not now, and there will never be, a more critical American policy decision than the one to call China's or Russia's technological bluff. There is no more important fact in central Asia, in the potential long term stress between Orthodox Slavs, and central Asian Muslims, than the reality that Russia has an enormous, and sophisticated pool of nuclear engineers, and the Muslims do not.

I predict that the man with the greatest potential to influence human history in the 21st century is the Iraqi or Iranian, or Egyptian nuclear engineer. Can the blonds produce a system that will give to them a 19th century security, and the wogs, a 19th century wog vulnerability?

America's vulnerability because of nuclear weapons has not received as much attention as it should have for a number of reasons. First, while 50 years is historically a brief time, a blink; for the individual human life span, it is a long time. The 10-year-old in 1950 is 60 at the end of the century. All the old conversations are memorable for their setting, and the people, many of whom are gone; rather than their content. Who the hell cares what was said? It all runs together. Politicians are supposed to sound tough and stand up to bullies. No one remembers if they said that nuclear weapons would make Americans more secure.

Second, within the club of foreign policy experts, and politicians, the goal went from being alone, to being "first." There was a catastrophic change for the blond democrats in that shift. But the catastrophe was missed, as attention focused on how vulnerable the other side was. But "they" had always been vulnerable. The Anglo-American drive to go everywhere and do everything was predicated on that.

Third, and related to the second, the only academic groups that were heard as the vulnerability inevitably took shape were physical scientists and economists. Their monopoly reinforced the existing view of nuclear weapons: They were just conventional weapons with a little more horsepower. The public accepted the fact that a lot means more than a few, and that America has to be sure it can afford to build a more sophisticated model.

American intellectuals have emotionally accepted the fact that the Russians and Chinese are "different" because of nuclear weapons. What now? As nuclear technology becomes better, leaks become more dangerous. The look away factor carries risk. But can any policy make a difference in the trajectory of the development of the systems?

However things may work in Russia, an attempt to check the power of China in Asia has to have a down side in the ability to close out the nuclear weapons age, or at least, to put controls on it. Blond threats to China insure a continuation of the relatively inexpensive, but highly sophisticated engineering game.

Nuclear weapons are the great residue of the Cold War. It was a war Americans think they won, because they did not, and do not, believe that the war was simply the continuation of an old, old ethnic war.

Slavs were the really big ethnic winners of the nuclear age. Absent nuclear weapons, the Slavs have all the questions about living next to the Germans that they always had.

The Chinese were the second greatest beneficiaries of nuclear weapons. The Chinese nuclear engineer has forever ended any chances that the blond democrats will be able to deal with China as just another rogue state.

No one sees the end of history. It is a fortunate generation that sees the answer to one major historical question. The most important historical events revolve around ethnicity. The blonds always had the same creative and attractive characteristics. And they were always racists.

The most important question resolved by the 20th century was resolved in 1955. The Slavs discovered how to live next to the Germans. It is no surprise that even after the collapse of Communism, an elderly, intelligent, peaceable Russian scientist is quick to insist that nuclear weapons must survive.[467]

From a global perspective, 1948, with Germany and Japan defeated, the world looked much like 1900. There really was no serious military threat to the English speaking blonds. But by the Cuban missile crises in 1962, just 14 years later, when serious American intellectuals were concerned whether mutual suicide was a few days away, ethnic realities were different around the globe.

While the mushroom shaped cloud has become the great symbol of the age; the delivery system, and the instrumentation to place the energy precisely where it would do the most damage, are major constituents of the nuclear weapons package. Economic problems will not stop the advance of nuclear weapon. Fundamentally, they represent talent, not hardware, and the single most reliable predictor of the spread of nuclear weaponry is IQ data. Given a more or less normal IQ distribution, the only real question about the spread of nuclear weapons has to do with the percentage of 15-year-old boys in the 11th grade.

The Russian engineer turned peripatetic money-grubbing traveler escaping a faltering post Communist Russia might, indeed, provide help to America's enemies. Also, the stream of newspaper stories about China helping threshold nuclear powers engineer their way over the top probably will continue.[468] But, finally, the central problem is, and will remain home grown talent.

The blond contempt for that talent has lead directly to the present. It would be interesting to visit 1950's college political science texts to see whether they predicted that the day would come when America would be vulnerable to destruction in 40 minutes from two nuclear powers. One suspects not. One suspects that they sounded like Secretary McNamara sounded in the early 60's: The U.S. lead in nuclear weapons was so long, the American technological base was so impressive, the rest of the world would never catch up. This assumed advantage led directly to announcements which labeled arms control moral weakness.[469]

The Reagan presidency is widely credited by conservatives as achieving the destruction of communism and the Soviet Union. The American leadership has relied on America's technology and economic strength to allow it to prevail since the beginning of the nuclear age. John Foster Dulles may have been the first post World War II Secretary of State to predict the collapse of communism for its economic weaknesses.[470] With economics and enough will, the American establishment has consistently believed that it could scale the nuclear mountain. But if one simply concentrates on what happened to American security in America during the last half of the 20th century, there is no doubt that America itself became more vulnerable by orders of magnitude, and from two, rather than just one potential enemy.

That dramatic decline in security went hand in hand with certitude that more technology subsidized by a much bigger economy and smarter people would create, finally, a secure world. Consider what a popular newsmagazine reported on an MIT study of Russian aeronautical scientists in 1956. The elite were as good as any in the world. But the elite group was extremely small and not supported by a Soviet cadre which lacked the "engineering instinct" developed in the U.S. and Germany. What of the future? The "experts" doubted that they would ever become truly self-reliant without massive changes in Soviet education.[471]

Would the authors of that article, would the MIT observers, would Secretary Dulles, have predicted that by the end of the century Russia could destroy the United States in 40 minutes? Would they have predicted that China could develop the engineering instinct to do the same?

The record of American pro-nuclear intellectuals has been amazingly consistent. Punditry has more or less tracked the aforementioned 1956 piece for over 40 years. Reports on Communist China have sounded the same.

Indeed, one does not have to retreat as far as the 1950's, ancient history to many Americans, to see a dramatic change, for the worse, in American security. The blast is old hat. The contest in recent years has shifted to instrumentation engineering. In the past 20 year period, the ability of both the Chinese and the Slavs to begin murdering the blonds in an orderly process, by starting the fire in one city rather than another, has improved exponentially. More, the improvement has been so dramatic; there may no longer even be any safe place to put American officials and American communications equipment underground. The same U.S. publications which celebrated Russian and Chinese backwardness, compared with U.S. standards, missed the point.

Russian engineers were responsible for the debate about the wisdom of putting missiles on railroad cars. The same engineering talent may have made it pointless to think about putting American officials or communication equipment inside a mountain. They may have forever ended the blond dream about directing the charred remains of the World from a series of caves. What had been an impregnable fortress developed the potential to become a pile of hot radioactive sand.

America has maintained a very clear and dramatic economic and technological superiority over both Russia and China since the beginning of the nuclear age. But this fact can not change the fundamental reality that America was dramatically more vulnerable in 1995 than in 1955.

Is Slavic and Chinese technology nuclear technology good enough? Maybe not as good as American technology, but good enough to put fear into the blond soul? Remaining "good enough" does not depend upon Russia or China matching the American consumer economy. It depends upon steady progress by a very specific engineer in a very particular product.

Over the past half century the purpose of nuclear weapons has changed inside the blonds' heads. At first, they were about stopping a horde from invading Northern Europe; then they became a brake for an evil ideology, then they became an instrument to do good everywhere.

The blond objection to Slavic Orthodox Christians in Serbia, post 1990 was not that they were communists, but they were fanatics. Woodrow Wilson would have put it the same way at the beginning of the century. The blond intellectuals would not, and will not, call it Serbian cowboys and Indians.

As the technology improves, the ethnic dimension will run deeper. There will be no successor to communism. There is no need for one. The lesson the communists taught is now clear. Everyone has learned the point: 15-year-old boys are in school, and they will stay in school.

America became vulnerable because America's blond 3-year-old is finally part of the betting pool. How long she will remain part of the pool is fundamentally an engineering matter, which is to say a talent, question. But it is also a political issue.

As Christians, as democrats, as capitalists, as free men and as racists; the blonds have always had an agenda for China, which the Chinese never had for the blonds. How should blond America proceed with that agenda?

Most major political questions that seriously divide the electorate are complex, involve numerous variables, and permit no conclusive answer. The fact that nuclear weapons are such a high-tech achievement reinforces that sense of confusion, of hedging one's bets, of not being sure. Their phenomenal technical sophistication seems to promise a seamless and boundless contest stretching far into the future. The complexity reinforces the incremental approach: Do what we did last year, plus a little more.

But what is different about nuclear weapons is while they are complex, and involve numerous variables; they also present a starkly simple choice. The wrong answer will necessarily involve a massive increase in insecurity and terror for everyone in every country for as long as anyone can see. What Russia and then China demonstrated is that societies can come from a technological no-where land, to a worldwide threat very very quickly, if they have the right 11th grader.

The view here is that no one can win the engineering contest called nuclear weapons, and that the present vulnerability on all sides was predictable in 1955. Arms control is not a theology; it is a necessity forced on the world by a reality that is best captured by IQ data.

In a peculiar way, the elements that make the IQ argument distasteful to liberals; its biological basis, its rigidity, are precisely the features that shake up the international order. The Slavic/German, Chinese/Anglo-American relationships are now different because of nuclear weapons.

1945–1955

Looking back one sees how dramatic the decade 1945–1955 was. For all their economic ineffectiveness, backwardness and authoritarian political style, the Russians changed the world for the blonds forever in just 10 years. In 1955 when they exploded their first hydrogen bomb, they had, once and for all, solved their blond problem. Inside the blond world, the sheer high tech marvelousness of the bomb was now tempered by another vision.

Because airplanes were the only effective delivery mechanism in 1955, the blonds responded by pushing the pedal on their own offensive systems, and by developing a defensive warning system across Canadian and U.S. territories. The manpower, energy and capital that it took to create those 1940's and 1950's early warning systems are now as forgotten and foreign as the effort to build the local castle moat. Time and engineering have filled the warning system with sludge.

The development of the ICBM changed R.O.T.C. exams across the country. In an instant there was no value in memorizing what all those initials representing all those early warning systems meant. This inability to develop a defensive system, or at least a system that anyone would trust in a serious confrontation with an opponent with hundreds of the things, is another insight into the uniqueness of nuclear weapons. From time to time one reads about the need/promise to develop the ability to locate and destroy nuclear weapons, but the fact that these calls have been mostly just ignored by the political leaders of both parties indicates that as a practical matter almost everyone recognizes the grim reality.[472]

The first general theorem about defensive systems for nuclear weapons: As a security measure for the blonds on the North American continent, offensive nuclear weapons did not work. Half a century after Hiroshima, there is a search for defensive systems because what the blond intellectuals thought in 1950 about nuclear weapons did not turn out to be true. There is simply no question that 50 years of energy, money and talent have resulted in a blond vulnerability that would have horrified Roosevelt's and Churchill's generation.

Now, the inevitability of more vulnerability everywhere as the 11th grade gets big around the globe will require that people see certain ethnic realities clearly. Germans have always thought a certain way about Latins and Slavs. Englishmen have always thought a certain way about Celts. The Anglo-American opinion about Asians was consistent for generations, or at least until the Toyota. One imagines that Europeans have thought a certain way about Arabs for a long time.

Nuclear weapons play a role in that world. The stand-off, a rough approximation in the death count after 40 minutes of nuclear war, is more of an irritant, more of an affront, to the blond establishment, than to the Slav or Chinese leadership class.

Habits die hard partly because the forces that establish habits have a great strength and a great truth about them. The blonds are honest in seeing what they see. It is also true that the blond leadership in Washington, D.C. at the beginning and at the end of the 20th century had a better view of the Chinese and the Slavs than the Chinese and the Slavs had of them. Insularity was never the characteristic of the great fighter.

Given a world that is relentlessly ethnic, the early years of nuclear weapons will be seen, world-wide, as one of the most important brief periods in human history. The 14 years, 1941 to 1955, will take on more imaginative freight as the years pass and the terror grows. Any particular dates have an arbitrary quality, but the entry of America into World War II and the explosion of the first Russian hydrogen bomb 15 years later are as good bookends as any. How close in time, yet how revolutionary those 15 years were.

Everything changed, because everything changed for Englishmen, Germans and Americans. The democratic blonds would find that they could not fold nuclear weapons into their traditional policies. The forces, which went into play during those 15 years, will play out for centuries. Finally, the student could get at the teacher.

Had America, during that 15 year period, been much more accommodating, or much more brutal; or much more open to close alliances with certain governments that it found abhorrent, or much more openly aggressive on the sole issue whether non-blonds would be permitted to have nuclear weapons; it might have been possible to maintain a nuclear monopoly; to change history. But by 1962 for the Slavs, and 25 years after that for the Chinese, the die was cast. Engineers do not forget how to solve the problem that they solved yesterday.

American intellectual and political leader missed the really critical nature of these years because they thought that being "ahead" meant something much more dramatic than it meant in the real world. Given the nature of the product, the quality of the engineer, and the consistent size of the planet, the Chinese and Russians had to be either seduced or terrified out of the line of work. The blonds did neither. The result is a vulnerability that would have both amazed and terrified the Greatest Generation.

There is weariness even among some conservative intellectuals about the urgency of SDI as it apples to Russia. They recognize that in the event of a really large scale nuclear conflict, no defensive system would be worth anything. The kind of arguments which were given even 20 years ago have collapsed under the weight of the engineering, which is to say the weight of a very particular 11th grader grown older.

The real thrust of the conservative pro SDI argument by the new century was not directed at Russia. It was principally a concern about the "rogue" states, with China occupying some indeterminate and shifting status between real and rogue. Once China crossed that spectacular threshold where they could threaten the blond world at home, their status as wog began to shift. One can be sure that as the number of Chinese nuclear weapons advances, China will look less rogue and more real.

Notwithstanding what hardheaded tough minded conservatives may think, ethnic minorities can not be protected if their tormenter is big enough, determined enough, and has four or five nuclear weapons.[473] The Cherokee experience is alive and well.

Luce called it "The American Century," but if one reflects on what Luce meant one sees that Luce meant what the British imperialist meant. Calling it the American Century was misleading. He really meant the Anglo-American Century Now and Forever, and all in the name of universal values. This undeniable commitment to universal, democratic and abstract values is connective tissue between the British Imperial impulse, and America under the nuclear gun. One sees in Luce's essay the complete identification the American political leadership class always had with Great Britain. Most of the world where Great Britain empired see the same identification. How could it be different? Innocent enough.

However, once Russia and China have nuclear weapons, that identification has to underscore the determination of the Russian and Chinese political leadership to keep the things. However blond Protestant American intellectuals parse the deaths of the opium trade, they will never see those deaths with the same steel resolve the Chinese leaders, corrupt and dictatorial or not, have when they see them. It is in that cube of reality called nuclear weapons that British Imperialism and American democracy unite. We are in an ethnic world.

The great problem for Anglo-American policy in the 20th century was identified as German dictatorship. For most of Europe it was simply identified as Germans. But in most of the world, Germany looks rather tame. If one compares the numbers of people of color killed by the democratic blond Englishmen, and the less democratic blond Germans over the three centuries prior to 1930, there is no doubt which blond would take the award.

The Chinese or Slav sees a real disconnect between what the blond democrat is requiring "over there" and the qualities it took to make England, England; America, America; or Australia, Australia. Acknowledging the fact that the blonds always voted, it looks like blond America is insisting on universal non-ethnic values everywhere, everywhere, everywhere. Everywhere — but Plymouth.

Luce was not articulating a new position, and he was not advocating a division. He believed that if the English-speaking blonds stayed united, and were sufficiently determined, they could make the world well. If he was idealistic in his approach to political arrangements, he was also clear eyed about the great characteristics which the English-speaking blonds shared. He shared the beliefs of thousands before him, who never articulated those beliefs as well as he did. His magazines celebrated the same nuclear technological marvels that all the other important blond public intellectuals supported.

The problem was that he and they failed to see what a specific 11th grader meant for them and theirs. They really did not appreciate what the writers on IQ were saying. And there was and is no way to understand what really happened to American and British security without understanding what a cohort of Chinese and Slavic young men who could write a 775 on the math SAT mean in a nuclear world.

Orthodoxy and the WW II Generation

The English-speaking blonds always felt a certain way. It is understandable but the reaction of other people is understandable too. If one made a careful analysis of all the spots where the blonds punished intermarriage between coloreds and whites prior to 1941, the claim that America actually practiced isolationism prior to Pearl Harbor is more than hypocritical.

American interventionists have never been honest about Pearl Harbor. Is it fair to simply dismiss the Japanese claim that Pearl Harbor was partly a justifiable reaction to the fact that the blonds were going to do in Asia what they had done in Alabama? China was Exhibit number 1 for the Japanese.[474] But it was not the only exhibit. Consider Hawaii, surely an Asian entity. One of the first quasi-official acts of the blonds as they appropriated the place, was to exclude Asians.[475]

Americans look innocent at Pearl Harbor in 1940 because white people won the war, and tell the story of the war. But when one realizes how close in time the black ships, and aggression and murder in Hawaii and the Philippines occurred, one wonders how the Japanese could possibly have thought anything except that they might be next? The blond intellectuals today would insist that this would not be a fair analysis of what was likely to happen to Japan. But consider. Consider the possibility that the first detailed plans for an actual invasion was not completed by Japanese for America; it was completed, as early as 1911, by Americans for Japan. The plan had been war-gamed numerous times throughout the 1920's and 1930's.[476] I do not argue that there were actual plans to attack Japan in 1941. But I argue a more general question. If one pulled out all the plans developed by English speaking blonds between 1500 and 1941 to attack other populations, were there any instances where the blonds had as many detailed plans as they had for Japan where, eventually, they did not attack?

It took the World War II generation to really nail the orthodoxy of intervention to the pulpit rail of America. The confluence of both fascism and communism as modernizing techniques, and American determination to prevent Russia from just gunning down German civilians in the street probably made a nuclear stand-off inevitable in Europe.

However, after a half century of engineering, nuclear terror has emerged as a challenge to the orthodoxy. Henry Luce's successor knows the blonds, democratic and idealistic, will not land soldiers in Mainland China to protect Tibet. Nuclear weapons have emerged from instrumentalism, to the prize itself.

Force, and the threat of enough force changes the way people speak and think. The World War II generation developed a style of thinking about international affairs which may have always been present in American life to some degree, but 1941-1945 saw the interventionist ambition become an unchallengeable tenet of patriotism.

Sooner or later nuclear weapons will force an American generation to make a bigger break with the World War II generation than would have been imaginable in the 1950's. General Lemay, General Patton and General Montgomery themselves would have second thoughts once the wog had the potential to kill the blond 3- year-old in her father's house. I do not know which generation will articulate the obvious, that the World War II generation overreached on the nuclear weapons question, but sooner or later, it has to be spoken.

The democratic blonds can not force a universalistic ethic, which they themselves did not practice, on an ethnic world. No population will sacrifice literally everything to make other people good. If Berlin in 1945 proves a point, so does Hungary, Korea, Vietnam and Serbia.

For 50 years the American editorial writer filtered nuclear weapons through a lens which blurred the reality. They could ignore what being a target meant for a time, but finally the engineering became so good in so many places that it has to be addressed. What has happened? What is likely to happen?

There is no possibility that Russia or China will stop educating their 15-year-olds. There is no possibility that they will lose their ability to make and improve nuclear weapon systems.

There is a kind of nostalgia about what America's place in the world once was.[477] But the 1950's will never return. One observer, reviewing why the West has become so much more vulnerable than anyone would have guessed at the beginning of the nuclear age, opined that nuclear weapons are easier to build than the establishment once thought.[478] The emphasis is backwards; it points towards a discrete bundle of stuff and technique, and away from the issue that makes the game this particular game: the quality of talent in the game. There is an understandable reluctance of American leaders to bluntly discuss with the American people the "real" state of affairs, which is to say the engineering state of affairs.

The wars with Iraq taught a lesson, but they did not teach the lesson conservatives think they taught. They demonstrated, with precision, that a technologically advanced U.S. could destroy the army of a small and technologically unsophisticated nation with amazingly few American casualties. In retrospect, it is understandable how some democrats could see, here, the true foundation of a New World order: an exhaustive menu of computerized equipment that could kill the opponents' soldiers but not the opponents' civilians. The blond democrat believes that with enough battlefield electronics he can finally realize the dream which was, in part, the dream of the first British imperialist warrior: Peacekeeping.[479]

Nuclear weapons are the antidote of the lessons of Iraq I and II. Here again, one sees how different nuclear weapons are from the technological marvels just below them on the ladder of force. Matching the U.S. in the production of tactical battlefield wizardry is like matching America in Wal-Marts. Absent America's economy it can not be done.

But because strategic nuclear weapons engage the blond on the blond's territory by putting the blond three-year-old into play, the test for strategic nuclear weaponry is more modest than the test for tactical nuclear weaponry. Your tactical nuclear weapon has to be better than the blond tactical nuclear weapon or you die on the battlefield. Your strategic nuclear weapon just has to be good enough. Not as good as the blond strategic nuclear weapon, but good enough to dampen the blond enthusiasm. Good enough to keep the blonds at home. Strategic nuclear weapons make it possible to keep the tactical magic out of your country.

Once upon a time Russia and more recently China could have been the stage for an Iraqi style exhibition. Nuclear weapons change that. It is not possible that Chinese or Russians political leaders would not have reflected on that as they watched the drama at the OK Corral in the Gulf. One assumes that other potential nuclear powers, "rogues," must have seen the same reality. Nuclear weapons are unique: They suffocate those layers of highly sophisticated weaponry just below them in the technology ladder. How different the discussions will be about North Korea if it becomes clear that the rogue has developed the capability to deliver nuclear weapons into the American heartland.

To be what America wishes to be, which is, as the Chinese Communists point out, the worldwide hegemonic power; it has to be able to neutralize nuclear weapons. No one believes that America will bet New York for a whole laundry list of alliances, goals and ambitions. When a sophisticated conservative academician appears to claim that because America has a faster rate of economic growth it should be able to successfully assert hegemony, he misses the point of the second half of the 20th century.[480]

America's imagery of itself as the nave isolationist was always at odds with reality. Certainly it was not the reality prior to World War II. Consider the obituary of General Matthew B. Ridgeway who died in 1993 at the age of 98. The sheer number and diversity of places where he went, often to use force, would have impressed the Vikings.

The son of a Regular Army artillery officer, he was born at Fort Monroe, Virginia, on March 3, 1895. In 1925 he was the commander of a company in Tsientsin, China. In 1930 he became a military technical advisor to Theodore Roosevelt Jr., the Governor General of the Philippines. In the late 1930's he went to Brazil. In 1943 he was in North Africa. In the late 1940's he was in the Caribbean. In the early 1950's with his appointment as commander of U. N. forces in Korea, he assumed the post for which older people would remember him. Later he was appointed to Tokyo.

One imagines that had the General had a cousin in Great Britain, the geography would have been different, but just as impressive. The English-speaking blonds have always traveled.

Can that travel continue? In a nuclear age?

The point is not America's collapse. America has the great strengths that it always had. The American economy is still the world's largest, Marxism as a European phenomenon has collapsed; American engineers are still some of the worlds most inventive and original. It is still morning in America on any number of indices. But in an important way, if one concentrates on the years 1947-1972 one sees that, on the nuclear front, America became vulnerable far beyond what

Henry Luce, Prime Minister Churchill, President Truman, President Roosevelt, and the rest of the blond English-speaking sainted greatest-generation would have though possible at the end of World War II.

The metaphor, the American cruise missile as the 21st century version of the 19th century Anglo-American man-of-war, has a very blond bounce and enthusiasm about it.[482] But if I am right, and the heart of the nuclear age is the 11th grade, the population that will pay the most for extending the metaphor into the real world is the next generation of blonds.

Compare the security of those revelers celebrating the victories of World War II in Times Square with the vulnerability of their grandchildren in Times Square today. Compare where the American soldiers could go with impunity in 1945, with where he can go today. The vulnerability for the North American continent increases each time a Chinese, or Russian, or Muslim, or North Korean engineer learns a little more. The tissue between biology, IQ, and nuclear weaponry can not be cut.

The Americans, like the British before them, and for many of the same reasons including geography, wealth, racial identification, democracy, idealism and a strong tendency toward hypocrisy wish to be good policemen. But the inevitability of ethnicity in this world means that the ambition finally confuses everyone, including the policeman himself. The Chinese, Islam, Orthodox Slavs, India or Pakistan just can not concede that the U.S. is the world indispensable policeman once the U.S. begins making demands on them in their neighborhood.

What does "world leadership" mean in a world of nuclear weapons? Does it mean, can it mean, that the U.S. will literally risk 50 million deaths, massive areas of the continent destroyed for millennia, because of an idealistic impulse to do good? Nuclear weapons insure that the responsibilities of the cruise missile will be limited in a way that the man-of-war was not.

I agree with substantial parts of the work of certain academicians who have focused on the implications of nuclear weapons, and who have warned against certain basic American assumptions buried within the WW II Orthodoxy. They properly underline just how fast Chinese nuclear technology has developed, and how vulnerable certain American interests have become. Paul Bracken[483] focuses on American bases in Asia, Samuel Huntington deals with strategic issues within a discussion of "civilizations."[484]

Huntington's concept of civilization, a structure related to culture, but different, may have particular relevance in the future of nuclear weapons. However, it could be dangerous to push the concept too far. It looks excessively intellectual, refined and somewhat removed: It would be dangerous to scrap the more basic, visceral, specific, and bloody term "ethnicity." When Russians look at Germans, or Chinese at Anglo-Americans, they remember specifics.

Bracken is right to concentrate on Asia as a different and particularly dangerous place now that nuclear weapons are there. But his analysis is highly dependent upon the kind of imagery that conservatives use to justify completely opposite strategies and goals. There are numerous references to international business, technology, issues of organizational structures, and information transfers; all of which may be insightful and true enough, but miss the true story of the relentless march of nuclear technology in Asia over two generations: that 11th grader. The professor favors the abstract over the familiar. His final analysis of the issue also blurs the hard reality. He properly corrects the assumption that the U.S. versus China contest is about side-by-side comparisons of tanks, missiles and planes. Rather, he says, they are about missiles versus bases. In fact, finally, they are about missiles versus people; people there, and now, people here.

American intellectuals have always had a much greater abhorrence about dictatorships over there, than racism over here. Consider what Mark Twain must have witnessed in black-white relationships in pre-Civil War America. Consider what Mark Twain, as a young man, must have witnessed and heard about the blonds and Mexicans, or the blonds and Indians, in California. Consider his remark that if the only thing that can destroy the czardom is dynamite, one should give thanks for dynamite.[485] How American it sounds. How modern it sounds.

Continuing the Anglo-American policeman orthodoxy in practice requires that America be immune from nuclear terror. One read in the 1990's about the risk that the proliferation of certain configurations of computers posed to America's nuclear supremacy.[486] All such articles featured a more or less desperate sense of urgency, and an impressive string of initials and models.

In the 1940's a similarly urgent story could have featured technology about heavy water, or chemicals, or exotic metals. Ten years later the story would have focused on rocket thrust. Ten years after that instrumentation became the magic under review.

But, after 50 years of more or less the same ending, technology after technology, there is no excuse for the intelligent reader to just put the paper down with a furrow across his or her forehead. Fifty years are worth something. It has been long enough, and expensive enough and dangerous enough for people to think about the project precisely as a 50-year experiment. At the end of a half-century of the experiment there is no doubt that America is more vulnerable, by orders of magnitude, than it was when the experiment began.

As electronics begin to replace industrial processes around the world, the trend line favors America's enemies at America's expense. Within the nuclear weapon story, the dynamic progressively shifts away from the large industrial blond economies and toward the rogue states that can match that really gifted engineer.

It is useful to tally nuclear weapons in two columns: one about economics, and one about the 11th grader. The Third World has a monstrously difficult task in making a bomb that can kill 10 million blonds. The first few missiles are agony. But as time goes on, the product line is finally in place. Then the job becomes more restricted. The importance of the capacity to create Wal-Marts recedes. Instrumentation issues, a discrete reality, matters of pure engineering, become more important.

The Americans, no less than the English, will always be able to develop a scenario that "going over there" is necessary to forestall an attack over here. The past five hundred years are enough history to demonstrate the point. The blond optimism about nuclear technology in the middle of the 20th century is partially an echo of the age-old British enthusiasm for going over there.

If the nuclear story is about technological systems, economics, and bravery; America's liberal and conservative interventionists are right. SDI is just one more technological marvel that the intelligent, energetic, optimistic blonds can master. In which case, every effort to put some control or restrain on nuclear weapons is a mistake. Even the prospect of a treaty dries up money and interest in SDI research.[487]

Conversely, if the nuclear threat is about what I say it is about; IQ and the 11th grade, every step along the nuclear road is one more step of blond Anglo-America forcing its own young toward a collision with biological reality and a real world oven. The future will demand that America declare itself on that dichotomy; practical problems require real world real time decisions. The nuclear game has a resemblance to that baseball game played in late May right after school by the sixth grade boys. When it begins the players are aware that the days are nice, long, warm, and summer vacation is just a few days away. But, too soon, early September, the sun begins to sink and parents and homework call. The 1950's were "School's out!" time for nuclear weapons. But in 1955, up in the heavens, a real world time line was staring to descend to earth. That time line forces a theoretical economic and biological issue into a real world, practical, day by day, problem.

At the start of the Third Millennium nuclear weapons might be considered in three loosely connected bundles: the blast, the delivery, and the instrumentation. They form the heart of the incredible vulnerability America has taken on in three generations following WW II.

A fourth bundle is possible: Put the platform for the missile "up there." If, a generation from now, America wakes up to find that that oven is five minutes away, it has only its blond optimism about its own abilities, and its contempt for the abilities of the Slavs and the Chinese, to blame.

6

Blonds and Slavs: Theory Meets Reality

Resolved, That we regard it as an insult to the people of Texas, who have gallantly achieved their liberties by the sword of revolution, to make the consent of Mexico a prerequisite to their re-annexation to the United States; and that an attempt to procure the assent of Mexico, now convulsed with insurrection and torn with contending factions, each claiming to wield the rightful powers of government, would be as fruitless as unnecessary, and uncalled for by justice and law of the case.

The New Hampshire Legislature[488]

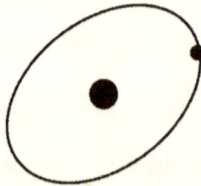

Tonight, when the Slavs close their eyes just before falling asleep, they can see in their imagination, millions and millions of beautiful little three year old blond girls with blue eyes throughout a wide and long land mass running from eastern Europe to the English Channel and then across the Channel to England and then, finally, to the Atlantic Ocean. And then, just in the last few seconds before dreamland, they see all those beautiful little girls on fire and on fire in 18 minutes. They then fall asleep for the best night's sleep that they have had for two thousand years.

It is a tribute to the blonds that that vision is what it took to keep the blonds at home: to their intelligence, their idealism, their fighting ability and their understandable racial identity. It is a tribute to a very specific 15-year-old Slav algebra student that he could give it what it took.

I am 63 years old and am part of a blessed generation. My generation has seen the resolution of as big a question as God, History, Evolution; pick one, as the human race has ever had presented to it. We may have been happy, we may have spent 50 years on medication; we may have been popular, we may have been hermits; we may have become rich beyond our youthful dreams of the 1950's, or we may be looking for supper in a Dumpster in an alley. But most generations are born, live and die without seeing a single really important issue resolved. A few see middling important issues resolved. A handful is like our generation and sees the resolution of one of the issues that will be central to human experience for all time.

On one side of the line first graders learn their lessons in a Slavic language, on the other side, in a Germanic language. Who draws that line?

It is precisely the intelligence and freedom of the blonds that makes them the threat that they are. Put more Protestant German families in Southern Brazil, and Brazil has to look like Alabama. What bothers the blonds bothers the blonds, and it has nothing to do with civics class.

Nuclear weapons are an engineered, artificial, political, focused response to advantages that are free, natural, aesthetic, social, moral and ubiquitous. Outside the blond world, political bureaucracies created nuclear weapons. Nuclear weapons force the blonds, more than any other population, into a different and more dangerous world.

What one sees with British soccer fan hooliganism: destruction, humiliation, and sometimes death, is what one would have seen with the Vikings a thousand years ago. Whether it is a crime or a joke is a matter of ethnic perspective. Clearly the racism is both informal and dangerous for the people living next to the British. The racism carries a great military advantage. The Vikings have remained constant.

My favorite comment about the fall of communism and the constancy of nuclear weapons was made by William F. Buckley Jr., perhaps America's most celebrated anti-communist conservative. He labeled as "strange" Prime Minister Tadeusz Mazowiecki's suggestion that Soviet troops might remain in Poland if its western border with Germany became an issue.[489] In fact it is not strange. It is largely what Eastern European history has been about. It is about blonds and non-blonds living together. Nuclear weapons have changed the game, because they have transformed certain populations that have historically been targets of the blonds. They turn the blonds into targets.

I suggest that for certain purposes one may understand the blonds best by considering Germans and Englishmen as the true representatives of the type, and then listen closely to what they have had to say about their near neighbors, Irishmen and Slavs. While an Asian or African might have trouble distinguishing them; it is here that one really sees the great racist core of the great fighter, and one can begin to abstract those characteristics that nuclear weapons would eventually begin to quarantine.

First, the blonds never needed a bureaucracy. Conversely the wogs would never have the ability to handle the blonds without a bureaucracy. For hundreds of years English intellectuals must have believed about Ireland what Kipling believed. There was no country there. That was a number of disorganized bands preying on each other.[490] Would the Germans on Eastern Europe or Anglo-Americans on Mexico have sounded different?

The main event sells fight night. The Germans and the Slavs have known each other a long, long time. When the big night came, it would make a difference on score cards across the planet. The blonds who speak English never saw German's position in Europe through Germanic eyes, even though they had more in common with the Germans than with the rest of the continent.

On the continent, religion and force stopped the Germans from doing what the blonds did everywhere else. No matter how democratic, modern and scornful northern Germany may have been, it could not break the Catholic Church in Germany. More important, because the English-speaking blonds would enter fight night as a unit, and because the Slavs are much more effective fighters than the Mexicans, the German ethnic cleanser could not do what the American ethnic cleanser could do.

On the European continent, a frankly Germanic political entity carried both the threats of democracy and of racism in the same way a victory by an English-speaking population in North America did in the 17th and 18th centuries. The Germans as blonds represented both in a visible ethnic way.

Those American intellectuals that welcome the Pope's apology for the familiar bundle of events: Inquisition, slavery and the Holocaust miss the point in the same way the Vatican misses the point. The inquisition, slavery/racism and the Holocaust all have ethnic dimensions. If the inquisition and religious repression generally fails, if religious freedom becomes established on the Continent, the blonds are free. On the North American continent, what feels right to the blonds is unchecked; people that look like Thomas Jefferson use black women as sperm receptacles. In Europe, the German, free from a foreign religion, was a reality that would have to be addressed by a Slav, sooner or later.

For American conservatives Hitler represents political authoritarianism at an extreme level. To the Slavs Hitler represents Germans unvarnished. It may not be Anglos and Mexicans in the American Southwest in the 1840's, but it is close enough.

Were the Germans in the grip of a dictatorship which they could not be expected to throw off?[491] Or was Hitler giving the Germans the foreign policy that the German people really wanted? Which is to say, the same policy British New England in the 19th century wanted in Northern Mexico.

Were nuclear weapons inevitable? There is a sense in which nuclear weapons bridge the gap between the personal and the social. There may have been as many happy informal childhood memories between seven year old Slav and German boys though the centuries, as there were between black and white seven year old boys in the American South. There were numerous instances where Germans moved east, just as Americans moved south, into Mexico, at the request of the wog maximum leader.

Anglo-Americans must have known many Mexicans in a civil, even a friendly way, just as Germans must have known many Slavs. However the seven-year-old wog gets older and finds out in the personal the reality of the polity. The blonds have an ethnic contempt for him, and the blonds want the land. Given the racial sensitivities of the blonds, it could not have worked any other way.

Once the Slavs have nuclear weapons, no one cares what Hitler really represents. The only thing that counts is what the Slavs think he represented.

For half a century blond American intellectuals told Americans that the struggle between the Soviet Union and the United States was brought on because of an aggressive ideology. Communism collapses. Nuclear weapons remain in place, and Americans and Russians continue to spy on one another.

Communism provided the bureaucracy that gave the Slavs the focus that the Germans never needed. The same is true of Chinese communism. The blonds great strengths, coupled with their informal racism, always provided as much focus as they would ever need.

Skinner's dictum that the real point of psychology is to be able to predict the single event reflects his ambition that psychology should emulate physics. But it violates his own theory. It presupposes a mental apparatus, separate and apart promulgating scientific goals. The observation that science is simply what scientists do would have been more consistent with his theory. The weather scientist is as much a scientist as the atomic physicist, and IQ solutions can be as good a solution, where statistical solutions are appropriate, as behaviorist accounts.

Statistical probes, such as social distance scales, could have predicted Germany's behavior toward the East in the 20th century. The same probes could have predicted the ability and interest of the United States to expand at the expense of Mexico in the 19th century.

In the working out, democracy has underlined and strengthened racism. Democracy and strength in a blond society have repeatedly insured that, sooner or later, the blonds will try to get what they want from their neighbors.

It is inevitable that a world where the Slavs have nuclear weapons will feel unnatural to the blonds generally, but particularly to the Germans. Similarly, but to a lesser degree, the Americans will perceive the Chinese with nuclear weapons as a kind of low boil continuous irritation: a violation of natural order and good manners. The 19th century felt somehow right to the blonds, in the same way that a James Bond movie in the twentieth century felt right.

Nuclear weapons float on very real ethnic tectonic plates. Probes of ethnicity are more like what the weather scientist does than what the atomic physicist does. What the analysis lacks in precision, it makes up in impact in the real world. The last half of the 20th century saw the beginnings of a product that will be with the human race for hundreds of years. For the first, brief, infancy of the weapon, a plausible argument could have been fashioned that it would serve ideological ends. But by the time of the weapon's adolescence an acute observer could have predicted what happened. The youngster would serve ethnic interests.

One saw in the various celebrations marking the 50th anniversary of VE Day, how much Britishness and Protestantism matter to America's fundamental nature. Similarly, in Eastern Europe, one saw with the break up of Communism how much Orthodox Christianity and a common Slavic background matter.

Certain Eastern European populations identify with Russia, and are willing to acknowledge Russia as the elder brother. Those decisions, in turn, will play a role in the geography of nuclear weapons: One will hear of agreements, formal and informal, between Russia and its younger brothers. After it all sugars down, some imaginative editor will print a map overlaying the boundaries of the nuclear map with the map of Orthodox Christianity established nine hundred years ago. Pundits will say, "Of course. How could it be otherwise?"

By 1995 it was clear that the collapse of ideology had not ended nuclear weapon research and had not closed out the threat of annihilation. Indeed one read that a more openly ethnic and more Orthodox reality was being born, and that the nuclear bomb was a central pillar of the new political arrangement.

One did not hear that final sigh of relief about the end of Communism from America's intellectuals, which 50 years of books about ideology by those same intellectuals would have predicted. Rather one sensed a disappointment, exasperation, anger and apprehension about what a frankly Christian Russia seemed to be tolerating, protecting (?) in Eastern Europe.

The site of the former Yugoslavia was bound to be the site of interminable ethnic conflict. Even where Germanic populations do not figure prominently in the conflict, the Germans are the people who are always potentially there, playing a role. The first and most important chapter in the tome on nuclear weapons is entitled, "Germans and Slavs, Now and Forever."

Inevitably, one mark of ethnicity is a certain amount of agreement across national boundaries. Not on every issue, and not all the time. But most of the time, and on most of the really important issues.

Who would deny that Germans and Englishmen are at least cousins? Were World War I and II, a murderous mutual assault engulfing two generations, violations of truisms about ethnicity? From a distance it certainly looks like they were. But there may be much bigger and more dramatic differences between Englishmen and German than the outsider would imagine. It would be very interesting to hear a series of focus groups of Englishmen and Germans describe each other. By comparison, the focus groups of each on Brazilians, Egyptians, Japanese, Italians and Indians would be boring and predictable. Racism flattens and simplifies social relations generally. But Germans and Englishmen have no objection to each on that plane. It would be fascinating to hear each group explain the other's behavior in the twentieth century.

The blonds have never stayed home. Blond internationalism inevitably becomes interventionism. The true isolationist is the classical peasantry in a series of isolated, familistic, authoritarian villages. That just is not the blond; Germanic, British or American. One is not surprised that the English discovered Africa, the Americans discovered the Japanese, and the Germans discovered the Slavs. Never the reverse.

What the blonds discovered did not impress them. The unofficial pre-modern history of Europe includes some impressive anecdotal evidence about a handful of blonds capturing the political center of very large agricultural empires.[492] There was a blond European empire in Russia, Eastern Europe and parts of the Mediterranean, which preceded and presaged the British Empire. Hitler saw the Hapsburg political entity as a specifically Germanic empire. When one reads about joint Slavic and Italian delegations at a "Congress of Oppressed Austrian Nationalities," one assumes that the day to day unofficial contact between the blonds and the wogs remained more or less consistent through the centuries, in the Germanic as well as the English blond empire.[493]

The blond English speaking intellectual would see very different authors behind the drama "1914" and the drama "1941." The discontinuities overwhelm the similarities. In the Slavic Orthodox world the fundamental sameness overwhelms everything else. They would see much bigger toys the second time around, but the Germans remain the Germans. That is the key to understanding how long nuclear weapons will survive, that there are no demons in the story, just people. Hitler's remark that Germans did not intermarry with Slavs, had a parallel in the 19th century in the United States as the blonds forced freedom into Mexico, northern Mexico became blond, and interracial marriage warranted imprisonment.[494]

Labeling the outbreak of the First World War the "greatest single catastrophe" in the history of the Europeans peoples misses the war's essential nature.[495] It was fated to happen. It happened everywhere the blonds bumped up against what were not them. The alternatives to the wars structuring the British Empire are Brazil or a true isolationism, like that of Japan for several centuries. Neither really suits the blue-eyed people.

One just assumes that the relationship between the U.S. and Mexico will be prickly. One assumes the same about Germany and Russia.

The combination of bemusement and aggression, which has always marked the dividing line between the blonds and their neighbors, is understandable on a number of levels, and is unlikely to disappear. Today that is just one of the characteristics that promise an increased nuclear threat for the blonds as well as everyone else. Another is the selective hypocrisy that always traveled with genuine idealism. For over two hundred years, the blond English speaking people have interfered in other peoples' race wars in a way that no one interfered with their race wars.

If there was blond establishment post World War II analysis of prejudice, Gordon W. Allport wrote it.[496] One sees the long arm of the World War II generation and its ability to set the terms of debate on a variety of social questions. It is when one transfers that analysis of prejudice to Eastern Europe and nuclear weapons that one sees how misleading and dangerous that Allport's analysis, America's analysis, was.

Allport emphasizes cognition, the person within; acting or reacting to ethnic or religious differences. He identifies six major approaches to a theory of prejudice, and labels his interpretation as eclectic. He acknowledges value in all of the six and certain truths in the resulting theoretical structures, even where there is some theoretical tension.

The six: historical influences, sociocultural, situational, psychodynamic, phenomenological (what the prejudiced individual in fact sees), and earned reputation (in many instances groups have the reputations they have for good reasons), has an arbitrariness about it. Many social science classification schemes share that trait but still can be useful.

But nearly a half century after Allport pronounced the theory one sees an omission. Between the middle of the 20th century and the beginning of the 21st century, one went from assuming biology would not be mentioned, to assuming it would appear as 1 or 2 on almost any list. What might a sociobiological insert look like?

It might refer to the behavior of fish or birds or reptiles. Certainly it would footnote chimpanzee behavior. Beyond that?

Assume that humans are the result of millions of years of juvinilization. It just is not possible to imagine that the process could have worked that long without a preference for the process, or the results of the process, within the organism itself. The Germans in Europe are a more attractive representation of the contest than the Japanese are in Asia, but they may each have their respective reputations as racists for solid biological reasons.

Interestingly, Allport uses the Germans, and not the Slavs, as an example of neurotic conformists and fanatical ideologues.[497] Would anyone, besides English speaking blonds, have made the same judgment? I do not think so.

The kind of intelligent non-ethnic specific social science represented by Allport just is not good enough to handle the world that is now coming at North American society via nuclear weapons. The American intellectual establishment, overwhelmingly protestant and Jewish has refused to accept the bedrock ethnic reality of nuclear weapons.

The following is most instructive sentence ever written on the longevity of nuclear weapons: A specific Slav 11th grader tied to a specific product has transformed a millennia old, confusingly episodic, intermittent, patchy, blurred, extensive social cloud; into a small, precise, clean, crisp, focused behavioral clock. The Slav has developed the ability to kill every German in Germany in 20 minutes. The 11th grader has put free men everywhere on notice.

Nuclear weapons have survived the fall of Communism: In this they have helped our understanding of the world. Just as they demonstrate, in an exaggerated way, the role of intelligence in developing economies; so they show with a bright light, ethnicity, the ancient relationships between Slavs and Germans. Dr. James B. Conant's belief that communism would collapse, because of its own inefficiencies, sometime in the 1980's certainly does seem prescient; but if he thought that that collapse would celebrate the end of nuclear weapons, he suffered from a serious naiveté.[498]

Professor Conant's opinion of the Russians apparently was not much different than Professor Einstein's: They walked around as members of "hordes."[499] Now Conant and Einstein are two of the most eminent names in the history of nuclear weapons. Both were concerned about the future of nuclear weapons. But neither one was interested in thinking about Russians as engineers. They did not think that they had to ask "Is there something about Russians which would make it not only conceivable but inevitable that they would have the ability to turn the American landscape into a nuclear fireball by the end of the 20th century?" That "something" is at the heart of what the entire world has witnessed in the last half of the 20th century and will witness again and again if nations do not place limits on their nuclear programs.

The top of the Russian IQ distribution can do a lot of engineering. When upwards of 90% of the blond populations were in school, compared to less than 50% of Russians there was no penalty for regarding the Russians as hordes. It was inevitable that the grandchildren of Einstein and Conant would live with the reality of thinking them hordes, once 90% of Russian children went to school.

Over the very, very critical short term of 1945 to, say 1963, a few years that really made a difference for the future of German/Slav relationship for the next thousand years, the American leadership class saw what was being created in Russia, but failed to make any reasonable generalizations about the experience.

Accordingly, the experience was bound to repeat itself with populations which were increasingly more of a stranger to the blonds than the Slavs.

One of the great anomalies of Anglo/American nuclear diplomacy is that underneath the roars of triumphalism, one sees a steady and consistent progression of nuclear power away from opponents who are more like the blonds toward populations that are more distant; strangers.

Certainly the Germans, America's first deadly enemy during the nuclear age, were more like Americans than any of the populations which would replace them in the role as demon. Similarly, now that Christianity has replaced Marxism as the dominant belief system in Russia, it is clear that American Catholics and Protestants have more in common with the Russians than they do with the Chinese. Will Islam follow China as the next serious nuclear power? Does anyone doubt that there is a longer, more intense, more bitter rivalry between the West and Islam, than between the West and any of the powers which preceded Islam in the nuclear novel?

Had something been worked out with the Germans in 1944 or 1945 it might have been possible to stop the Russian, the relative stranger from gaining nuclear weapons. Had something, been worked out with Russia it might have been possible to stop the Chinese, the more distant stranger, from gaining nuclear weapons. If something could be worked out with the Russians and the Chinese, it might be possible to prevent Islam, the implacable thousand year opponent of Europe from gaining nuclear weapons. This potential horror is the final result of a policy that completely discounted ethnicity, in favor of threats to enforce universalisms that were not practiced by the blond democrats themselves, during their relentless march to take over three continents.

American intelligence agencies have long predicted the spread of nuclear technology. Consider the 1961 proposal by the chairman of the Joint Chiefs of Staff, General Lyman Lemnitzer, that America make an unprovoked nuclear attack on Russia in 1963, the last time when Russia could be attacked without provoking nuclear retaliation.[500] While the normal response may be to recoil in horror, the ability of the blonds to continue to do in the 21st century, what they had done in the 17th, 18th, 19th and 20th centuries rests precisely on the blonds' ability to shield their own populations from destruction.

I would argue that seen in the proper context the Cuban Missile Crises was the first major demonstration that nuclear weapons would dampen the blonds' ambitions more than any other population. It would be interesting to read classified documents of the late 1950's and early 1960's, up to the time of the crises. Were there policy makers who advocated a preemptive nuclear strike? By the time Russians pulled their missiles out the American leadership class had, for the first time, concentrated on what a nuclear weapon exploding on the home front really meant. I suspect that there was a dramatic decrease in speculation about the desirability of a preemptive strike once the excitement died down.

American leaders think that they have a mandate to contain Communist China, to contain a nationalistic Orthodox Russia, to contain a fundamentalist Islam, to make the world well through threats based on superior nuclear technology. The seriousness with which they approach the mandate could probably first have been seen in classified discussions about whether or not America should use nuclear weapons against Russian civilians. I would predict those discussions are there. Up to about 1962.

A nuclear stalemate, once established, was fated to last for generations. The image of a long protracted standoff does not fit well with American optimism. It fits perfectly with the view that nuclear weapons are engineered products, and that once a country develops a very big school system, very impressive talent begins to become visible.

Nuclear weapons, alive inside the ancient text of human civilizations, impress with their youth and their potency. Just three generations old, they affect everyone's thinking on every important point of conflict. Once a minor country gets them, it becomes a major country. See under "China."

One wonders how Russians viewed Germany when no one had nuclear weapons, compared to how they view Germany now, when the Russians have thousands of them. One wonders how the change has affected the Germans. In Asia how did the natives parse the end of the Vietnam War? Did nuclear weapons figure in their interpretation of events?

World War II probably strengthened a set of assumptions that the English speaking blonds had had for generations; from times far back, centuries before America existed. The assumptions and the strengths supported each other. The role of policeman is not a new one. What is new is that a series of rogues are developing the ability to follow the policeman home.

Nuclear weapons cut across a long long blond ethnic tradition. To the extent the ancient assumptions have been passed to the new generations, there will be long periods when the world just will not "feel right."

Nothing could have stopped the blonds from taking North America and Australia from the aborigines. Given the opinion the Germans have long had about Slavs, much of the 20th century might have been predicted.

It is very difficult to develop data that would be useful to the development of political "science." But a paper, which would have been useful in predicting the fate of Yugoslavia, appeared in 1977.[501]

The authors tracked the movements of the Yugoslav peasantry into cities, a process that is taking place everywhere. The researchers found that the religious identity of the city made a critical difference in determining the peasant's destination. They did not behave in an economically rationally manner and just move to the nearest and most convenient center of opportunity.

The humorous, good-natured description of Yugoslavia as a nation of two alphabets, three religions, four languages, five nationalities and six republics, was replaced by a more natural, more ethnic, more brutal, more honest reality.[502]

Differences can be too numerous, too big, and too strong for a single national thread to hold.

As bad as the bloodshed has been, it could have been worse. In fact maybe the great lesson about Yugoslavia might be that, a few decades ago, the carnage might have led to a European wide war.

If one imagines the sore bursting in Eastern Europe at the end of the 19th century, rather than the end of the 20th century, one realizes that at the end of the 20th century a key participant is missing, a neighbor who has both ethnic and political interests. A big and intelligent neighbor. Of course. Germany.

If Germany is not a player, Russia is. Russia is there whether or not the American establishment likes it. It is just the way the world is, and it makes a difference.

In any struggle involving either Germany or Anglo-America against Orthodox Slavs, it is inevitable that the Russians will play the role of the elder brother to the Orthodox. The real role of the elder brother is not to protect the younger, smaller brother from a chastising or even a whipping when the younger brother deserves it. The real role of the elder brother is to get involved when the smaller brother seems to be at serious risk from really superior forces. Particularly if there is a threat the bully might eventually turn on the elder. You can tease, push and bully your friend's smaller brother; if you commence to break his arm, you have lost your friend and gained an enemy. When 13 Security Council members voted to prohibit Serbia from supplying material to its proxies, one sees what ethnicity means when Russia vetoed the resolution.[502]

Do nuclear weapons play a role? Assume that Roosevelt had forced England and Russia to accept something less than the complete destruction of Germany. Assume further that, in 1955 or 1956, two of the most important years in history, the Germans tracked the Russians down the nuclear road and exploded a hydrogen bomb. Bosnia would look very different at the end of the twentieth century.

The British and American Empires grew big behind the argument that if aggression is not stopped early, it will inevitable become worse. The non-blond 11th grader who can write a 780 on the math SAT is the final answer to that type of reasoning. The logic of the blond interventionists is as good as it always was. A nuclear-armed Russia and a nuclear-armed China, however, restrain that logic.

Serbia will not mark the final attempt to locate just where Russia's younger brothers live. There will be English speaking voices sounding the alarm with frequent references to the "lessons" of the European twentieth century. There always were. There were warnings before World War II, before Munich, before World War I before the Spanish American War. Interventionism within a relentlessly ethnic world demands a certain psychology in a substantial part of the imperial population.

In a sense, the British Empire was the accretion of islands through a stream of logic: One can never be safe enough. One expects the same publication from the American foreign policy establishment that one expects from the British foreign policy establishment: Warnings about the dangers that may occur if one stays home, and does nothing.

The ability of the blonds to literally threaten total war, total destruction, was lost during the last half of the twentieth century. In this the world is more different for the blonds than it has ever been. Democracy will not be required as a precondition of peace. Moreover, there is no need for the Russians of the Chinese to avoid the kind of role along their borders that England played, and the U.S. played along their borders.

There may be conflicts where Russia plays a "non-constructive" role, by the standards applied by Americans. But if one looked at the history of U.S. involvement in Latin America one would not be surprised. In the real world, to have an advantage is to use it.

Orthodox Slavs have the great non-negotiable guarantor of peace: They have nuclear weapons, and the Germans do not. Perhaps the most telling incident about the determination Russians will likely display to maintain nuclear supremacy over the Germans is from World War II. When the Germans offered to trade Stalin's own son, a fighter pilot who had been captured, for a German officer, Stalin refused saying that he did not trade field marshals for soldiers. The son died in a German prison camp, and the man's son, Stalin's grandson, praised Stalin for the sacrifice for the sake of the Russian war effort.[504]

Where American fears aggregate around "Munich" Russian fears revolve around Germany. "Extremism in defense of liberty is no vice," like every general political statement, carries its own ethnic message. The Russians are not bothered by high sounding political slogans. They are bothered by the specific and recurring nightmare that the Germans have liberty and the Russians do not have nuclear weapons. "Muscular Protestantism" sounds one way in Minnesota. It sounds very different on that Slavic/Protestant division in Europe. "Liberty" has always been the blond's flag. Ethnic survival has always been written on the flag of the blond's neighbor.

The blond intellectual's attempt to portray political systems in a circle, that fascists and communists might touch each other, rather than a left/right linear scale has much to recommend it. The Communists in Russia and China did share some ambitions with religious conservatives and political fascists in South America, who also rightly claimed that they were forces of modernization.

But there are serious qualifications with the circle imagery where nuclear weapons are concerned. The Catholic Church is one. While it operates to inhibit democracy, it also operates to inhibit the development of the ultimate weapon. Where the Catholic Church provides the fundamental lens for the political eye to view the world, there will be limits on the use of force. Argentina and Brazil probably could become nuclear powers. But a religious authority would trump any ambition in that direction. A Communist Russia, China, or North Korea has no similar damper.

It is impossible to imagine Roosevelt and Truman as non-Protestants. They were supreme realists and not tied to any authority above the nation state system. The Chinese and the Slavs saw what Roosevelt and Truman were willing to do to win.

The Chinese and the Slavs also do not have any institution claiming authority over the nation state system. Once nuclear weapons become part of their nation state arsenal, they can match the blond down to earth realism with a down to earth realism of their own. Accordingly, while from the blond Lockian/Jeffersonian perspective the communist and fascists may share some formal political practices, one will never be a nuclear threat; the other will always be a nuclear threat.

October 31, 1517 is the beginning of a certain relationship between the blonds and the colored peoples. Or maybe it would be truer to say that it strengthened and increased a trend that had existed for centuries. Once Luther nailed his 95 proposals to the church door, sooner or later the colored people would learn that there was no escaping the need to develop something to deal with the blonds.

The blond democrats hammered the communist bureaucrats for over half a century for self-serving hypocrisy. But that bureaucracy changed the blond world forever. Attempts by the blonds to change the Slav world by force, post 1955, began to carry a very big risk.

The Russian Communists' claim that they dramatically increased the Russian level of education deserves to be considered honestly. The claim is that prior to the 1917 revolution more than one-third of the work force was illiterate.[505] By 1970, about 60 percent of the industrial work force, and more than one-third of the collective farm workers had a least some secondary education.[506] In 1928 about a half million Soviet citizens had received university and specialized secondary training: Twenty years later the number was almost 15 million.[507]

Now the communists, like the democrats, ignore the differences that become visible when these sorts of rapid expansion of educational opportunities take place. An IQ distribution which resembles the U.S. distribution ensures that some impressive talent would become visible very fast when the transition took hold.

Who could forget that movie scene when the cave man's crude projectile becomes an intercontinental ballistic missile? The trail from Stone Age's ability to kill one man at a time to the twentieth century's ability to kill millions follows the curiously artificial, but also curiously biological path, through the 11th grade.

Russian ethnicity was finally bound to trump internationalism. It fits with the way people are. Margaret Thatcher and Ronald Reagan may have thought that the Russian Communist Party was a broken relic of an evil past, but if one agrees with the sociobiological analysis advanced here, what is impressive about the Bolsheviks is how powerful their legacy has been: They educated the Russian peasantry. They were responsible for Queen Victoria's children, people that look like Ronald Reagan and Margaret Thatcher, spending their lives 40 minutes from an oven for as far as the world can see. They left the Slavs with enough terror on a 50-foot cylinder to force the Germans to accept a border that the Germans did not make.

Of course that is not the only border the Russians share with strangers. The difference is that the border with the Germans affects how the Russians can handle all their other borders.

Within a few years after the fall of communism in Europe it was clear to everyone that the term three generations of American intellectuals had used to classify the problem, "Ideology" would not contain an adequate explanation for the second half of the 20th century. More important, ideology would not provide a reliable guide to predict what lay ahead for nuclear weapons.

The Communist Party may never have represented the real interests or the real yearnings of the Russian people, as non-Russians saw it, but there can be no doubt that on the critical issue it was the communists who did what had to be done to solve the most basic question the Slavs would ever face: the German question. They put the 15-year-old Russian boy into school. Given the reality that sooner or later, the blond regard for the Russian was bound to become front-page news, the communists did what the Russian people needed them to do.

Nuclear Weapons: Slavs, Germans and the End of Act One

The Anglo-American foreign policy establishment sees Anglo-American foreign policy towards the Continent as a piece: a determined struggle against an authoritarian hegemony which could finally threaten England herself. Napoleon, the Spanish Inquisition, Hitler and Stalin all look alike.

A second look, one that began with populations, would feature different realities. The dividing line, for some purposes, would fall on other seams. England played a leading role in defeating Spain's, France's and Germany's dream of a continental state. The reality today is a Slavic continental state, with nuclear weapons, and all that implies.

There was a long pre-history for Germans and Slavs. The Germans always carried certain racist feelings toward Slavs.

The Germans, given their antipathy towards populations which did not look like them, could not fight or do as much algebra as they could, always carried the potential to build a Europe as blond as North America or Australia. But a Catholic Europe, to which they, however fitfully, belonged, was bound to limit the blond's geography, because it affected the inside of some German heads.

The blonds were always free; Luther made the freedom more complete. The Slav explosion in 1955 is the behavioral riposte to Luther's publication of October 31, 1517.

The blonds were free for four hundred and forty years, a great time of testing for much of the planet. Once the blonds had their own church, it was inevitable that the primary political reality would become racial characteristics. The Catholic Church's directive to the blonds is the same as to the Jews. "Disappear." The Vikings do not find the directive any more congenial than the Jews.

The Catholic Church represented a terrible threat to the blonds. An Italian institution, it made it likely that if Luther, or someone like him, had not been successful, the blonds would become Africanized.

But with Luther's success, problems came for a wide variety of Africans in a wide variety of places. In 1955 a Slavic bomb exploded and a revolution commenced: There were Africans out there who visit the blonds at home.

Nuclear weapons are the end of a long, long ethnic game. Nuclear weapons are a specifically Russian trump. No one knows exactly what that relationship between Russians and Germans will look like, but it is certain that a non-nuclear Germany will not attack a nuclear Russia. The Russians are as aware of that as the Germans.

A minimum defense for Russia today, surely would have looked like as maximum a defense as any Russian Czar would have wished. They can murder Germany in 20 minutes and they can force Anglo-America to bet their own progeny should they decide to play the traditional English role and interfere with borders that Russian leaders consider essential.

The German push east was as inevitable as the American push west. When Boston heard that white people who spoke English has taken a big tract of land from brown people who spoke Spanish, Boston exploded with joy. One sees the blonds pushing west into Europe 2,000 years ago. When they were successful, the home villages behind the line celebrated.

Was the blond push east, qualitatively different? The world did not come equipped with borders. They represent blood. For the blonds, and for everyone else. Stalin and Hitler were intelligent men, but 19th century men. They could not have had any feel for how nuclear weapons would grow, but they did know that it would make a difference for generations if the Germans won or the Slavs won. Did either of them, in the fire of the 1940's, believe the struggle was anything other than a racial struggle?

Racial identity is the rock upon which nuclear weapons stand. Anglo-American foreign policy will have to accommodate it. Reagan and Thatcher were a partnership that looks like Churchill and Roosevelt. Except for nuclear weapons. They shared the same good looks, the same determination, the same intelligence, the same idealism, the same ambition, and the same racism. Churchill and Roosevelt could go everywhere. Reagan and Thatcher could not.

The 15-year-old Slav who is really good in math class will force Anglo-America to recognize some fundamental basic truths about Europe. It is a place where ethnicity plays a dominant and continuing role, because the competition is much more even than it was in Great Britain, North America, New Zealand or Australia. The blond could not appropriate land with a push. It had to be a war. When the Slavs won the war with Germany, with help from the blonds who speak English, certain particulars, ethnic particulars, became locked in granite. The more perceptive establishment writers recognize this.[508]

Legislators and warriors, who imagine that an adversary with nuclear weapons will behave like one without, are on the wrong planet. Calling the understandable Russian effort to keep NATO forces at a reasonable distance, the "New Imperialism" is an invitation to a never ending series of confrontations with Russia that can not be won, and that will work against the ability to control nuclear weapons.[509]

The basic reality of both World War I and World War II was ethnic. If the Germans lost, the Slavs won.

If one pulls Islam out of the debate, Eastern Europe is basically a bitter, angry, seam where populations are, or basically identify with, either Slavs or Germans. What Hitler observed shortly after World War I about the Germanic mother and the Slavs, was still true in Eastern Europe in the twenty-first century. The blond mother has the same good eye for foul looks and foul habits everywhere.[510] The problems the blonds have with Russian habits at the beginning of the 21st century are not much different than at the beginning of the 20th century, or, for that matter, at the beginning of the 15th, 12th or 10th centuries. In fact the problems are not much different than the problems the blonds have with most of the planet. The difference for Eastern Europe is that in Eastern Europe, post 1955, foul habits travel with a spectacular asset, a 15-year-old who can really do algebra.

Talent and ethnicity will determine how long the world with live with nuclear weapons. The American people shared an image of Russia and Eastern Europe between 1946 and 1985 as a unified political structure, consolidated by and serving the ideological goals of cohesive transnational Marxist elites. I have no knowledge of any particulars, but it was an ethnic stew for centuries and I strongly believe that as more information becomes available one will see that it was an ethnic stew for 50 years after World War II as well.

As records are opened and the true picture becomes visible, it will be clear that the people in the seam, including the leaders, behaved as they have for generations. The German bureaucrats had to bend; they knew Germany had lost the greatest war in history to a foe that was acutely aware that it was regarded as racially inferior.

The Germans lost some, they lost many; they knew that their options were severely limited, many of them were sincere Marxists; but what will be impressive as the records become available is how consistent, how intelligent, how dogged and united the bureaucracy was on a single issue: Keep the Slavs out of Germany. There is suggestive data. What was the percentage of East Germany's student population who learned to speak a Slavic language? The bureaucracy was drawn from the same classes.

Russian leaders, also intelligent men, were aware of the Germanic resistance. Long term, what may one expect?

Following the collapse of communism one could glimpse a kind of frustration, annoyance, and anger in the American establishment that is fated to coexist with nuclear weaponry for a long, long time. The annoyance stems from the realization that the end of the ideological debate about Russian Communism meant much less than it should have meant for nuclear weapons.

The World Policeman and Nuclear Weapons

The Anglo/American establishment thinks that the American victory in the Cold War was complete.[511] The Russians then should act as defeated adversaries, something like Germany or Japan in 1945.

But it is precisely because of the complete destruction of Germany, and the associated reality of the Russian nuclear program, that the Russians will be a continuing irritation to America, and possibly something much more. With Germany prostrate, and an engineer who can cook not only Berlin, but Indianapolis, the Russians have become aware that do not have to reprise Germany 1940, 1914, 1800, 1000, 500, etc. The Russians will not abandon that security. They are free to be Russian, and to use force against Islam in areas they consider Indian Territory, in a way that Germany was not free to be Germans and to use force in areas that Germans considered Indian Territory.

The Russians may have aggressive designs on some of their neighbors' interests, but it would be naïve to think that some of Russia's neighbors would not like to appropriate land which is considered Russia's by both Americans and Russians. Consider that polls show that in January 1993 only one third of the Russian population told pollsters that it was a misfortune that the Soviet Union had disappeared, but by the end of the year almost one-half regretted the change, and nearly 75% thought that the change had been a mistake.[512] Doubtless much of the regret has to do with economic problems, but it would be a mistake to think that many Russians do not want a strong Russia. Given the twentieth century, the Russian people are aware that the size and shape of Germany is intimately related to the Russian nuclear weapon program.

The Russians are aware that as long as they have some kind of check on the United States, they will be able to use force to protect their interests against the three great ethnic opponents that they face along their borders. First, and most important, they have to be sure that the millennia old struggle with blond racism in Germany is, once and for all, over. The Germans have aesthetic, intellectual, and organizational reasons to be racists. If the Germans do not have the right to be racists, who does? However, the Russian nuclear arsenal guarantees that the racists will stay on the Germanic side of the line.

The second and third areas concern Islam and China. Islam could be the great wild card of the nuclear age. One reads of Islamic challenges to the U.S. in the Middle East, to Russia in central Asia, and efforts to develop an autonomous Islamic state in areas China has long considered hers, and one wonders. What if one Islamic State comes up with the same 15-year-old they found in a shack in North Korea? Who knows how much force might be needed, where, and how fast?

Is the nuclear weapons story a technological chapter in the book about the relationship between the blonds and everyone else? Or is the blond/wog story a chapter in a big technology book?

History will finally give the answer, but it is fascinating to imagine a kind of parallel universe between Asian Muslims playing Cherokee to Russians now in the role of Germans. Now, the Muslims have the foul habits, the disadvantaged aesthetic and the authoritarian mysterious religion.

Germany saw itself as a bulwark between the Christian West and the Horde. Russians see themselves as bringing civilization to the Central Asian Islamic tribes. What if Islam does not see it that way?

I do not believe that the parallel universe will ever come into existence however. Russians have interests but once they are satisfied, Russians will be willing to stay home. Anglo/American civilization really does have a uniquely intense certitude about its own universality. Democracy here has a dangerous edge. The American penchant for being the world's policeman has to look threatening to Russia. Is it possible that even senior Russian scientists and governmental officials who basically admire the U.S. do not agree that some credible threat must be maintained against the U.S.? I believe that they do agree on the point. There is a threshold nuclear arsenal the most modern, democratic, sophisticated Russian will insist on maintaining.

They have been able to maintain this threat since the time of the Cuban Missile Crisis, and they will be able to maintain it in the future. Blond intellectuals failed to learn the most important lesson from that very first crisis at the dawn of the nuclear age. The Russians never intended to risk their society for Cuba. They could blink without anyone imagining that they had suffered a real diminution of authority where it mattered.

The real lesson of the crises is that at the beginning of the new century, the world can look back and see how valuable nuclear weapons are to the non-blonds. In 1962 the United States had over 300 intercontinental missiles as well as numerous submarines capable of firing nuclear warheads. By contrast, Russia could threaten the North American continent with but four to six ICBMs, and about 100 short range missiles that could have been fired from submarines only after they had surfaced.[513] Indeed the advantage was so dramatic that a study was completed about the wisdom of a preemptive first strike, which concluded that it was possible that the United State's could very well lose only a couple of coastal cities after completely destroying the Marxist Slavic world. Some observers thought that one of the reasons that the Soviet Union put missiles into Cuba in the first place was to give their shorter-range less sophisticated missiles a launching pad nearer to the American mainland.

Now, compare the realities in 1962 with the realities at the beginning if the new century. The U.S. can still destroy Russia, but it is also true that Russia can destroy the U.S.

Establishment American pundits treat the years between 1962 and the year 2000 with triumphalism. But if one looks at the engineering realities, the facts reveal a trend that has worked more against U.S. security than Russian security. Two Questions: First, was the trend predictable? Second was there any lesson for the future for the American leadership in that 38-year period?

Russia does not need Cuba as a launching pad for one reason. The Russian engineer became so good at the death business that his product, from 10,000 miles away, at the end of the twentieth century, was better than the product from 90 miles away shortly after the middle of the century.

The great American orthodoxy on international affairs will not just vanish. But Cuba and Vietnam were both challenges and calls for reformation on nuclear weapon theory.

The orthodoxy insists that the blonds must extend to the east as far as they can. The orthodoxy is a guarantee that the Slavs will maintain an up to date nuclear weapons program. The threat that NATO might be a shield for a restive Germany is obvious, and must play a role for Russian leaders. Less obvious is the threat that NATO might become a shield for an ambitious Islam.

Is Turkey a source of support for Islamic separatists now within the Russian orbit?[514] As a non-Arab Islamic State, Turkey represents an opportunity for the United States and a potential concern for Russia. Not the concern that a resurgent Germany might be, but another reason to maintain a very big sophisticated nuclear program.

The view here, that nuclear weapons are a great asset for Russia and China, and a very new and different type of risk for the blonds, explains why, even though their technology is far inferior to the blond technology; it is good enough. One can be sure that Russia and China will never completely stop their nuclear weapons program.[515] They know that to be able to do to their Indians what was done at Plymouth; they have to be free of the world's policeman.

The pre-nuclear world will never return. The engineer will not unlearn what he has learned. The issue can not be fixed with a few extra point of GDP put into the Department of Defense. A world with a small Germany and a big Russia, and a small Japan and a big China is simply a different place than the alternatives.

At the beginning of the twentieth century the English-speaking blonds could have had a big Germany or a big Russia. What England and America could never have had was a Germany and Russia living alongside each other without racism, without mutually exclusive claims of authority, and without the threat of armed conflict. The seam between Germans and Slavs was similar to the seams between blond America and Latin/Indian Mexico, or protestant England and Catholic Ireland.

After 1964 the choice was gone and the reality was a big Russia, a Russia with the ability to visit New York. After experiencing the bloodiest two wars in history, Europe at the beginning of the twenty-first century has some similarities with Europe at the beginning of the twentieth century.

The Germans are a good-looking, democratic, honest, creative, intelligent and gifted people. England recognized a threat in a unified Europe under Germany. One is not surprised to read that the English and American upper class did not want a coup which would topple Hitler and open the way to a negotiated settlement of World War II. They wanted more: To teach the Germans, as an ethnic group, a lesson that the population itself would never forget.[516]

But "lessons" in the nuclear age are expensive. The German objection to Englishmen and Americans revolved around issues of political interference. The German objects to the Slav because of the way he looks and acts. The observations that Germanic populations make about Russians can correctly be labeled as racist.

Anglo-America insisted that Hitler represented an idea that had to be destroyed in Germany. Russia does not care about German ideas. It has to insist that it be allowed a military superiority to destroy Germans. They do not think this is civics class.

It was inevitable that the blonds would not be able to confront a nuclear Russia in the way they could have confronted a non-nuclear Russia. Should that be said loud and clear, or should it be avoided, blurred, ignored?

The problem with blurring that fundamental issue is that it may pose a risk in dealing in areas where America really does face a threat to its real interests. Movies depict wars on a map, one sees struggles featuring populations gaining and losing ground. But geography does not have much to do with the possibility of wars between nuclear-armed powers.

The important lessons of the nuclear age, post 1955, is a very different lesson from the lesson taught at Munich. The nuclear lesson is that even the blond democrats have to pick their spots.

The great victory of the 20th century in the Slav head is the victory against racism, which is to say Germany. The conservatives who favored the expansion of NATO [517]and the liberals, who would approach the issue more slowly, miss the point.[518] The point is ethnicity. The blond idealism has a very real sincerity and strength to it, but the policies, to work, would require a world of ideas, but no people.

Nuclear weapons in the hands of the Slavs, and not the Germans, comprise a really dramatic answer to the endless debate whether or not history is cyclical.

Once the Russians have 2000 nuclear weapons, one can not imagine a scenario which would make the Slav/German history anything but a centuries old straight line that terminates with the ability of the Slavs to cook Germany and no comparable power held by the Germans.

Once one sees both the ethnic and engineering realities behind nuclear weapons; one sees that the United States has become vulnerable into the future as far as the eye can see. Some time in that period America may feel that it has to invade one or more countries that are actually affecting American interests. Which countries do we know that she will not invade? Simple. The one with the nuclear weapons that can be delivered to the kindergarten, the one down the street from the White House. That means that it is in America's interest to try to work something out with those powers which can make the delivery now: Russia and China.

One can confidently predict that more and more countries will have the technological ability to develop nuclear weapons. "Proliferation" avoids the reality. The potential threat in the Middle East does not come because the U.S. sells something to Russia or China, and then Russia or China sells it to Iran.[519] Engineers everywhere are fated to get better.

We know that for all practical purposes, the Russian and Chinese engineers are good enough to keep the world's policeman off their dirt. How good are all the other engineers? No one knows, but suppose that at some point an Iranian peaceful nuclear energy program moves forward, and Iran establishes that Iranian engineers are good enough.[520]

A program designed around assumptions that the U.S. engineer will do such superior work that great engineers from other countries will not be able to threaten the American heartland will continue to fail, as it has failed for half a century. Behavior is the key. American optimism on the issue will prove to be as misplaced as the American optimism in the 1940's and 1950's that the wogs will not be able to engineer access to the American heartland.[521]

Great engineers do great work. An IQ test could have been used as a window into seeing whether there were any potential great engineers in the Russian schoolroom. What happened to American invulnerability between 1964 and the end of the century was that the great engineer trumped geography. They do not need Cuba as a launching pad.

The engineering will inevitably become more impressive than it now is. Moreover, there are places in the world where nuclear weapons could play a much more volatile role than they play now.

It is more than just possible that there are Russians who think that a Middle East in turmoil strengthens Russia. Russia is the world power which could become a worldwide focus of Islamic resentment and fundamentalism in a way which would not be likely as long as Israel and the United States are perceived as the great Satan. The great engineer can trump geography, but geography promises that Christian and Islamic populations will be each other's irritant for a long long time. Further, where the Russians perceive their interests within a family of Slavs to be at risk from an expansionary Europe, it is helpful to have an area where the U.S. also has a potential vulnerability if you choose to supply America's enemies with hardware and a specific 11th grader grown older.

SDI: The Blonds Safe?

> If comedy is cyclical, tragedy is linear and predictable.
>
> Nicole Bensoussan[522]

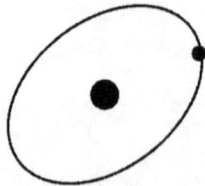

I know what nuclear weapons are. The other 5 billion people on the planet are wrong. The first task is to spot the functional realities.

Where does a discussion of SDI belong? With a discussion about technology? About freedom? About history? About religion? Or about ethnicity and the 11th grade?

SDI, an SDI which really works, or more accurately, an SDI which everyone knows really works, is an absolute requirement for the blonds to continue to maintain their ancient posture toward the wogs. The bell will never go off signaling that China and Russia have accepted that Americans will be secure while they will remain vulnerable. The contest finally is not between technologies; it is between technicians. When one watches the top of the deck of one thousand million Chinese, or the best science students out of two hundred million Slavs, concede permanent defeat in an intellectual contest, one is not witnessing a lot of engineering: One is witnessing a miracle.

At the beginning of the twenty-first century, children from different ethnic groups all over the world attend algebra and history classes. This was not true for any century preceding the twentieth. For the purpose of understanding why SDI, a defensive weapon, will not prove any more successful than offensive nuclear weapons; one must take a morning off and look in on schools in villages throughout the wog world.

For the wogs, the key in algebra class is to identify a handful of young men who will prove themselves so adept at abstract quantitative reasoning that they will be able to cook Winston Churchill and Thomas Jefferson in their homes in Viking country. Which is to say, to be able to begin to exclude over 90 percent of the boys taking algebra from that classroom that will be the heart of their nuclear weapons program 8 years hence.

The key in history class is behaviorally very different. An undifferentiated, dirty, low skilled, parasite ridden, impoverished horde of illiterate peasant boys has to develop a more or less common past. They have to see each other in a world driven by ethnicity. Part of that history is seeing Winston Churchill, Lord Kitchener, Siegfried, Daniel Boone, Margaret Thatcher, F.D.R. and Thomas Jefferson as a package.

The important point in history class is to give an ethnic group a coherent past. It is not propagandizing: It is inherent in that class. History has a point of view. What would the text look like on the Indian reservation if it had not been written by a White?

Now that children all over the world are in school, what does that Slavic 11th grader in Russia hear about the Germans? What does that Chinese 11th grader hear about Englishmen and Americans? What are they fated to hear? Can anyone imagine that they could hear anything else? Without an outside powerful religious institution challenging the state, there will be no institutional challenge to the cultural anthropology that the Chinese, the Slavs or the other wogs learn. It was clear, after the dust had settled following the collision between American and Chinese planes, that some Chinese "men on the street" were authentically more anti-American and aggressive than the Communist leadership.[523]

The process of national identity is inevitably different in the peasant world than in the blond world. Great fighters carry their country with them. The peasantry has its country assigned to it by bureaucrats, via the 11th grade. China was announced to thousands of Chinese peasants by the central government, in a way that Germans, Englishmen and Americans never had to have their countries announced to them.

The Russian and Chinese 11th grades will be the most important factors in determining the wisdom of developing an American SDI program. Because the best algebra students in each county are roughly equivalent; a defensive nuclear program for America is likely to lead to a weapon system that will break down the defensive system. For the North American continent, it could be as much a mistake as an offensive nuclear program. Everything depends upon whether the Chinese and Russians can be talked into accepting the program.

No one believes that a nuclear defense system against Russia or China will ever be so good that the blonds would be willing to risk the total destruction of their civilization. In European military history, nuclear weapons represent a resolution of the debate between Catholic Europe about that minutia of rules for wars, and blond Protestant Europe's rejection of the notion of a code for war as inherently absurd. In the nuclear age the Catholic version will prevail. In the working out there will be no price worth a nuclear confrontation. There will be rules for conflicts between populations that have nuclear weapons.

This means something concrete to the Russians, in very concrete specific places. Is the Russian presence in Chechnya a monument to traditional Russian ruthlessness?[524] Or is it just another validation of the way the world is; not much different than the blond presence in what had been Australia, North America, Mexico, or Africa? Force and the threat of force formed the nation state everywhere. Moreover, great powers behave like great powers. When the Communists forced the blonds out of Georgia, Armenia and Azerbaijan one saw national power serving an ethnic end.[525]

Nuclear weapons do not change the status of the struggle as an ethnic struggle. What nuclear weapons do is to change the characterization of the struggle as the "Great Game" inside the head of western housewives. Once the blond housewife sees what she has to bet, the characteristics that suggest "game" begin to recede.

Compare two pieces from Boston area newspapers: one dealing with the Chinese in Tibet, and one dealing with the blonds at Plymouth. The editorial on the Chinese calls forth imagery of Buddhist compassion dealing with the steel of Chinese imperialism and promises the familiar promise of the arc of history uniting, finally, with the shining ideal of justice.[526]

The story about Plymouth features an Indian who was invited to speak at Plymouth's 350th anniversary gala. The speech he planned to make included a report from a book published in 1622 in England that said that Pilgrims took as much of the Indian's provisions as they could carry, and that they robbed the Indians' graves.[527] The descendants of the Pilgrims did not let him make the speech.

Now, why should a 1622 publication in England lie about the event in a report about and to Englishmen? The point, finally, is not about bad people in two places. The point is that nation building everywhere looks a certain way in a relentlessly ethnic world.

The two great calls to battle for Anglo American intervention revolve around "stability" and "justice." They necessarily serve different interests. Adopting both of them promise a lot of work, and an inevitable clash with the other great powers who would like to do, more or less, what Englishmen and Americans did in the formation of England and America.

Germany's role in World Wars I and II do not look to be rational to Anglo-America because there was nothing that Great Britain or the United States desperately wanted in 1914 or 1937 that they did not have. They could go anywhere and do everything. And they were invincible on their dirt.

Germany and Russia never had a comparable psychic wealth. They always had each other. Taking land from Scotsmen, or Irishmen, or Indians, or French Canadians, or aborigines, or even 10 million Mexicans is one thing. Taking it from a couple hundred million Slavs is a wildly different thing. If you guess wrong about your ability to put the Slavs on reservations, it becomes a problem for a long, long time. Particularly if they can locate a 15-year-old Sakharov. The intensity of the ethnic conflict inevitably underlines and strengthens nationalism. Once Russia survived Marxism, some degree of Pan-Slavism was as predictable as the New Hampshire legislature's reaction to the success of the blue-eyed people in taking over half of Mexico.

My guess is that somewhere, in some journal written by an Italian priest, a few years after Luther began his revolution, there is an eerily prescient observation about nuclear weapons at the end of the 20th century. While this priest knew that the Germans knew the Italians, he also knew the blonds. The blonds, whether they spoke German or English would never be satisfied to live in one space. Once they had their own religion, something would have to be developed to keep them in defined parts of the planet.

SDI is simply the same nuclear arms race with a new label. The Russians think that they have, once and for all, won what was perceived by both them and the Germans as a centuries old race war. The most important prize in that Russian victory is a cylinder pointed at Germany which, should it go off, will, for all practical purposes, amount to a genocide. It is a tribute to the blond aesthetic, social morality, intelligence, organizational skill, and determination that that is what it took to be safe as a neighbor next to the Germans. The Russians will make every imaginable sacrifice to maintain that cylinder in working order. SDI threatens that Slav victory.

When should one begin the story of nuclear weapons as a game in which everyone understood that this was going to be real competition? One might begin it before or immediately after World War II. Certainly there were sophisticated observers inside the military and technical programs who were aware of Russian attempts to develop a nuclear weapon well before the end of the Korean War. In fact, I was 10 in 1950 and I can remember a discussion in the early 1950's between my father and a neighbor about a newspaper report on Russian efforts to build nuclear weapons that could eventually threaten the U.S.

The first part of the game featured bigger and bigger bombs. That

phase essentially ended in the mid 1950's after Russia demonstrated that it had the technical expertise to develop a hydrogen bomb. The fact that the U.S. could produce a bigger and more technically advanced bomb than Russia just became uninteresting. The Russian bomb was big enough. There was something else about that Russian bomb. It focused a lot of attention on the competition. Intellectuals who otherwise were not much interested in politics, paid attention the day that the news reports featured what Russian engineers could do.

Compare Cuba in 1962 and Eastern Europe in the 1990's. In 1962 the American Secretary of State said that Russia blinked because of American power. Now, update that story to that morning in 1999 when Russia landed a few hundred paratroopers in that airport in the former Yugoslavia at the request of the Serbs, to the rage of General Kitchener's big son. Did the thousands of nuclear weapons that the Soviet Union amassed during those 40 years make a difference? Did the change serve an ethnic end? Did geography make a difference? I suggest that the few hundred troops the Russian landed at that airport in the teeth of Anglo-American opposition established an ethnic reality the blonds did not want to recognize.

It is easy to overlook how long, considering the total duration of the nuclear arms race, that SDI has been around. More than likely there were references to defensive systems from the 1940's. However, assume for the sake of argument that President Reagan's speech in 1983 was the modern beginning of SDI as a major political program.[528] I would argue that that period of time represents a more substantial amount of time, compared to the length of the nuclear arms race than is generally recognized.

For my purpose, 1955, the demonstration that Russia could build a hydrogen bomb, was the year when the blond establishment should have recognized the competition for what it was: a game played by a handful of young men with phenomenal talent. It established the Slav nuclear engineer as an excellent engineer.

Now, divide the offensive side of nuclear weapons into three categories: the blast, the delivery, and, finally, the instrumentation. Sit back, take a sip, and consider how fantastic the engineering became on both the Russian and

American side in each of those three categories in that brief period between 1955 and 1983. One began that period with people talking about essentially saving the country, by being able to control the damage of the blast. One began that period by people measuring the ability of bombers to get through defensive systems, in Northern Canada, thousands of miles away, a matter involving hours. One began that period by wondering if the Russian instrumentation would put the energy on the North American continent, or in the middle of the Pacific Ocean. Just 28 years after 1955 everyone was satisfied that Russia could, in less than an hour, drop that energy in the middle of Washington, D.C.

By contrast, begin the story of SDI as a visible active political program in 1983, and consider what has been achieved in terms of really reducing American vulnerability in roughly 20 years. Nothing. There have been promises: One read in 1989 about fantastic particle beam shields in space by the mid-1990s.[529] One read in 1989, just 6 years after President Reagan's proposal, that SDI is precisely the type of program which plays to American strengths in technology: communications, miniaturization and instrumentation systems.[530] But no one bets their family on a menu of competitive advantages. One bets the family on a product that one knows, without doubt, will protect one's family. From this perspective, the reality is that a defensive system remains as illusory at the beginning of the 21st century as in the 1980's.

What is the difference? Why did the progress in offensive weaponry proceed so quickly, while progress in defensive systems is so delayed? The blond optimist will argue that the difference is that America was forced to play the game with unfair and unnecessary constraints. The optimist will argue that adhering to treaty provisions meant that America could not turn its great potential loose: The only way to solve the problem is to take all constraints off and, if need be, put defensive systems into space.

I suppose that we will never know until all the constraints are off, but I think that the difference is competing against nature, a landmass and time on the one hand, and, on the other, competing against another gifted engineer. The issue simply is not a stationary as opposed to a moving target. The issue is competition.

The competition to the blonds is coming from places no one would have predicted in 1955. The idea that China, not to say North Korea, could develop a weapon which could hold the blonds at bay by threatening the 3-year-old blond at home, would have been just unbelievable in 1955.

The American interventionists have the same mind set about strategic relationships that British imperialist had. Arrange friendly nations in various geographical locales into alliances to be able to check a real or potential enemy from dominating that area. From the perspective of the natives, the implicit and unspoken moral rational for that policy was and is that democracy enjoys a status that justifies a blond presence, racists or no. In a world defined by different populations that assumption becomes a problem. It was inevitable that something like SDI would be proposed to continue the basic strategy.

John McCain's proposal for a Pacific alliance joining the United States, Japan, and South Korea and others to develop a nuclear defense from the Aleutians to Australia fits with the general blond history.[531] Non whites will see a different reality behind his proposal than will whites. America is sensitive to the actions which indicate that a developing China is doing more than just developing inside China; that it is doing something outside China, it is projecting influence or power outside its own boundaries. That projection means, at a minimum, not becoming more vulnerable to America than she is now.

To the heirs of British imperialism the projection seems to be inherently aggressive.[532] Conservative Americans honestly do not see that the initial projection of force by white people into Asia is bound to be perceived by Asians as much more unnatural and aggressive than anything that China is likely to do. Moreover the simple fact that the Asian powers are geographically much closer to the launch pad than Americans makes a huge difference in the chances a defensive system could actually supply security. The simple physical fact that Asians are within a few minutes of the energy source requires a system be faster and more effective by orders of magnitude than a system that could work as long as it had 40 minutes of notice.

The perspective urged here would treat Japanese, Chinese and Koreans as a single group. They all came out of peasant backgrounds, they all present a familiar familism to the blonds, and, most important, they are all good at algebra.

Comparisons between Japan, an island power next to a continent, and Great Britain's situation are common enough. But the more important truth for nuclear weapons concerns their differences.

While the Japanese may carry some of the racist assumptions that the English carry, there is a tremendous aesthetic difference. It would be impossible not to understand some of the British racism, indeed the blond racism generally, with some measure of understanding, on that ground. The Japanese themselves understand that they do not carry that advantage.

Also, there are different realities between Asia and Europe on the two "continents." One is not surprised to read that Margaret Thatcher retired and able to speak freely expresses some concern for the future of the Europe, because the Germans have a taste for dominance.

The comparison that would have Japan play Germany to China as France may have a core of truth.[533] But it is not the best comparison.

Contrary to what some experts may believe, China armed with nuclear weapons is unlikely to make Japan, the only country which has tasted nuclear weapons, more belligerent. It is more likely that the Japanese would become more resentful of a blond power that will attempt to deal with China as it dealt with China in the 19th century.

Japan sees the relationship between the Black Ships and Pearl Harbor in a very different way than the Vikings see it. At least one reason that Japanese expressions of guilt about World War II are much more muted than the German guilty plea, is that, logically enough, the Japanese see the role that the democratic blond racists played in setting the stage for World War II in Asia. To the Japanese, the German in Asia spoke English.

The dramatic difference in the numbers of 15-year-old boys in school in Asia at the end of the 21st century, compared with the beginning of all previous centuries is the key to why the relationship between Asians and the blonds has become very different. One wonders what Chinese leaders think about what has been accomplished within their lifetimes. They can get at Buckingham Palace. Surely they must see the difference that talent made. Whatever Liberals or Marxists might say about inherited IQ differences, they should at least consider the possibility that Russia and China became secure from the blonds precisely because biology plays a large role in determining IQ.

IQ differences became visible the instant the peasant 15-year-olds stepped into a classroom. Pundits, who find the implications of a genetic component in IQ in an increasingly technological world to be depressing, miss the larger point of how liberating this reality must be to East Asians.[534] The fact that North Korea may have the ability to take out an American city does not seem depressing to North Koreans.

More generally, by the middle of the 21st century it will be clear that East Asians have accomplished an economic change without parallel in the modern world. Much has been made about whether Asia success represents something about Asians or something about economic development, and what, if anything, this success portends for the U.S.

On purely economic grounds, apart from military considerations, blond America will not be worse off if East Asia does well. Boston and Route 128 have been and are totally impressive centers of technological innovation and creativity. Today, somewhere on Route 128 a 60-year-old is driving home who remembers, with regret, when Massachusetts was number 1 and California tried harder. Well, O.K., a much larger population and a bigger capital base finally meant something when they were wedded to world class educational institutions. It is a truism of economics that in the big picture no one really lost because California did very very well, and 128 did very well, and no one loses long-term because Japan and Korea, and increasingly China do well.

Once the competition involves not just economic bragging rights but invincibility, on the one hand, or vulnerability for millions of people on the other, understanding what is happening with nuclear weapons becomes a life and death issue. The simple fact is that China may in the foreseeable future become a society of over a billion people who are roughly half as wealthy as Americans, without developing a Western style democracy.[535] Observers who express some doubts about "Westernized" the Japanese have become, and who at least consider it possible that they may identify more with China as she inevitably begins to take up more space in the world, could be right.[536] And it may lead to increasing areas of disagreement and anger between Asians and the blonds. For example, as Japan began to match American levels of aid to poor countries; it was inevitable that sometimes the blond establishment would have reservations about the identity and intent of the donee states.[537]

I have never seen a study of how Americans really feels about Japanese economic success, but it seems to me that they resent it in a way that they do not resent Germans success. One assumes that issues of racial identity are part of the difference. One assumes that the Asian former colonies of the blonds may exhibit some of the same dynamic. IQ data promise a protracted period of East Asians doing well.

At first, IQ data was just another page in the same book that the blond people had been writing for a long, long time. Eventually, everyone, but particularly East Asians, will see how different this page is. The critical mistake the blond intellectual made was to assume that the page simply reinforced what the blonds had known for hundreds perhaps thousands of years.

The entity which the IQ psychologists track is at the center of the nuclear arms race. As that truth becomes visible, one wonders how the blond populations will react.

The nuclear age beginning roughly at the mid-twentieth century has witnesses a material reality murdering an idea. In 1955 or 1956 when I was in high school, an English teacher, of English descent, and an Anglophile, would encourage the class to debate whether England should leave those places where the populations were not democratic or were not ready for democracy. The blond racism always traveled with an impressive idealism. The succeeding 40 years of the century after I graduated established the reality that an Asian engineer could keep both the idealism and the racism off of Asian soil.

The key issue for SDI is to be sure that the abstractions and generalizations that the blond intellectual applies do, in fact, fit the problem at hand. One sees references to the Kellogg-Briand Pact of 1928, along with predictable and mostly accurate references to America's technological leadership.[538] The one foreign policy issue on which hard right conservative and establishment Wall Street types agree is that arms controls do not work.

However, the view presented here is that if arms controls do not work, nothing will work. The world will be treated to a future where nuclear weapons will be stationed in space. Russia and China will never agree to become the blonds' targets.

The pundits who claim history teaches lessons about nuclear weapons make two category mistakes. They abstract and reify "History" as if it were data.

Second, they place nuclear war on a continuum with other wars. These are serious mistakes.

A common deep biological reality underlies Japan's economic success, China's growth rate, and North Korea threatening to develop nuclear weapons. It is interesting that Americans perceives all three as pointed at them. American conservatives who note with understated relief that Japan has economic problems too, will discover that, over a long period of time, the Japanese advantage in algebra class will not go away.[539] When Japanese students are dramatically better than American students in math, economic consequences are inevitable.[540]

In China, math proficiency has obvious military implications precisely because of nuclear weapons. The English speaking blonds had been aware of Asians with some measure of curiosity, interest, a combination of humor coupled with disgust, and a great deal of puzzlement before the Asians were aware of them. Force was inevitable once the blonds began entering Asia. That is not to say that force was not part of Asia prior to the blonds; force is inevitable in the interactions between different ethnic groups. Force is part of the India/Pakistan equation. Force may be part of the continuing China/Japan debate. When one reads that Japan scrambles fighter planes to make sure that China is aware of its claim to some uninhabited islands, one sees that ethnicity promises a trend toward force.[541]

But what is different about the blond force in Asia, is its curious combination of real idealism, and real racism. Generalizations can be made about the informal relationships between the blonds and the Asians, which would look curiously like the relationships between Slavs and Germans. Border disputes are usually, first, informal personal disputes, assaults, ranging from slurs to murders.

Nuclear weapons travel over borders. The real surprise on nuclear weapons involves Korea. Over the years North and South Korea may develop a working rapprochement which will incorporate a nuclear weapons program. Would anyone be surprised, given an ethnic world and long memories everywhere, that the first potential target on the Korean list would be somewhere near Tokyo?

Why Korea? What is there about this poor isolated country which makes them a potential nuclear threat, even to the North American continent? It is a fact that American intellectuals certainly know at some level, but almost deliberately turn and shift their gaze. Korea offers an opportunity to completely re-think the realities of nuclear weapons.

Conservative analysts convinced that the American nuclear policy has been successful, plead for the return of Teddy Roosevelt, a firm hand, more muscular Protestantism. But Teddy Roosevelt never had to bet Teddy Roosevelt's three-year-old at home, millions at a pop. Other columnists, treating North Korean nuclear weapons as an extension of North Korean economic life, believe that its trading partners have an enormous leverage over its policies.[542] But, what are North Korea's nuclear weapons?

Whether true or not, the story about CIA agents encouraging Japanese officials to convert gambling machines to use magnetic cards, instead of cash, to lessen the flow of Japanese gambling money into North Korea as a way to exert leverage on its nuclear program, reinforces the image of American officialdom trying to control a behavioral problem, through the manipulation of stuff.[543] The fact that the Japanese were (also) stunned by the CIA's demonstration at the amount of progress North Korea has made with its nuclear program demonstrates that the ability to underestimate the validity of IQ data is not a Caucasoid monopoly. No one, blond or not, knows how to handle that gifted Third World engineer employed in a nuclear weapons program.

Analysts, who point to deterrence and the end of the Cold War in Europe as the model for American action against North Korean nuclear weapons, miss the essential truth of the most important long range result of the Cold War.[544] The American school bus is 40 minutes from Chinese and Russian nuclear missiles.

They will remain 40 minutes away, or they will move closer. They will not move further away. They serve an ethnic end. Similarly, the North Korean nuclear program serves an end that North Korea must consider as ethnic.

The notion that we are in a world of competing cultures is more accurate than the view that the world is composed of competing political ideologies; but it underestimates the intensity with which the Chinese and Russians will cling to nuclear weapons. If nuclear weapons are the canvas, the world is painted in ethnic tones. Now this does not mean that nothing can be done. But anything that can be done to lessen the risk, even for the blonds themselves, will be very difficult. Sending the Seventh Fleet through the Taiwan Strait every time there is a disagreement over the status of Taiwan, guarantees that the gifted 15-year-old Chinese turned 28, will continue to work on nuclear weapons.[545]

One reads that no machine can or will replace the committed soldier in deciding disputes among nations. General Patton's chain of being beginning with Samson swinging the jawbone of an ass, through the elephant, armor, the long bow, gun powder, and lately (1933) the submarine, all finally, giving way to the man, has an appeal and a ring of truth for the great blond fighter.[546]

However, once nuclear weapons became the machine, the fundamental ethnic dimension of the truism can not be missed. A blond John Henry can not beat that machine. The only question is whether he will come to that realization when the machine is 40 minutes away, or 5.

The word "game" applied to nuclear weapons competition has a certain blond look about it. It has a kind of playfulness about it, a modest nod in the direction of John Wayne.

The British upper class, certain that its role was to be very different than any other upper class, both because of ethnicity and achievement, took some steps simply to keep the real or potential enemy "off balance." Any country that seeks to be able to affect events literally everywhere has to play that "game."

The problem is that now other nations clearly see the ambition that Anglo-Americans have, and they see that they have to keep Anglo-America off balance. Nuclear weapons can do that. Engineering talent can do that.

One sees that even the blonds' lack balance dealing with a nuclear armed threat. Would the Russians have landed 300 paratroopers on that airfield without a nuclear arsenal behind them?

When a voice for American interventionism, to insure that Russia does not behave like a great power in Russia's neighborhood, summons Congress to build ABM, one sees the familiar but in a very different and dangerous setting.[547] American, like Englishmen will run heroic risks, but to imagine America will bet New York City to keep Russian troops out of Ukraine is absurd.

A revisionist's account would consider America's involvement in Vietnam a success, despite the agony, and the debacle at the end, on the grounds that it gave some nascent democracies time to develop. There may be something to it, but from the Asian perspective the main lesson was what was visible. The blonds left.

A working accommodation to avoid war might have been possible in Asia, among Asians, without the introduction of nuclear weapons. The blond conflict with Japan, the most self-aware, perhaps most intelligent Asian, was probably inevitable given the behavioral logic that accompanied Anglo-American racial sensitivities. One is not surprised to read that Macao, unlike Hong Kong, had a large population of mixed race Europeans and Chinese. [548] The Japanese imperialists must have been aware of that.

It may be true that in East Asia liberal democracy remains what it was at the beginning: an Anglo-American import.[549] But this is not at the heart of the continuing nuclear weapons story in Asia. The fundamental issue is ethnicity. The Chinese will never give up nuclear weapons because the Chinese have to be sure that Queen Victoria will not be back.

When one reads the blond establishment on the nuclear threat, one is struck by how confident and consistent it remains in the teeth of a deteriorating security situation. Margaret Thatcher, in a list of reasons why the United States must have SDI includes the ability of the West to threaten everyone everywhere.[550] She does not see what a racist threat this has to be to China, indeed to all the non-blond populations who knew the British in their salad days. Any account of the British Empire written in English would begin with what a threat Russia and Spain posed; never what a threat the blonds posed. Any account in English of the beginning of the nuclear age, would sound the same.

The basic dance of ethnicity and the bomb was set in a 30 or 40 year period in the second half of the 20th century. The Slavs gained more from the development of nuclear weapons than any other population. The Chinese were second. They will not surrender their ability to force the blonds to bet the blond children the next time the blonds get the urge to kill people to do good.

Given their history, and their talent, the economic issue is simple enough: Do the Chinese have enough of an economic base to continue the nuclear weapon march? Compare the estimate that the Russians had only 4 long-range ballistic missiles capable of hitting the North American continent in the early 1960's with the estimate that China had 60 medium range missiles and 8 single-warhead strategic missiles in 1991.[551]

The relevant statistics are available in the popular conservative press.[552] The allies spent 40, 000 man-years to make the Hiroshima bomb in the 1940's; an equivalent in the 1970's took India 2,500 man-years. What the American conservatives fail to see behind the change is the relevant variable. The issue is no longer whether the wog has access to American or Western talent: It is whether he can grow his own talent. See North Korea.

How are Korea and Vietnam connected in the head of the American blond intellectual? Is it geography? Is it history? Is it political behavior? Is it America? Is it China? Is it more universal: The nature of man? Of war? Of ethnicity?

When did they look the same? When different? When the Japanese and French went home? One wonders how they looked to the blond intellectual when Teddy Roosevelt and the Great White Fleet started to tour. How will they differentiate in the blond head when America finds out, if it does, that North Korean engineers have access to the blond nursery school?

Did Americans consider using nuclear weapons on Korean civilians? Did Americans consider using nuclear weapons on Vietnamese civilians? Did the fact that America had become vastly more vulnerable to nuclear weapons in the 1970's than in the 1950's play a role in the length of time the idea was actually under consideration?

Was it possible that Asians during World War II became surprised at the ferocity of British and American fighters?[553] Was it possible that the populations on the receiving end of the imperialist impulse to do good ever thought the imperialists were anything other than ferocious? When the Japanese saw the percentage of Filipinos America killed just a generation before Pearl Harbor, they must have known what would happen if a withdrawal of the blonds from large sections of Asia could not be negotiated.

The explanations for the blond wars against the wogs changes wogdom by wogdom, circumstance by circumstance, but there has been a singular thread that ties the faintest stirrings hundreds of years ago at the beginning of the British Empire to today. The blond intellectual identifies the same political identity. These were not wars against people; these were wars against evil people: dictators. The cohesiveness, ideology and ambition of the Marxists heightened everyone's awareness of the dictator, but there was not much that was said in English about the communists that was not said in English about Roman Catholic bureaucrats, Moslem bureaucrats or Orthodox bureaucrats, for centuries.

Bureaucracy is a given in peasant societies. The difference between the traditional bureaucracies and the fascist and communist bureaucracies of the 20th century is that the 20th century varieties really were agents of modernization on that most critical behavior: They put the 15-year-old into school. They stepped between the peasant father and the peasant child. That role was never required in blond societies.

The nuclear age has given the wog bureaucrat an asset totally and completely out of scale to any asset any non-blond bureaucracy controlled in any prior confrontation with the blonds. The bureaucrat now controls what a 28-year-old An Wang engineers.

The image then is of a non-democratic bureaucrat solving the blond problem through the abilities of a particular engineer. The nuclear reality expresses that, but the long future that can be predicted for nuclear weapons rides on a deeper and more durable reality. The gifted engineer is ethnic too.

The continuing behavioral spine of nuclear weaponry is made up of outstanding high school students who became outstanding college students, who became outstanding engineers, who became junior administrators, who finally run the show. They know each other, they like each other, they respect each other. They are aware of the traditional blond attitude and behavior toward them. The Russians know the Germans. The Chinese know Anglo-America.

They continually look for, and continually find, through the help of school administrators the one indispensable ingredient in the nuclear program: the very special 15-year-old. The 15-year-old as he moves through the system will take on his elders' beliefs. He will have an ethnic perspective of life. At 15 he has the beginnings of that perspective. He will believe in the nuclear program. He thinks that he is one of the saviors of his people, the savior who solved the blond problem by developing the real final solution: the ability to just kill everyone.

The Russian nuclear engineer wants what the Russian bureaucrat wants. The Chinese nuclear engineer wants what the Chinese bureaucrat wants.

The great value of Vietnam is how long it lasted. A settlement could not be negotiated, but the blonds left anyway. Did nuclear weapons have anything to do with 1975? If one focuses on nuclear weapons to judge American statecraft of the 1950's, what does one make of John Foster Dulles and President Eisenhower? Was Dulles' enthusiasm for the brink of war in the middle of the twentieth century partly responsible for what Chinese engineers are engineering at the beginning of the twenty-first century?[554]

According to one source, a review of top secret State Department memoranda concerning Korea showed that American policy makers in the 1950's did not share the horror of nuclear weapons that had become a given by the end of the century. President Eisenhower reportedly felt the use of nuclear weapons would be worth the cost if they could help achieve a substantial victory.[555] Could the dramatic increase in horror around nuclear weapons in America have anything to do with the fact that Americans are now targets?

One way to view the road from Korea, 1950, to Vietnam, 1970, and then Korea 2000, is though the nuclear lens. The picture changed dramatically because the capability of Chinese engineers changed dramatically. The blonds have always been able to visit China. What happened in that 50 year period is that it became clear that the Chinese engineer could visit London and Washington.

The incredible, and totally unpredicted, economic success of East Asians is related to their scores on tests of quantitative ability. Academic talent makes a difference. The difference translated to nuclear weapons makes a world more different for the blonds than anyone else.

For the nuclear weapons game, those successes have cultivated doubt, and maybe apprehension, in the blond intellectual's head. The first reaction in the American press to the reality that everyone could soon wake up to a bright shining morning when the North Koreans had nuclear weapons was predictable: This is an emergency. It was the same reaction in the 1950's with Russian technology and in the 1970's with Chinese technology. People adjust, but the world was still changed. See Vietnam.

One will read of American delegations traveling back and forth in an effort to find a "reasonable" compromise with North Korea. Announcements will be made announcing the final happy breakthrough, again and again. But if some dramatic agreement is not reached, it is inevitable that it will be clear one day that North Korea has access to a nursery school right outside the White House. The heart of the North Korean nuclear program is not an emotional extravaganza by a fevered aging bureaucracy.[556] It is North Koreans in the 11th grade.

The Proliferation/SDI Dance

Remember the tough-minded triumphal declarations of the Reagan foreign policy team of the 1980's. There was a Team B that would explicitly disavow arms control treaties in favor of a nuclear weapons policy that would put Russians under increasing threat.[557] Now, there will never be a consensus on what was achieved and what was lost. But the position urged here is to call attention to one undeniable change that largely became visible between the beginning of the Reagan presidency and roughly 1995. On one issue, nuclear weapons engineering, America was more vulnerable at the end of the period than the beginning.

Nuclear weapons have always had much more to do with engineering than politics. At the end of the Reagan presidency China could start a nuclear fire in Indiana. And Russia would be better at starting the fire.

Liberal and leftist nuclear scientists did not do anyone a favor when they invented their Doomsday Clock. The clock demonstrates that the Left and Reagan Republicans walk hand and hand briskly into the future, confused, sharing the same dangerous misconceptions, under the same growing ominous cloud. Connecting the hands of the clock to the intensity and volume of the visible political reality misses the consistent, steady, predictable advance of the quiet, hidden, potent behavioral engineering substrate.

SDI represents the continuation of two assumptions that have always supported the nuclear weapons program. The first is that the blonds are intellectually so superior that nuclear weapons do not represent a threat to them. The second is somewhat at odds with the first, but fits with the common assumption that nuclear weapons are just one more rung on a long, long history of weapons development: Psychological environmentalism transferred to the nuclear weapons story predicts that a wealthier economy and a heroic population will carry the day.

If one goes back to the 1950's in the Chinese nuclear weapons program; the "beginning" for all practical purposes, one can not but help notice a curious disparity between the sophistication of the engineers who would finally be able to knock down Los Angeles, and the political economic thinking that would determine Chinese economic activity generally for a generation. One heard of plans to develop a steel industry through backyard furnaces; at the same time nuclear scientists were learning how to apply techniques a few months old.

That lack of sophistication about economic and psychological conditions no longer applies in China. One assumes that they do see the asset that they have in the 15-year-old.

Nuclear weapons require a focus: There is no plane floating above the ethnic plane that we live on every day. One can confidently predict that the fall of communism in China will make as little difference to the Chinese ability to fashion nuclear weapons as it did in the Soviet Union/Russia. Moreover, the democratic English speaking world's insistence that everyone treat their neighbors better than the Pilgrims treated the wogs at Plymouth, or Anglo Texas treated Mexico, may help to force a specific alliance between an Orthodox Slavic Russia and an atheistic Communist China to keep the United States under a credible nuclear threat; an alliance that, absent nuclear weapons, would be unthinkable.[558]

The Chinese see what they have done with just a very few nuclear weapons. They are unapologetic about why they and the Russians, for all their ethnic, religious and historic differences, will cooperate to ensure that Anglo-America will not be able to threaten their children with nuclear weapons, without Anglo-American children being similarly threatened.[559] The fact that Russia and China, two countries who share a land mass where there is a potential for conflict over conventional population and resource issues may cooperate with each other, rather than with the U.S., demonstrates the importance of nuclear weapons. It also shows how determined some countries are to put some kind of limits on where the Vikings can go and what they can do once they arrive.

Political realities of the nuclear big three: The U.S., China and Russia have been permanently altered by nuclear weapons. In a sense, all of the moves within this triangle have been affected by what the 15-year-old did in algebra class in the second half of the twentieth century: For these three, when they deal with each other, there is no nuclear free zone.

At the end of the day the world is faced with a reality which will require decisions and action. The great engineer is as mobile as tanks or oil or money. What if China decides that its position will be advanced if there is a believable Muslim nuclear threat? A Muslim bomb could take pressure of it and put it on its two antagonists: India, with which it has a longstanding border dispute, and the U. S., heir to British Imperialism.

China would not have to actually give away her secrets. Her engineers could simply monitor and make suggestions about the program the Muslim engineers are pursuing. China may be criticized for this, but here as everywhere, the circumstances are important. Assume the observers were right who claim that Truman and his advisors were really aware that Japan was willing to surrender without a nuclear attack?[560]

Israel and her supporters have advanced the idea that Israel should be seen as part of a democratic world, an expression of universal values and supported and protected on that basis. The real world of nuclear weapons makes that approach dangerous to both Israel and her supporters. It would be better to go to China and Russia and just admit that Israel has a very different status to Americans, and that she will be supported on that basis. In turn the United States will tacitly agree not to carry universal themes too dangerously close to legitimate Chinese and Russian interests.

While on the personal level no population has been more self-consciously ethnic than Anglo-America, the American establishment's refusal to state that ethnicity has been and remains a legitimate source of violence by everyone, including the blonds, has become a problem to the next generation of blonds. The refusal to talk about blond ethnicity openly has been at the heart of British and American exceptionalism in international affairs. For blond intellectuals, Anglo/America floats above the ethnic world: In an ethnic world, but not of it.

One consequence of the blond refusal to see what Russia and China have to see, may be that the partnership between a self-defined Christian Russian state and an atheistic Marxist Chinese state will be more potent and dangerous to the blonds than the partnership between fascist Japan and Italy, and a racist Germany. One never knew how important the partnership was to either Russia or China when they were both Marxist states, but, given the centrality of nuclear weaponry, one sees how important the relationship is now.

Both have a very real stake in being sure that the blonds share some vulnerability to nuclear weapons. The engineering staffs in each country, big and good now, if they combine will become bigger and better.

The impression one gets from the national press on nuclear proliferation is of technology escaping from the West on little technology feet. Before the blond intellectual will understand why his three year old has become a part of the international betting pool, he will have to see the another image: a dirty little shack called a school, without plumbing or modern heating, in an incredibly poor agricultural village; part of the monotone. The 15-year-old boys in that village have been in that school, rather than the fields, for not more than 4 generations. It is an October morning; we are in algebra class. In one respect that class is like algebra class in an elite American school. Most of the boys look at the blackboard and say to themselves, "What the hell does that mean?" But there is one who says, to himself, "What is the matter with these guys?"

The boy becomes older, continues his extraordinary work in the rest of his high school career, goes to college, and remains at the head of his engineering classes. Certain adults are watching how he does with great interest. They are pleased when it looks as if he is as outstanding at 22 as he was in that village shack. Civil servants recruit him, and a comparative handful of young men from similar circumstances, into the nuclear weapons program. They have engineered the key for the lock of the future. Proliferation: the final answer for the Vikings.

Practical Problems Exist Within Time Constraints

The fact that nuclear weaponry has the behavioral look that it has makes for critical differences on the time dimension. In the nineteenth century catching up with the British Navy in the production of battleships might have taken the better part of the century for a country which was poorer than England, but growing economically faster. The battleships of the challenger rolled into the ocean over the backs of millions of peasants becoming an industrial labor force. The sheer mass of stuff that comprised the ship secured a tremendously long lead-time. And, if British sailors were more skillful or braver, the competition could not force the English to bet what they were not willing to bet. The British Empire became enormous for a lot of reasons, but a couple of the most important reasons were that the English had a lot of material before anyone else had a lot of material, and the English are willing to risk their lives to stuff it down the wog's throat on the wog's dirt. They are as brave as they claim to be. Those advantages meant the English never had to play the Game at home.

See how different nuclear weapons fit with time. In the year 2000 a Chinese official suggested that America was overreacting to the North Korean nuclear program because North Korea would not actually have a missile able to hit the U.S. mainland for another 15 years.[561] Assume that North Korea will be able to deliver a cylinder to Buckingham Palace or the White House by the year 2020. In a world without nuclear weapons little Korea could never threaten the U.S. and England; and the U.S. and England could always threaten North Korea.

Assume that the North Koreans saw the need to have that ability when President Eisenhower with a big blond grin threatened to bomb them with nuclear weapons in the early 50's. They will not have matched the Anglo/American hardware but they can force Americans to bet what the American housewife really does not want to bet.

Once the threat of delivery becomes real, it makes a difference in how the policeman acts in that particular wog's corner of the world. The problem with continuing the assumptions and policies underlying America's nuclear weapons program is that over time the rogue that can match that 15-year-old algebra student may threaten to make trouble in a place where America really can not paper over a serious difference.

We have all heard numerous times how dangerous our times are because a nuclear weapon can be smuggled into New York in a briefcase. Well, maybe or maybe not. Typically the greybeard making the observation either wishes that the United States would make a greater effort in the nuclear weapons field, or the reverse: They would prefer the United States forget about building an expensive space based defensive system since we are all so vulnerable right now.

Both miss the point. The big very visible railroad in space carrying nuclear weaponry closer and closer to the American heartland has a kind of hidden parallel track that is spiked into the earth: The railroad on earth is labeled miniaturization. The missile in space and the bomb in the briefcase have the same father: engineering talent and they ought to be approached with the same tactics and the same explanations.

A bomb in a briefcase that can change human history represents thousands and thousands of man hours from men with very different specialties who share the same characteristic: the ability to write a 785 on the math SAT. It is tough to come up with thousands of man hours of engineering talent at that level. Nations can do it and giant corporations can do it. A collection of fanatics with a pick up truck and a briefcase can not do it. The point is that the talent has to be controlled.

For a gentile, reading the Old Testament when one is over 50 is very different from reading the Old Testament as a teenager. As a teenager one sees the Jews, an interesting group, doing a lot of fantastic things: wars, miracles, winning some, losing some; and a curious God, sometimes very visible, sometimes not, sometimes very familiar to a model that one has internalized, sometimes not.

At 50, or better 60, one sees a stage play with certain specifics highlighted. Ethnicity, as a topic, takes up more space; one is less sure how to fit God into the story. Equally important, 30 to 40 years have pushed Time into the adult's head. Time has become an important actor. One's life, like high school, is not forever. The Old Testament was a long long story but it was not forever. And one of the unavoidable reactions for the gray-haired reader is the awareness that after innumerable battles, losses, wins, disappointments, successes; Time finally revealed a specific result. The Jewish God is still there. The competition was not simply defeated; it disappeared.

The story about nuclear weapons is like that story in two respects: It is a big story, and it will be a long story. How it ends, matters.

The threat that China represents to Anglo-America is more than a threat that it may export hardware to America's enemies.[562] If one uses the British per capita GDP as a kind of consistent historical scale to measure industrialization and modernization, one concludes that the process can proceed very rapidly. From the dawn of industrialization, in, say, the first half of the 18th century to the end of the 20th there were innumerable arguments, centering around culture, IQ, religion, appearance, etc., which were used to explain why Great Britain was so much wealthier than most of the world. The middle third of the twentieth century saw school systems everywhere begin to capture very high percentages of the school age boys, and the economic figures, particularly in Asia, began to look very different.

Their great early success pointed the blond democrats toward the others' fanaticism, rather than their own. For example, one reads that Sudan, over a hundred years ago, was the site of the same Islamic fanaticism one reads in the paper today.[563] How do we know that? Egypt, then virtually a British colony, joined with Britain to conquer Sudan once and for all and to put an end to resistance to British aggression in the area. "Fanatical" Dervishes armed with primitive spears attacked an Anglo-Egyptian force only to be mowed down by machine guns and other modern weaponry. In Afghanistan, the British succeeded, by force, in taking over the country's foreign policy. The British, punishing Afghanistan for resisting, captured Kabul and burned down the Great Bazaar. The blonds read that resistance to British imperialism and racism was fanaticism, not that the British aggression represents fanaticism. As long as there were no ways to get at the policeman, his aggression is defined by his vocabulary. As long as there is no way to get at the policeman, the wog's resistance is also defined by the policeman's vocabulary.

The explosion of the first Soviet hydrogen bomb should have been a signal to the blond intellectual that a New World Order really was in the making. Post 1955, populations that could come up with the special 15-year-old in big enough numbers, would be able to define fanaticism for themselves. The difference between what the second modern world policeman faces from what the first world policeman faced, is not terrorism by a handful of fanatics roaming the streets of New York with hidden bombs, in a way they did not roam the streets of London. The difference is that there are non-blond engineers in the world who can make the policeman disappear.

Behaviorists were able to give shape to a different way of viewing human behavior as they set up shop in a laboratory and moved our gaze from what Skinner labeled "topography" to the probability of a given response.[564] One sees how different nuclear weapons are when one looks at a clock.

If one performs a simple mental adjustment, one can not avoid the dramatic increase in vulnerability for the blonds on the North American continent in a brief 45-year period after 1955. If one tries to represent what happened to American security in that period, in terms of 1955 technology; one would move 1955 bombers loaded with atom bombs from an airfield hidden behind a mountain range deep inside the Asian land mass to an airfield in Nova Scotia.

Perhaps more ominous, some of the bombers on that Nova Scotia airfield carry the Chinese flag. And there are fears that, in a few years, North Korean bombers may taxi on to the runway. No one could doubt that had President Eisenhower been told that Nova Scotia would offer its airport to Russian bombers loaded with nuclear weapons, war with Canada would have been inevitable. The horrifying became acceptable because it occurred day by day in small engineering increments, because the U.S. was also improving its offensive capabilities, and because the launching pad remained the same.

It took two generations for the wogs to move the delivery of Doomsday from over 10 hours to 40 minutes. How many generations will it take to move the delivery from 40 minutes to 5 minutes?

With apologies to Winston Churchill, no one sees the end of the story of nuclear weapons; no one even sees the beginning of the end. But we have seen the end of the beginning. The beginning was about talent and ethnicity.

I do not know if there is a God or if there is a Devil; but if there is a Devil I know what his favorite engineered product is. All things are no longer possible for any ethnic group. Nuclear weapons carry an existential message. The democratic blonds have to make serious decisions about what kind of a world they can have, and about what they can and can not do.

In the acres of space between the view expressed here and the establishment view about what nuclear weapons are, the most important point involves a shift of perspective. When one sees nuclear weapons as behavior; one sees nuclear weapons as a practical, day by day problem for the blonds; a problem that will not go away for generations. Nuclear weapons will cross that seam in middle class America's head which separates distant, intellectual and political problems from the day to day security and financial issues which define real life.

Some day, generations removed from the immediate threat, people may debate how nuclear weapons fit with European imperialism. Was it a chapter from an economics text? Or was it a story about ethnicity: a snapshot of how a planet divided between a peasantry and a great fighter has to look once the peasantry puts its young men in school and develops a "big enough" economy?

The two great engines that will power nuclear weapons into the future are academic talent, and ethnicity. One may predict that they will be as potent when the product is for defensive purposes as when it was frankly and honestly for attack.

Certainly September 11, 2001, will be a much more important date in the future of nuclear weapons than the pundits first publicly recognized. Large segments of the college educated, blond, professional, secularized, nominally Protestant public saw that the laws of physics operate on American soil. Many of those intelligent people could imagine something that they could not have imagined moments earlier. America had a real, visible ethnic enemy who threatened Americans in a personal and direct manner. If certain groups became intense target of American resolve, inevitably other groups began drawing a pass. There would be less generalized hectoring against the Slavs and the Chinese for human rights violations. As Americans perceive that their long-term enemy has a specific ethnic identity, there will be more attention to keeping other parties friendly, or at least neutral.

One of the gifts nuclear weapons have given the world is that they operate as a window that allows us to see through the fog into a deeper, more basic reality concerning large scale human violence. Ethnicity is the biggest figure in that reality. As such, it will operate to neutralize, blur and excuse the mistakes and terror that the twin modernizing forces of the 20th century, fascism and communism, committed. The Slavs and the Chinese know that whatever mistakes the communists made, they began a process that would keep the blonds off their dirt.

How does Islam fit with the move of the peasantry into the modern world? Certain particulars would seem to be at odds with modernization, particularly the status of women. But other particulars may prove to be the foundation of a new, and potent, and clearly anti-Western movement.

A fair amount of punditry was expended on what might happen to nuclear designs, equipment and material in Pakistan if the political leadership declines to follow America's lead. If one listened carefully, one heard an echo of the old familiar concern about proliferation. But once one sees that the nuclear weapons game is not about stuff, but about talent one sees that the more basic question concerns what happens to Pakistani talent if Islam topples the pro-American government.

One can only speculate about how Islam and nuclear weapons will move into the future. The beginning of the nuclear weapons story did not feature Islam, and the beginning of nuclear weapons is all we know.

Reverend Robertson and Reverend Falwell were criticized for suggesting that the horrific result of September 11 carried a message from God, but Americans invoke the name of God so often and so publicly when things go well, that it would have been inappropriate to have absolutely no mention of God when America's enemies are successful.

Religion has an ethnic dimension, inevitably. In a sense, for Protestants Christianity began with Luther's conscience. Once that conscience was free, the German-Slav game, an intense, localized and brutal version of the general worldwide blond-wog game, was bound to affect the entire planet. A private informal racism has given the blue-eyed people a permanent agenda. For the four centuries following Luther, and on three continents, Luther's neighbors have had to contend with the spectacular strengths and determination of that conscience.

But, after 1955, the blonds had to bet what they never thought they would have to bet. The blond three-year-old girl with blue eyes now shares the same role and the same status as all the other three- year-olds: Target.

The vulnerability of the English-speaking democratic blond people that developed in the last half of the 20th century because of certain behavioral particulars of nuclear weapons is the central event of those 50 years. How does the reality, Mutual Assured Destruction, grow in the future?

I believe that religion plays a critical, if sometimes hidden, role in how one handles the possibility of nuclear war. Nuclear weapons change the nature of war in a very crucial particular that invades the religious domain. Providence has been utilized to explain both defeats and victories from the time of ancient Israel to the present. Sometimes a righteous God will interfere for the favored side, sometimes He will not. His people remained His people but that did not preclude some terrible, but just defeats, including the loss of Israel. In non-nuclear conflicts, one side looses but the other side wins. Somebody inherits the earth. With a nuclear war, no one inherits the place.

I am an agnostic. Agnosticism has been a kind of intellectual step-child between the enormity of the Jewish/Christian/Moslem God morphed into various shapes over different millennia and among different ethnic groups, on one side; and the atheistic positivism that modern social science requires, on the other.

But agnosticism may not be a bad entry to approach nuclear weapons. Certitude, a belief issue, has the potential to become dangerous as it is tied to a monstrous action issue. Constructing a nuclear wasteland is so excessive, so extreme, and so different, that, finally; it is a religious question in a way that previous wars just were not.

I do not know if the is a God, or if there is a Devil. But if there is a Devil, I am positive that I know his favorite engineered product.

As a start, an agnostic says that, deep down, one is not sure; one is simply trying to fit together the pieces of an enormous puzzle. One wonders how so much order could have simply emerged in the universe. And the tough pattern is not the physics; it is the inside of the human head. We feel that there is some transcendent value to human existence. We accept that we will die. But no one accepts millions of three-year-olds dead in minutes in massive nuclear fireballs, across continents, around the globe.

NOTES

Chapter 1: Peasant Societies as Learned Behavior

1 Charles J. Lumsden and Edward O. Wilson, *Genes, Mind and Culture* (Cambridge: Harvard University Press, 1981), 92.

2 B. F. Skinner, *Beyond Freedom and Dignity* (New York: Alfred A. Knopf, 1971), 122.

3 Edward O. Wilson, *Sociobiology: the new synthesis* (Cambridge: Harvard University Press, Belknap Press, 1975), 551.

4 James C. Scott, *The Moral Economy of the Peasant: Rebellion and Subsistence in Southeast Asia.* (New Haven and London: Yale University Press, 1976), 159.

5. Christopher Hitchens. "Now, Who Will Speak for Rushdie?" *New York Times.* 17 February 1989, A39.

6. K.C.Wu, *The Chinese Heritage.* (New York: Crown Publishers, Inc., 1982), 393.

7. Karl A. Wittfogel. *Oriental Despotism: a comparative study of total power.* (New Haven: Yale University Press, 1957).

8. Edward O. Wilson *Consilience: The Unity of Knowledge.* (New York: Alfred A. Knopf, 1998), 253.

9. B. F. Skinner, *About Behaviorism.* (New York: Alfred A. Knopf, 1974), 243

10. John Kenneth Galbraith. *The New Industrial State, 2d ed. rev.* (Boston: Houghton Mifflin Company, 1967; New York: New American Library, 1971), 138 (page citations are to the reprint edition).

11. Wu, *The Chinese Heritage.* 108.

12. Marvin Harris, *Cultural Materialism: The Struggle for a Science of Culture.* (New York: Random House, 1979), 32-33.

13. Ibid., 32.

14. Ibid., 38.

15. Ibid., 15.

16. Ibid., 39.

17. Ibid.

18. Lumsden and Wilson. *Genes, Mind and Culture.* 249.

19. Ibid., 16.

20. Ibid., 18

21. F. Vogel and M. R. Chakravartti. "AO Blood Groups and Smallpox in a Rural Population of West Bengal and Bihar (India)," in *Natural Selection in Human Populations. : The Measurement of Ongoing Genetic Evolution in Contemporary Societies.* ed. Carl Jay Bajema (1971, John Wiley & Sons, Inc., reprint ed., New York: Robert E. Krieger Publishing Co., Inc., 1977), 150 (page citations are to the reprint edition).

22. Samuel L. Popkin. *The Rational Peasant: The Political Economy of Rural Society in Vietnam.* (Berkeley: University of California Press, 1979), 105.

23. Judith E. Smith, "Italian Mothers, American Daughters: Changes in Work and Family Roles," in *The Italian Immigrant Woman in North America.* ed., Betty Boyd Caroli, Robert F. Harney and Lydio F. Tomasi (Toronto: The Multicultural History Society of Ontario, 1978), 207.

24. Anita Chan, Richard Madsen, and Jonathan Unger. *Chen Village: The Recent History of a Peasant Community in Mao's China.* (Berkeley: University of California Press, 1984), 14

25. Wittfogel, *Oriental Despotism.* 18.

26. Wu, *The Chinese Heritage.* 79.

27. "Disasters-Earthquakes; Floods; Tornadoes," *World Almanac & Book of Facts 1981.* (New York: Newspaper Enterprise Association, Inc.), 748.

28. David P. Barash. *Sociobiology and Behavior.* (New York: Elsevier, 1977), 2.

29. Jane E. Stevens. "Old ways restored after 'experts' fail," *Boston Globe.* 31 January 1994, 25. 30. Alan Ryan. *review of The Woman in the Cowshed: An Inquiry into Well-Being and Destitution.* by Partha Dasgupta, *New York Review of Books.* 11 May 1995, 24.

31. Barash, *Sociobiology and Behavior.* 124.

32. Ibid., 125.

33. Wilson, *Sociobiology.* 4.

34. Richard A. Easterlin and Eileen M. Crimmins. *The Fertility Revolution: A Supply-Demand Analysis.* (Chicago: The University of Chicago Press, 1985), 146.

35. Frederick Osborn. "A Return to the Principles of Natural Selection," in *Natural Selection in Human Populations.* ed. Bajema, 370.

36. Lumsden and Wilson. *Genes, Mind, and Culture.* 99.

37. E. R. Nye, "Natural Selection and Degenerative Cardiovascular Disease," in *Natural Selection in Human Populations.* ed. Bajema, 196, 197.

38. D. H. Stott, "Cultural and Natural Checks on Population-Growth," in *Culture and The Evolution of Man.* ed. M. F. Ashley Montagu (New York: Oxford University Press, 1962; reprint 1972), 364-365 (page citations are to the 1972 reprint edition).

39. John Erik, "China's Policy on Births," *New York Times.* 3 January 1982, E 19.

40. Donella H. Meadows et al. *The Limits to Growth: A Report for the Club of Rome's Project on the Predicament of Mankind .* (New York: Universe Books, 1972; reprint, New York: A Signet Book, 1972), 121 (page citations are to the reprint edition).

41. Amit K. Bhattacharyya. "Role of Rural-Urban Income Inequality in Fertility Reductions: Cases of Turkey, Taiwan, and Morocco," *Economic Development and Cultural Change.* 62, no. 1 (October 1977): 127.

42. Nick Eberstadt, "The Health Crisis in the USSR," review of Rising Infant Mortality in the USSR in the 1970s, by Christopher Davis and Murray Feshbach, *The New York Review of Books.* 19 February 1981, 23 n. 3.

43. Bruce F. Johnston and Anthony J. Meyer. "Nutrition, Health, and Population in Strategies for Rural Development," *Economic Development and Cultural Change.* 62, no.1 (October 1977): 6.

44. Frederick S. Hulse. "Some Factors Influencing the Relative Proportions of Human Racial Stocks," in *Natural Selection in Human Populations.* ed. Bajema, 134.

45.   Peter Kolchin, *Unfree Labor: American Slavery and Russian Serfdom.* (Cambridge: Harvard University Press, Belknap Press, 1987), 73.

46.   Johnston and Meyer.   "Nutrition, Health, and Population in Strategies for Rural Development," *Economic Development and Cultural Change.* 62, no.1 (October 1977): 4.

47. Easterlin and Crimmins. *The Fertility Revolution.* 90

48. Ibid., 5.

49. Adi Ignatius, "Beijing Boom: China's Birthrate Rises Again Despite A Policy of One Child Families," *Wall Street Journal.* 14 July 1988, 16.

50. Meadows et al., *Limits to Growth.* 76.

51. B. F. Skinner, *Contingencies of Reinforcement: a theoretical analysis.* (New York: Meredith Corporation, Appleton-Century-Crofts, 1969), 199.

52. B. F. Skinner, *Recent Issues in the Analysis of Behavior.* (Columbus: Merrill Publishing Company, 1989), 118.

53. Alan Macfarlane. *The Origins of English Individualism: The Family Property and Social Transition.* (Basil Blackwell, 1978; New York: Cambridge University Press, 1979), 168.

54. Ibid., 185.

55. Ibid., 178-179.

56. Fernand Braudel. *The Mediterranean and the Mediterranean World in the Age of Philip II, trans. Sian Reynolds, vol. 1.* (New York: Harper & Row, Harper Torchbooks, 1975), 240 (page citation is to Harper Torchbooks edition) .

57. Ibid., 241.

58.   Alistair Horne, *A Savage War of Peace: Algeria 1954-1962.* (New York: Macmillan Ltd., 1977; reprint, New York: Penguin Books, 1977), 101. (page citations are to the reprint edition).

59. Iurii Krizhanich. *Russian Statecraft: The Politika of Iurii Krizhanich.* trans. John M. Letiche and Basil Dmytryshyn (New York: Basil Blackwell Inc.1985), 163.

60. Mikhail Bakunin. *From out of the Dustbin: Bakunin's Basic Writings 1869-1871.* trans. Robert M. Cutler (Ann Arbor: Ardis Publishers, 1985),182-183.

61. Sergei Mikhailovich Kravchinskii. *The Russian Peasantry: Their Agrarian Condition, Social Life and Religion.* (1888; reprint ed., Westport, Connecticut: Hyperion Press, Inc., 1977), 27 (page citation is to the reprint edition).

62. Harris, *Cultural Materialism.* 40.

63. Danilo Dolci, *Report from Palermo, trans. P. D. Cummins.* (The Orion Press, Inc., 1959; reprint, New York: The Viking Press, Inc. 1970), 215 (page citations are to the reprint edition).

64. Chan, Madsen and Unger. *Chen Village,* 13, 44.

65. Fox Butterfield. *China: Alive in the Bitter Sea.* (New York: Times Books, 1982; reprint, New York: Bantam Books, 1983), 15. (page citations are to the reprint edition).

66. Chan, Madsen and Unger. *Chen Village,* 172.

67. Scott, *The Moral Economy.* 17.

68. Butterfield, *China.* 240.

69. "Slave sisters reunited after 41 years. " Nashua (New Hampshire) Telegraph, 3 May 1984, 43.

70. Kolchin, *Unfree Labor.* 365.

71. Robert C. Stuart and Paul R. Gregory. "A Model of Soviet Rural-Urban Migration," *Economic Development and Cultural Change.* 62. no. 1 (Oct. 1977): 84.

72. G. Kh. Shakhnazarov et al.. *Social Science.* ed. Charles and Catherine Baroch (Lexington, Mass.: D.C. Heath and Company, 1973), 137.

73. Lester E. Klimm, Otis P. Starkey, and Norman F. Hall. *Introductory Economic Geography.* 2nd ed. rev. (New York: Harcourt, Brace and Company, 1940), 448.

74. Ezra F. Vogel, "Rice-price time in Tokyo: rural political clout," *Boston Globe.* 9 August 1982, 2.

75. Yoshimi Ishikawa. *Strawberry Road.* trans. Eve Zimmerman (Tokyo: Kodansha International Ltd., 1991), 13.

76. Park Chung Hee, paraphrased by Kyung Cho Chung. "What Made the Revolution Succeed," in *Sources in Modern East Asian History and Politics.* ed. Theodore McNelly, (New York: Appleton-Century-Crofts, 1967), 268 (hereinafter cited as East Asian History).

77. Kasum Nair, *In Defense of the Irrational Peasant: Indian Agriculture after the Green Revolution.* (Chicago: University of Chicago Press, 1979), 91.

78. Butterfield, *China.* 251.

79. Ibid., 250.

80. Enno Von Lowenstern. "The Man Who Pulled West German Out of Poverty," *Wall Street Journal.* 21 November 1989, A18.

81. Horne, *A Savage War of Peace.* 63.

82. Dolci, *Report from Palermo.* 188.

83. Meadows et al., *Limits to Growth.* 154.

84. Kolchin, *Unfree Labor.* 69.

85. Ibid., 152.

86. Ibid., 153.

87. Kravchinskii, *Russian Peasantry.* 29.

88. Ibid., 48.

89. Albert B. Martinez and Maurice Lewandowski. *The Argentine in the Twentieth Century.* trans. Bernard Miall (London: T Fisher Unwin, 1911), 157.

90. Ibid., 156.

91. William Mathewson. "China's Rural Unemployed. " *Wall Street Journal.* 6 December 1990, A12.

92. John Wang, "China's Jobless Youth: A Mounting Problem," *New York Times.* 30 September 1979.

93. Editorial, "Down on China's Farm," *Wall Street Journal.* 3 February 1995, A12

94. Alice Kessler-Harris. review of *The First Century of Unemployment in Massachusetts, by Alexander Keyssar. New York Times.* Book Review, 4 May 1986, 36.

95. "Labor Letter," *Wall Street Journal.* 23 April 1991, 1.

96. Edwin O. Reischauer. *The Japanese Today: Change and Continuity.* (Cambridge: Harvard University Press, Belknap Press, 1977. Reprint, 1988), 46 (page citations are to the reprint edition).

97. Ibid., 60.

98. Wu, *Chinese Heritage.* 67-69.

99. Ibid., 131.

100. Ibid., 134.

101. Ibid., 135.

102. Ibid., 436.

103. Mao Tse-tung, "Report on an Investigation of the Peasant Movement in Hunan," East Asian History, 218.

104. Chan, Madsen and Unger. *Chen Village,* 22.

105. Popkin, *The Rational Peasant.* 91.

106. Ibid., 155-156.

107. Scott, *The Moral Economy.* 78.

108. Popkin, *The Rational Peasant.* 103.

109. Nair, *introduction to In Defense of the Irrational Peasant.* xvii.

110. Ibid., 130.

111. Ibid., 131.

112. Ibid., 81.

113. P. M. Barford. *The Early Slavs: Culture and Society in Early Medieval Eastern Europe.* (Ithaca: Cornell University Press, 2001), 8.

114. Kolchin, *Unfree Labor.* 161.

115. Ibid., 159.

116. Ibid., 165.

117. Ibid., 217.

118. Ibid., 205.

119. Kravchinskii, *Russian Peasantry.* 5.

120. Ibid.

121. Krizhanich, *Russian Statecraft.* 113.

122. Kravchinskii, *Russian Peasantry.* 111.

123. Letiche and Dmytryshyn. *Russian Statecraft.* xliv.

124. Kravchinskii, *Russian Peasantry.* 1

125. Leo Cellini, "Emigration, the Italian Family, and Changing Roles," in *Italian Immigrant Woman in North America.* 278.

126. Carlos Rangel, *The Latin Americans: Their Love-Hate Relationship with the United States.* trans. Ivan Kats (New York: Harcourt Brace Jovanovich, 1977), 185-186.

127. Ibid., 27.

128. Martinez and Lewandowski. *Argentine in the Twentieth Century.* 134.

129. Klimm, Starkey and Hall. *Economic Geography.* 208.

130. Martinez and Lewandowski. preface to the Third Edition. *Argentine in the Twentieth Century.* xviii.

131. Ibid., 128-129.

132. Ibid., 131-132.

133. Mark Jefferson. *Peopling the Argentine Pampa.* American Geographical Society, Research Series No. 16 (New York, 1926), 33.

134. Ibid., 36.

135. Ibid. 140.

136. Ibid., 27.

137. Fernando Bastos de Avila S.J.. *Economic Impacts of Immigration: The Brazilian Immigration Problem* . (1954; reprint, Westport, Ct.: Greenwood Press, 1970), 11 (page citation is to the reprint edition).

138. Robert Darnton. "The Meaning of Mother Goose," *New York Review.* 2 February 1984, 41, 44.

139. Kravchinskii, *Russian Peasantry.* 159.

140. Dolci, *Report from Palermo.* 165.

141. Ibid., 193

142. Nair, *In Defense of the Irrational Peasant.* 7.

143. Chan, Madsen and Unger. *Chen Village.* 69.

144. Kolchin, *Unfree Labor.* 106.

145. Chan, Madsen and Unger. *Chen Village.* 216.

146. Dolci, *Report from Palermo.* 202.

147. Scott, *The Moral Economy.* 13.

148. Dolci, *Report from Palermo.* 126. Chan, Madsen and Unger. *Chen Village.* 13.

149. A. Grenfell Price. *White Settlers in the Tropics.* American Geographical Society, Special Publication No. 23 (New York, 1939), 127.

150. Popkin, *The Rational Peasant.* 250 n.

151. Anna Ferro-Luzzi. "Environment and Physical Growth," in *Genetic and Environmental Factors during the Growth Period.* ed. C. Suzanne (New York: Plenum Press, 1984), 182.

152. Price, *White Settlers in the Tropics.* 208.

153. Ibid., 208.

154. Richard M. Morse. "Manchester Economics and Paulista Sociology," in *Manchester and Sao Paulo: Problems of Rapid Urban Growth.* ed. John D. Wirth and Robert L. Jones (Stanford: Stanford University Press, 1978), 8.

155. Nick Eberstadt. "Women and Education in China: How Much Progress?" review of *China as a Model of Development.* by Al Imfeld, *China's Economy and the Maoist Strategy.* by John G. Gurley, and *China's Economic Revolution.* by Alexander Eckstein, *New York Review of Books.* 19 April 1979, 41.

156. David Hackett Fischer. *Albion's Seed: Four British Folkways in America.* (New York: Oxford University Press, 1989).

157. Editorial, *Boston Globe.* 17 January 1998.

158. Fischer, *Albion's Seed.* 28, 30.

159. Ibid., 130.

160. Joanne Della Valle. "Chelmsford has a stable population, accessible location," *Boston Globe.* 28 August 1999, E1.

161. Fischer, *Albion's Seed.* 345.

162. Ibid., 532.

163. Ibid., 533.

164. Ibid., 634.

165. Ibid., 716.

166. Ibid., 717 n. 7.

167. Ibid., 718.

168. Jay Mack Holbrook. *New Hampshire Residents, 1633-1699.* (Oxford, Mass.: Holbrook Research Institute, 1979), iii.

169. Eberstadt, "Women and Education in China," 41.

170. Ibid., 42.

171. Barbara Crossette. "India's Descent," *New York Times.* Sunday, 19 May 1991, sec. 6, 27, 57.

172. Horne.*A Savage War of Peace.* 61.

173. Ibid., 110.

174. Bhattacharyya, "Role of Rural-Urban Income Inequality in Fertility Reductions," *Economic Development and Cultural Change.* 62, no.1 (October 1977): 124.

175. Chan, Madsen and Unger. *Chen Village.* 115.

176. Reischauer, *Japanese Today.* p. 187.

177. Rangel, *Latin Americans.* 82.

178. Martin T. Katzman. "Sao Paulo and its Hinterland: Evolving Relationships and the Rise of an Industrial Power," in *Manchester and Sao Paulo.* 112.

179.   E. Levasseur. preface to the first edition, Martinez and Lewandowski, *Argentine in the Twentieth Century.* xxxvi.

180. Jefferson, *Peopling the Argentine Pampa.* 100.

181. Dolci, *Report from Palermo.* 74.

182. Ibid., 215.

183. "Portugal," *The World Almanac and Book of Facts.* 1981, 570.

184.   Tadeusz Bielicki and Zygmunt Welon.   "The Operation of Natural Selection on Human Head Form in an East European Population," in *Natural Selection in Human Populations.* ed. Bajema, 94.

185. Shakhnazarov, et al., . *Social Science.* 137.

186. Kravchinskii, *Russian Peasantry.* 74.

187. Wu, *Chinese Heritage.* 401.

188. Ibid., 399.

189. Chan, Madsen and Unger. *Chen Village,* 17.

190. Frederick S. Hulse. "Some Factors Influencing the Relative Proportions of Human Racial Stocks," in *Natural Selection in Human Populations.* ed. Bajema, 131.

191. Butterfield, *China.* 254.

192. Ibid, 240.

193. Nicholas D. Kristof. "Far from Tiannanmen: Color TV and Contentment," *New York Times.* 7 October 1990, 1.

194. Kaare Svalastoga. *Social Differentiation .* (New York: David McKay Company, Inc., 1965), 45.

195. Kravchinskii, *Russian Peasantry.* 23.

196. Letiche and Dmytrshyn. *introduction to Russian Statecraft.* xlv.

197. Shakhnazarov et al.. *Social Science,* 138.

198. Kravchinskii, *Russian Peasantry.* 77.

199. Chan, Madsen and Unger. *Chen Village.* 14.

200. Dolci, *Report from Palermo.* 151.

201. Emiliana P. Noether. "The Silent Half: Le Contadine Del Sud Before the First World War," in *Italian Immigrant Woman in North America.* 6-7.

202. Butterfield, *China.* 49.

203. Wu, *Chinese Heritage.* 351.

204. Kolchin, *Unfree Labor.* 328.

205. Robert F. Harney. "Men Without Women: Italian Migrants in Canada, 1885-1930," in *Italian Immigrant Woman in North America.* Caroli, Harney and Tomasi 93.

206. Kolchin, *Unfree Labor.* 212.

207. Chan, Madsen and Unger. *Chen Village.* 194.

208. "Japan-Myths behind the Miracle," ABC News Closeup, December, 1981.

209.   John L. M. Binnie Dawson.   "An Anthropological Perspective on the Evolution and Lateralization of the Brain," in *Evolution and Lateralization of the Brain.* ed. Stuart J. Dimond and David A. Blizard, *Annals of the New York Academy of Sciences.* 299 (1977): 441-443.

210. Ibid., 443.

211. Kolchin, *Unfree Labor.* 216.

212.   David Ignatius.   "A Divided People," *Wall Street Journal.*   9 September 1982, 16.

213.   Maxine Hong Kingston.   *The Woman Warrior: Memoirs of a Girlhood Among Ghosts.*   (New York: Alfred A. Knopf, Inc., 1976; reprint, New York: Vintage Books, 1977), 3 (page citations are to the reprint edition).

214. Dolci, *Report from Palermo.* 138.

215. Jay Mathews, "Custom, living conditions stifle romance in China," *Boston Globe.* 28 December 1979, 3.

216.   Steven W. Mosher.   "Why Are Baby Girls Being Killed in China?" *Wall Street Journal.* 25 July 1983, 11.

217. Leo Cellini, "Emigration, the Italian Family, and Changing Roles," in *Italian Immigrant Woman in North America.* ed. Caroli, Harney and Tomasi. 282-284.

218.   Arthur Kleinman and Byron Good.   eds., introduction to *Culture and Depression: Studies in the Anthropology and Cross-Cultural Psychiatry of Affect and Disorder.* (Berkeley: University of California Press, 1985), 16.

219. Arthur Kleinman and Joan Kleinman. "Somatization: The Interconnections in Chinese Society among Culture, Depressive Experiences, and the Meanings of Pain," in *Culture and Depression.* Kleinman and Good, 429-430.

220. Kleinman and Good. eds., introduction to Part II, *Culture and Depression.* 179.

221.   Anthony J. Marsella et al..   "Cross-Cultural Studies of Depressive Disorders: An Overview," in *Culture and Depression.* Kleinman and Good. 306.

222. Skinner, *About Behaviorism.* 129.

223. Lumsden and Wilson. *Genes, Mind, and Culture.* 312-313.

224. Wilson, *Sociobiology.* 562.

225. Thomas Sowell, *Race and Economics.* (New York: David McKay Company, Inc., 1975), 8.

226. Fischer, *Albion's Seed.* 364-365.

227. Ibid., 740.

228. Wu, *Chinese Heritage.* 353.

229. Letiche and Dmytryshyn. *Russian Statecraft.* 116.

230. Nair, *In Defense of the Irrational Peasant.* 81.

231. Scott, *Moral Economy of the Peasant.* 99.

232. Popkin, *Rational Peasant.* 77.

233. Alfred L. Malabie Jr.. "Off-the-Books Business Booms in Europe," *Wall Street Journal.* 24 August 1981, 1.

234. Roger Cohen, "Rome Eyes Merchants Reporting Less Income Than Their Employees," *Wall Street Journal.* 19 November 1984, 36.

235. Bradley K. Martin. "Tokyo Fights to Uphold System 70% in a Survey Consider to be Unfair," *Wall Street Journal.* 19 November 1984, 36.

236. Karel van Wolferen. *The Enigma of Japanese Power: People and Politics in a Stateless Nation.* (New York: Alfred A. Knopf, Inc., 1989; reprint, New York: Vintage Books, 1990), 22 (page citations are to the reprint edition).

237. Ibid., 211.

238. Robert Neff et al.. "Hidden Japan," *Business Week.* 26 August 1991, 34.

239. "Honest Japanese. " Parade Magazine, 7 April 1991, 19.

240. Frank Ching, "China Again Tries to End Secret Deals, Bribery Found at Every Level of Society," *Wall Street Journal.* 4 September 1981, 22.

241. Arthur Waldron. "China Now: Miracle or Kleptocracy?" review of *After the Nightmare.* by Liang Heng and Judith Shapiro, *Wall Street Journal.* 14 May 1986, 28.

242. Claudia Rosett. "How Peru Got a Free Market Without Really Trying," *Wall Street Journal.* 27 January 1984, 31.

243. Maria E. Estenssoro. "When an Economy Goes Underground," *New York Times.* 26 July 1987, 3.

244. Ibid.

245. Stephen Engelberg. "Poland's New Climate Yields Bumper Crop of Corruption," *New York Times.* 12 November 1991, 1.

246. Richard Parker. "Inside the 'Collapsing' Soviet Economy," Atlantic, June 1990, 68.

247. Walter C. Clemens Jr.. "Perestroika Needs a Work Ethic to Work," *Wall Street Journal.* 5 December 1989, A22.

Chapter 2: Morality as Strategy by Control.

248.   James C. Scott.   *The Moral Economy of the Peasant: Rebellion and Subsistence in Southeast Asia.* (New Haven: Yale University Press, 1976).

249. Samuel L. Popkin. *The Rational Peasant: The Political Economy of Rural Society in Vietnam.* (Berkeley: University of California Press, 1979).

250. Scott, *Moral Economy of the Peasant.* 5.

251. Wittfogel, *Oriental Despotism.* 143-144.

252. Scott, *Moral Economy of the Peasant.* 184-185.

253. Kingston, *The Woman Warrior.* 5.

254. Scott, *Moral Economy of the Peasant.* 38.

255. Edward O. Wilson. *On Human Nature.* (Cambridge: Harvard University Press, 1978), 162.

256. Popkin, *Rational Peasant.* 96-97.

257. Ibid., 139.

258. Ibid., 163.

259. Ibid., 129.

260. Ibid., 132.

261. Ibid., 145-150.

262. Ibid., 184, 242.

263. Ibid., 252-258.

264. Ibid., 39.

265. Ibid., 38.

266. Ibid., 27-28.

267. Ibid., 49-50.

268. Ibid., 104.

269. Ibid., 17.

270. Ibid., 19.

271. Ibid., 27.

272. Ibid.

273. Ibid., 74.

274. Ibid., 40-41.

275. Ibid., 78 n.

276. Ibid., 101.

277. Ibid., 98.

278. Ibid., 91

279. Scott, *Moral Economy of the Peasant.* 2.

280. Popkin, *Rational Peasant.* 69.

281. Scott, *Moral Economy of the Peasant.* 6-7.

282. Popkin, *Rational Peasant.* 21.

283. Ibid., 61.

284. Ibid., 3.

285. Scott, *Moral Economy of the Peasant.* 168.

286. Ibid.

287. Popkin, *Rational Peasant.* 108-109.

288. Id., 88-89.

289. Id., 43-44.

290. Id., 44 n.

291. Id., 108.

292. Scott,preface to *Moral Economy of the Peasant.* vii.

293. Popkin, *Rational Peasant.* 77.

294. Ibid., 84.

295. Ibid., 109

296. Ibid., 114.

297. Lester Thurow, *Head to Head: The Coming Economic Battle Among Japan, Europe, and America.* (New York: William Morrow and Company, Inc., 1992), 207.

Chapter 3: Urbanization and the 11th Grade:.
Demonstrating the Statistical Solution.

298. B. F. Skinner, *The Behavior of Organisms: An Experimental Analysis.* (New York: Appleton-Century-Crofts, Inc., 1966), 443.

299. Wilson, *On Human Nature.* 45.

300. Skinner, *Contingencies of Reinforcement.* 202..

301. Tony Horwitz, "Nilotic Nobel's Cairene Tales," *Wall Street Journal.* 27 October 1989, A4.

302. Alan Riding, "Problems of Mexico City: Warning to Third World," *New York Times.* Sunday, 15 May 1983, 12.

303. Seth S. King, "Food Sales by U.S. Called Peace Tool," *New York Times.* Sunday, 3 October 1982, 11.

304. Svetlana Alliluyeva. "Talk with Stalin's Daughter: Why She Left Soviet Again," interview by Raymond H. Anderson, *New York Times.* Sunday, 18 May 1986, 12

305. Aydin Yalcin, "The Sources of Terrorism in Turkey," *Wall Street Journal.* 22 June 1981, 20. Sari Gilbert, "Turkey suffers urban population boom," 29 December 1981, 3.

306. John K. Fairbanks. "The New Two China Problem," *New York Review.* 8 March 1979, 3.

307. June Kronholz, "City Limits," *Wall Street Journal.* 14 June 1983, 1.

308. Peter F. Drucker. "China's Growth Area, the Service Sector," *Wall Street Journal.* 3 March 1993, A14.

309. "China," *TIME Almanac2003.* (Boston: TimeInc.), 748.

310. Krizhanich, *Russian Statecraft.* 13.

311. Kravchinskii, *Russian Peasantry.* 3-4.

312. Arthur Lewis, "Development Economics in the 1950's," in *Pioneers in Development.* ed. Gerald M. Meier and Dudley Seers, (New York: Oxford University Press, 1984), 128.

313. Nair, *In Defense of the Irrational Peasant.* 95-96.

314.   Hazel Moir, "Dynamic Relationships between Labor Force Structure, Urbanization, and Development," *Economic Development and Cultural Change.* 62, no.1 (October 1977): 25.

315.   Margaret R. Wolfe.   "The Rural and Small-Town Experience with Commentary on Italians in Southern Appalachia, 1900-1920," *The United States and Italy: The First Two Hundred Years.*   Proceedings of the Ninth Annual Conference of the American Italian Historical Association (AIHA), ed. Humbert S. Nelli (New York: The American Italian Historical Association, 1977), 164.

316.   Avila, *Economic Impacts of Immigration.*   83.

317.   Rangel, *Latin Americans, 207.*.

318.   Freeman Dyson, *Infinite in All Directions.*   (New York: Harper & Row,1988; reprint, New York: Perennial Library, 1989), 275 (page citation is to the reprint edition).

319.   Meadows et al.. *Limits to Growth,* 153-154.

320.   Hee, "What Made the Revolution Succeed," East Asian History, 269.

321.   Scott, *Moral Economy of the Peasant.*   208-215.

322.   Riding, "Problems of Mexico City."

323.   Richard Critchfield.   "Reassessing Asian Villagers' Return From the City," *Asian Wall Street Journal Weekly.*   5 March 1984, 12.

324.   Richard Critchfield.   "Let Japanese Help Rural Java," *New York Times.* Sunday, 28 February 1982, E 19.

325.   Walter C. Clemens Jr.. "Perestroika Needs a Work Ethic to Work," A22.

326.   H. J. Eysenck, *The IQ Argument: Race, Intelligence and Education.*   (New York: Library Press, 1971), 43.

327.   David C. McClelland.   "Testing for Competence Rather Than for 'Intelligence', " in *The IQ Controversy: Critical Readings, ed. N.J. Block and Gerald Dworkin.* (New York: Pantheon Books, 1976).

328.   R.J. Herrnstein.   *I.Q. in the Meritocracy.*   (Boston: Little, Brown and Company, 1971), 127.

329. Leon J. Kamin, "Heredity, Intelligence, Politics, and Psychology: II," in *The IQ Controversy*. Block and Dworkin, 379.

330. Clarence J. Karier. "Testing for Order and Control in the Corporate Liberal State," in *The IQ Controversy*. Block and Dworkin, 348-349.

331. Salvatore J. LaGumina, ed.. *Wop!* (San Francisco: Straight Arrow Books, 1973), 172-173. The original source is Nathaniel S. Shaler, "European Peasants as Immigrants," *Atlantic Monthly.* 37 (May 1893): 646-655.

332. J. P. Guilford. *General Psychology.* (New York: D. VanNostrand Company, 1939), 530-531.

333. Paul R. Ehrlich and S. Shirley Feldman. *The Race Bomb: Skin Color, Prejudice and Intelligence.* (New York: Ballantine Books, 1978), 60. The original source is R. Pinter, *Intelligence Testing: Methods and Results.* (New York: Holt, 1923).

334. Arthur R. Jensen. *Educability and Group Differences.* (New York: Harper and Row, 1973), 34-35.

335. Arthur R. Jensen. *Genetics and Education.* (New York: Harper and Row, 1972), 170.

336. Stephen Thernstrom. *The Other Bostonians: Poverty and Progress in the American Metropolis, 1880-1970.* (Cambridge: Harvard University Press, 1973).

337. Ibid., 250-251.

338. Ibid., 174.

339. Ibid., 37.

340. Eli Ginsberg, "The Professionalization of the U.S. Labor Force," *Scientific American.* 240, no. 3 (March 1979).

341. Thernstrom, *The Other Bostonians.* 50.

342. Ibid. 132.

343. Ibid. 50.

344. Ibid. 139

345. Ibid., 141.

346. George J. Borjas. "The U.S. Takes the Wrong Immigrants," *Wall Street Journal.* 5 April 1990, A18.

347. Anthony H. Richmond. *Post-War Immigrants in Canada.* (Toronto: 1967), 40.

348. Ibid., 261.

349. Ibid., 106.

350. Thernstrom, *The Other Bostonians.* 146.

351. Ibid., 240.

352. William S. Egelman. "Traditional Roles and Modern Work Patterns of Italian American Women in New York City," *Italian Americana.* 2, (2000): 188-196.

353. Thernstrom, *The Other Bostonians.* 135-136.

354. Ibid., 50.

355. Ibid., 139-141.

356. Herbert J. Gans. *The Urban Villagers: Group and Class in the Life of Italian Americans.* (New York: Free Press, 1962).

357. Ibid., 124.

358. Ibid., 126.

359. Price, *White Settlers in the Tropics.* 72-73.

360. Jeremy Boissevain. *The Italians of Montreal: Social Adjustment in a Plural Society.* (Ottawa: Information Canada1970; reprint, New York: *New York Times.* Arno Press, 1970), 14-15. (page citations are to the reprint edition).

361. June Kronholz. "The Super Savers," *Wall Street Journal.* 5 October 1979.

362. Price, *White Settlers in the Tropics, .* 73.

363. Boissevain, *The Italians of Montreal, .* 17, 57.

364. Robert F. Foerster. *The Italian Emigration of Our Times.* (Cambridge: Harvard University Press, 1924; reprint, New York: Arno Press, 1969), 422. (page citation is to the reprint edition).

365. Jefferson, *Peopling the Argentine Pampa*. 172-173. In the 1880's the Bank of Buenos Aires had more depositors who were Italian citizens than Argentine citizens. Thomas Sowell, "Affirmative Action: From Bad to Worse," *Wall Street Journal*. 6 March 1990, A20.

366. Thomas H. Holloway. "Italians in Sao Paulo, Brazil: From Rural Proletariat to Middle Class," *Support and Struggle: Italians and Italian Americans in a Comparative Perspective*. Proceedings of the Seventeenth Annual Conference of the American Italian Historical Association (AIHA), ed. Joseph L. Tropea, James E. Miller, and Cheryl Beattie-Repetti (New York: The American Italian Historical Association, 1986), 124-125.

367. William Foote Whyte. *Street Corner Society: The Social Structure of an Italian Slum*. 2nd. ed. (Chicago: University of Chicago Press, 1955).

368. Ibid., 141.

369. Ibid., 107.

370. Gans, *Urban Villagers*. 83.

371. Samuel L. Baily. *Immigrants in the Lands of Promise: Italians in Buenos Aires and New York City, 1870-1914*. (Ithaca: Cornell University Press, 1999), 110.

372. Robert L. Thorndike. *Reading Comprehension Education in Fifteen Countries: An Empirical Study*. (New York: John Wiley and Sons, A Halstead Press Book, 1973).

373. Ibid., 129.

374. Robert B. Zajonc. "Family Configuration and Intelligence," *Science*. 16 April 1976, 232.

375. Andrew M. Greeley. *The American Catholic: A Social Portrait*. (New York: Basic Books, 1977), 51 n.

376. Thernstrom, *The Other Bostonians*. 146.

377. Leonard O. Packard, Charles P. Sinnott, and Bruce Overton. *The Nations at Work: An Industrial and Commercial Geography*. (New York: Macmillan Co., 1933), 431.

378. Braudel, *The Mediterranean and the Mediterranean World in the Age of Philip II*. 238-40.

379. Patrick J. Buchanan. *The Great Betrayal: How American Sovereignty and Social Justice Are Being Sacrificed to the Gods of the Global Economy.* (Boston: Little, Brown and Company, 1998), 178.

380. Paul Kennedy, *The Rise and Fall of the Great Powers: Economic Change and Military Conflict from 1500 to 2000.* (New York: Random House, Inc., 1987; reprint, New York: Vintage Books, 1989), 149 (page citation is to the reprint edition).

381. Ibid., 243.

382. Frederic M. Biddle. "Book on U.S. Competitiveness," *Boston Globe.* 15 May 1990, 57.

383. Meadows et al.. *Limits to Growth,* 116.

384. Steven Greenhouse. *"Workers Want Protection From the Promises of 1992," New York Times. Sunday, 25 June 1989, sec. 4, 2.*

385. *"Potential Power," Wall Street Journal.* 13 November 1989, 1.

386. George Will, "Italy's once-shaky economy now one of Europe's finest," *Concord (New Hampshire) Monitor.* 15 September 1989, B9.

387. "Beyond the earthquake: the problems of the Mezzogiorno. " *News from Italy.* (Fondazione Giovanni Agnelli, Torino, Italy) no. 4 (January 1981): 2.

388. Thernstrom, *The Other Bostonians.* 172.

389. Jensen, *Educability and Group Differences.* 63.

390. Smith, "Italian Mothers, American Daughters," 210.

391. Frank J. Cavaioli. "Charles Poletti and Fourteen Other Italian-American Governors," in *Italian Americans in Transition.* Proceedings of the XXI Annual Conference of the American Italian Historical Association, ed. Joseph V. Scelsa, Salvatore J. LaGumina, and Lydio Tomasi. (New York: The American Italian Historical Association, 1990), 142.

392. Jensen, *Educability and Group Differences.* 64-65.

393. Rudolph Pintner. *Intelligence Testing: Methods and Results.* (New York: Henry Holt and Company, Inc., 1923,1931), 450-51. (page reference is to the second edition).

394.   Rudolph Pintner.   "Comparison of American and Foreign Children on Intelligence Tests," *Journal of Educational Psychology.* 1923, 14, 295.

395.   Pintner, *Intelligence Testing.* 250.

396.   Ibid., 252.

397.   Horace M. Bond.   *"What the Army 'Intelligence' Tests Measured.* (1924)," in *The Bell Curve Debate: History, Documents, Opinions.* ed. Russell Jacoby and Naomi Glauberman (New York: Random House, Inc., Times Books, 1995), 597.

398.   . Eysenck, *The IQ Argument.* 120-21.

399.   Donna White and Brenda Panunto.   "Verbal and Nonverbal Abilities in English First and Second Language Children," *Psychological Reports.* 42 (1978): 194.

400.   Salvatore J. LaGumina, ed.. *Wop* (San Francisco: Straight Arrow Books, 1973), 148-153. The original source is Allan McLaughlin, "Italian and Other Latin Immigrants," *Popular Science Monthly.* 65 (August 1904): 341-7.

401.   Margaret R. Wolfe.   "The Rural and Small-Town Experience: With Commentary on Italians in Southern Appalachia, 1900-1920," in *Proceedings of the Ninth Annual Conference of the American Italian Historical Association (AIHA).* 165.

402.   Anthony V. Margavio.   "The reaction of the Press to the Italian-American in New Orleans, 1880 to 1920," *Italian Americana.* 4, no. 1 (Fall/Winter 1978): 78. The original sources are Annual Reports of the Commissioner-General of Immigration for the fiscal years ended June 30, 1899, through 1930. Those listed as having no occupation probably spent much of their time doing unskilled agricultural work. The figures do not simply indicate that Italian emigrants were agricultural laborers: They suggest the nature of the society the emigrant left behind.

403.   Dolci, *Report from Palermo.* xix.

404.   Svalastoga, *Social Differentiation.* 125.

405.   Packard, Sinnott, and Overton, . *Nations at Work.* 438.

406.   "Mezzogiorno: a challenge for Italy," *News from Italy.* (Fondazione Giovanni Agnelli, Torino, Italy) no. 28 (September 1988): 5.

407. "A place for Cinderella. " *News from Italy.* (Fondazione Giovanni Agnelli, Torino, Italy) no. 10 (July 1983): 3.

408. Baily, *Immigrants in the Lands of Promise.* 217-237.

409. Bob Davis, "Despite His Heritage, Prominent Economist Backs Immigration Cut," *Wall Street Journal.* 26 April 1996, 1.

410. George J. Borjas. "National Origin and the Skills of Immigrants in the Postwar Period," in *Immigration and the Work Force: Economic Consequences for the United States and Source Areas, ed. George J. Borjas and Richard B. Freeman.* (Chicago: The University of Chicago Press, 1992), 26.

411. George J. Borjas, Richard B. Freeman, and Lawrence F. Katz, . "On the Labor Market Effects of Immigration and Trade," in *Immigration and the Work Force.* ed. Borjas and Freeman, 214.

412. George J. Borjas. "Self-Selection and the Earnings of Immigrants," *The American Economic Review 77, no. 4.* (September 1987): 534.

413. Samuel P. Huntington. *The Clash of Civilizations and the Remaking of World Order.* (New York, Simon & Schuster, 1996), 87.

414. . Lester C. Thurow. "Converging Perceptions," *Boston Globe.* 6 February 1990, 28.

415. Thurow, *Head to Head.* 158.

416. Tony Horwitz, "Urban Harvest," *Wall Street Journal.* 8 September 1993, 1.

417. Stuart and Gregory. "A Model of Soviet Rural Urban Migration," c development and Cultural Change 84.

418. Roger Cohen, "Ethnic Japanese in Brazil Look to Tokyo,", *Wall Street Journal.* . 15 March 1989, A14.

419. David Shribman. "Quebec Premier Urges Vote for Stability," *Wall Street Journal.* 22 September 1989, A10.

420. "A Sermon of the Perishing Classes in Boston-Preached at the Melodeon, on Sunday, August 30, 1846," in *Speeches, Addresses, and Occasional Sermons by Theodore Parker.* vol. 1 (Boston: Ticknor and Fields, 1860).

Chapter 4: The Blond Invasion of Asia.

421. Walter A. McDougall. *Let the Sea Make a Noise.* (New York: BasicBooks, 1993), 207.

422. Nicholas D. Kristof. "Riddle of China: Repression As Standard of Living Soars," 7 September 1993, *New York Times.* 1.

423. Marcus W. Brauchli. "Migrants Fuel China's Economic Growth," *Wall Street Journal.* 17 August 1993, A10.

424. Jonathan Mirsky. "Democratic Vistas?" New York Review of Books, 13 August 1998, 31.

425. Paul A. Samuelson. *Economics, 10th ed..* (New York: McGraw-Hill, Inc., 1976), 876.

426. E. S. Browning. "Some Chinese Simply Won't Make a Move Without Fung Shui," *Wall Street Journal.* 19 December 1983, 1.

427. William Lewis, "The Secret to Competitiveness," *Wall Street Journal.* 22 October 1993, A14.

428. Urban C. Lehner. "Black and White," *Wall Street Journal.* 9 December 1982, 1.

429. David E. Sanger. "64% of Japanese Say U.S. Relations Are 'Unfriendly,' " *New York Times.* 6 July 1993, 1.

430. John K. Fairbank. "The Real Stuff," *New York Review of Books.* 14 April 1983, 16.

431. "Guest Editorial," *Wall Street Journal.* 4 December 1989, A14. citing *Democracy in America.* published in 1840.

432. Urban C. Lehner. "Belief in an Imminent Asian Century Is Gaining Sway," *Wall Street Journal.* 17 May 1993, A12.

433. Bill Powell and Bradley Martin. "What Japan Thinks of Us," Newsweek, 2 April 1990.

434. Robert J. Samuelson. "The Value of College," Newsweek, 31 August 1992.

435. Gavin Wright, "Where America's Industrial Monopoly Went," *Wall Street Journal.* 20 December 1990, A16.

436. Herbert Stein, "Memories of a Model Economist," *Wall Street Journal.* 23 November 1992, A14.

437. "New Faces at the Harvest. " *Wall Street Journal.* 1 October 1990, A12.

438. "The Return of Central Europe," *Chicago Fed Letter.* (The Federal Reserve Bank of Chicago) no. 33 (May 1990): 1-2.

439. Ibid., 2.

440. Mayo Mohs, "I.Q." *Discover.* September 1982.

441. Richard Lynn. *Educational Achievement in Japan: Lessons for the West .* (Armonk: M. E. Sharpe, Inc., 1988), 23.

442. Neil Ulman, "Brazil's Japanese Population Thrives, Helps Tokyo Forge Ties With Brasilia," *Wall Street Journal.* 24 September 1982, 39.

443. Jan Tinbergen, "Development Cooperation as a Learning Process," in *Pioneers in Development.* ed. Meier and Seers, 322.

444. Wilson *Consilience.* 182-195.

445. Thurow, *Head to Head.* 153.

Chapter 5: Sociobiology and Nuclear Weapons.

446. Robert Murphy, *Diplomat Among Warriors.* (Garden City: Doubleday & Company, Inc., 1964) 273, 275.

447. Tatyana Tolstaya. "Boris the First," review of *The Struggle for Russia.* by Boris N. Yeltsin, *New York Review of Books.* 23 June 1994, 3.

448. Krizhanich, *Russian Statecraft..*

449. Charles A. Radin. "Korean crisis poses threat of new arms race," *Boston Sunday Globe.* 12 June 1994, 28.

450. Seymour Melman. "Military realities vs. the 'missile gap' of '62," *Boston Sunday Globe.* 25 October 1987, A7.

451. George Gilder. "Secrecy Manias Only Backfire," *Wall Street Journal.* 1 October 1985, 32.

452. James Carroll, "US sowed a nuclear wind in North Korea," *Boston Globe.* 21 June 1994, 13.

453. David Warsh, "Social capital: powerful lens or passing fad?" *Boston Sunday Globe.* 25 September 1994, 81.

454. *Documents and Records Relating to the Province of New Hampshire, from 1686 to 1722.* ed. Nathaniel Bouton (Manchester, N. H.: John B. Clarke, 1868), 2: 30-31.

455. McDougall, *Let the Sea Make a Noise.* 291.

456. Ibid., 292.

457. Ibid., 291.

458. J. B. Bury, *The Invasion of Europe by the Barbarians.* (New York: W. W. Norton & Company, 1967, reissued 2000), 38-42.

459. McDougall, *Let the Sea Make a Noise.* 391.

460. Max Boot, "Will Bush Bury 'Bodybag Syndrome'?" *Wall Street Journal.* 11 September 2000, A44.

461. Jean Mayer, "A scientific solution," *Boston Globe.* 5 September 1992, 23.

462. Editorial, *Wall Street Journal.* 3 February 1992, A12.

463. Dorothy Zinberg. "War plants make peace," *Boston Globe.* 19 November 1994, 15.

464. John Diamond, "Air Force general calls for end to atomic arms," *Boston Globe.* 16 July 1994, 3.

465. Boeing ad, "Salute to America's global 'keepers of the peace'!" *Newsweek.* 23 April 1956, 17.

466. William J. Broad. "In Russia, Secret Labs Struggle To Survive," *New York Times.* 14 January 1992, C9.

467. Ibid.

468. Paul Quinn-Judge. "Algeria triggers nuclear headache," *Boston Globe.* 5 February 1994, 2.

469. Michael Novak, "The theology of arms control," *Boston Herald American.* 13 June 1979, 25.

470. Simon Serfaty, "Lost Illusions," *Foreign Policy.* 66 (Spring 1987): 9.

471. Science, *Newsweek.* 23 April 1956, 68.

472. Heather Wilson. "Nuclear Threat-Leadership Wanted," *Wall Street Journal.* 8 December 1993, A14.

473. William Safire. "NATO on the Brink," *New York Times.* 28 January 1993, A21.

474. McDougall, *Let the Sea Make a Noise.* 273.

475. Ibid., 391.

476. John Lehman, review of *Naval Battles of the Twentieth Century.* by Richard Hough, *Wall Street Journal.* 8 March 2001, A20.

477. Editorial, "A meaningful SDI mission," *Boston Globe.* 2 November 1991, 18.

478. Robert Jastrow and Max M. Kampelman. "Why We Still Need SDI," *Commentary.* , November 1992, 23.

479. George Melloan. "Gulf Lessons- for Good Guys, and Bad," *Wall Street Journal.* 18 March 1991, A15.

480.   Herbert Stein, "Lack of U.S. Will Isn't Economy's Fault," *Wall Street Journal.* 20 January 1988, 26.

481. Albin Krebs, "Matthew B. Ridgeway Dies at 98; Leader of U.S. Troops in 2 Wars," *New York Times.* 27 July 1993, A1.

482. Editorial, "Baghdad and Beyond," *Wall Street Journal.* 28 June 8, 1993, A16.

483.   Paul Bracken, "America's Maginot Line," *Atlantic Monthly.*   December 1998, 86.

484. Huntington, *Clash of Civilizations..*

485. Patricia Nelson Limerick. "Talking is better than silence," *USA Today.* 7 January 1985, 10A.

486. Carla Anne Robbins. "Out of the Box," *Wall Street Journal.* 14 December 1998, 1.

487.   Editorial, "Calling Jimmy Carter," *Wall Street Journal.*   23 September 1994, A14.

Chapter 6: Blonds and Slavs: Theory Meets Reality.

488. New Hampshire Legislature, Resolution by the Senate and House of Representatives, 1844, *Laws of the State of New Hampshire from November Session, 1842, to June Session, 1847, Inclusive* . (Concord, New Hampshire, Butterfield & Hill, 1847), 159.

489. William F. Buckley Jr.. "Strange Suggestion of Polish Prime Minister," *Manchester (New Hampshire) Union Leader.* 6 March 1990, 23.

490. David Gilmour, "The Man Who Would Be Good," review of *The Letters of Rudyard Kipling.* Volume 4: 1911-19, ed. Thomas Pinney, *New York Review of Books.* 25 May 2000, 41.

491. Amity Shlaes, "Unwilling Executioners," *Wall Street Journal.* 26 November 1996, A18.

492. Harold John Edward Peake. *F.S.A., The Bronze Age and The Celtic World.* (New York: reprint, Hacker Art Books, 1969), 107. (page citation is to the reprint edition).

493. Charlse Killinger. "The Italian Democratic Left and Woodrow Wilson," in *New Explorations in Italian American Studies.* Proceedings of the 25th Annual Conference of the American Italian Historical Association, ed. Richard N. Juliani and Sandra P. Juliani (Washington, D.C., American Italian Historical Association, 1992), 50.

494. *Mary Moore vs. The State.* 7 Texas Court of Appeals 608, (1880).

495. Paul Johnson, "The Road to Sarajevo," *Wall Street Journal.* 18 November 1991, A14.

496. Gordon W. Allport. *The Nature of Prejudice, .* (Garden City: Addison-Wesley Publishing Company, Inc., 1954; reprint, Anchor Books, 1958).

497. Ibid., 275.

498. Louis Menand, "The Quiet American," *New York Review of Books.* 14 July 1994, 18

499. Sidney Hook, "My Running Debate With Einstein," *Commentary.* July 1982, 41.

500. James Carroll, "America's dirty dance with nuclear weapons," *Boston Globe.* 30 May 1995, 15.

501.   Oli Hawrylyshyn.   "Ethnic Affinity and Migration Flows in Postwar Yugoslavia," in *Economic Development and Cultural Change.* 62, no.1 (October 1977).

502. Ibid., 93.

503. Albert Wohlstetter. "Bosnia: Air Power, Not Peacekeepers," *Wall Street Journal.* 9 December 1994, A16.

504. "Grandson starts movement to pave way for new Stalin," *Boston Globe.* 14 June 1995, 6.

505. Shakhnazarov et al.. *Social Science,* 137.

506. Ibid., 137-138

507. Ibid., 139.

508. Irving Kristol. "Russia's Destiny," *Wall Street Journal.* 11 February 1984, A12.

509. Therese Raphael. "Russia: The New Imperialism," *Wall Street Journal.* 22 June 1994, A20.

510.   Czeslaw Milosz.   "Swing Sift in the Baltics," review of *The Baltic Revolution: Estonia, Latvia, Lithuania and the Path to Independence.* by Anatol Lieven, New York Review of Books, 4 November 1993, 16.

511. Fareed Zakaria. "Offer Russia a Peace of Vienna," *New York Times.* 9 May 1995, A27.

512. Adrian Karatnycky. "Back to the USSR," *Wall Street Journal.* 30 June 30 1994, A10.

513. Melman, "Military realities," A7.

514. David Filipov, "Turk held for aiding Chechnya," *Boston Globe.* 12 August 1995, 2.

515. Colum Lynch, "US calls for total nuclear test ban," *Boston Globe.* 12 August 1995, 2.

516. Thomas Powers, "The Conspiracy That Failed," *New York Review of Books.* 9 January 1997, 54.

517.   William Safire, "Baltics Belong in a Big NATO," *New York Times.*   16 January 1995, A17.

518. Editorial, *New York Times.* 9 May 1995, A26.

519.   Kenneth R. Timmerman.   "Time to Stop the Iranian Nuke," *Wall Street Journal.* 21 April 1993, A14.

520.   Elaine Sciolino.   "Iran's Nuclear Goals Lie in Half-Built Plant," *New York Times.* 19 May 1995, A1.

521.   Albert Wohlstetter and Gregory S. Jones.   "Alternatives to Negotiating Genocide," *Wall Street Journal.* 3 May 1995, A14.

Chapter 7: SDI: The Blonds Safe?.

522. Nicole Bensoussan. "Tragic Vistas in Spike Lee's Jungle Fever and Do The Right Thing," in *Shades of Black and White: Conflict and Collaboration Between Two Communities.* ed. Dan Ashyk, Fred L. Gardaphe, and Anthony Julian Tamburri, (Staten Island, N.Y.: Italian American Historical Association, 1999), 237.

523. Hugo Restall, "China's 'Victimhood' Breeds Aggression," *Wall Street Journal.* 4 April 2001.

524. Claudia Rosett, "Defiant Chechnya Tests Moscow's Empire," *Wall Street Journal.* 9 December 1994, A12.

525. Robert D. Kaplan. "The Great Game Isn't Over," *Wall Street Journal.* 24 November 1999, A18.

526. Editorial, "The teardrop of Tibet," *Boston Globe.* 9 September 1995, 10.

527. Karen White, "Addressing a 25-year slight," *Brockton (Massachusetts) Sunday Enterprise.* 21 May 21 1995, 18.

528. Editorial, "SDI's Enemies," Manchester (New Hampshire) Union Leader, 10 November 1989, 31.

529. Id.

530. Editorial, "Secretary of Disarmament," *Wall Street Journal.* 28 November 1989, A14.

531. John McCain, "The Missile Threat the White House Ignores," *Wall Street Journal.* 22 May 22 1996, A22.

532. Editorial, "AWOL in Southwest Asia," *Wall Street Journal.* 6 December 1996. A18.

533. Arthur Waldron. "Deterring China," *Commentary.* October 1995, 21.

534. David Brooks, "Dark Gray Matter: How IQ Trumps Everything Else," *Wall Street Journal.* 20 October 1994, A20.

535. Editorial, "East vs. West," *Wall Street Journal.* 16 May 1994, A18.

536. Charles Horner. "Under the Rising Sun," *Commentary.* , July 1994, 31.

537. Editorial, "Japan's Iranian Interests," *Wall Street Journal*. 4 August 1994, A12.

538. Editorial, "Upside-Down Arms Control," *Wall Street Journal*. 26 September 1989, A26.

539. Editorial, "Japan, Eek.," *Wall Street Journal*. 1 June 1995, A14.

540. John Saxon, "Classroom Calculators Add to Math Illiteracy," *Wall Street Journal*. 16 May 1986, 24.

541. "Japan scrambles jets over island, "*Boston Globe*. 25 August 1995, 11.

542. Leslie H. Gelb. "The Next Renegade State," *New York Times*. 10 April 1991, A25.

543. Steve Glain and Norihiko Shirouzu. "Lost Gamble," *Wall Street Journal*. 24 July 1996, A1.

544. Arthur Waldron. "Here's How We Respond to North Korea," *Manchester (New Hampshire) Union Leader*. 14 April 1994, 37.

545. Editorial, "Asides," *Wall Street Journal*. 6 March 1996, A20.

546. "Notable and Quotable," citing a 1933 paper by General George S. Patton, in *Patton: A genius for War.* by Carlo D'Este; *Wall Street Journal*. 14 November 1995, A14.

547. Editorial, "Making Moscow Happy," *Wall Street Journal*. 16 May 1997, A18.

548. Matt Forney and Thom Beal,. "Macau's Return to China Stirs Little Interest," *Wall Street Journal*. 15 December 1999, A17.

549. Nicholas Eberstadt. "No Democratic Trend in East Asia," *Wall Street Journal*. 18 July 1989, A22.

550. Margaret Thatcher. "Notable and Quotable," *Wall Street Journal*. 13 March 1996, A14.

551. Kathy Chenault. "China says it will sign nonproliferation pact," *Boston Sunday Globe*. 11 August 1991, pp1,18.

552. William F. Buckley Jr.. "The Nuclear Quandary," *National Review*. September 20, 1993, 87.

553. John Lehman, "The Navy's Second Wind," *Wall Street Journal.* 1 June 1995, A12.

554. Chalmers M. Roberts. "Ike moved world from the brink to a summit," *Concord(New Hampshire) Monitor.* 13 October 1990, 12.

555. "Ike Mulled Nuking Chinese in Korean War. " *Manchester (New Hampshire) Union Leader.* 8 June 1984, 27.

556. John J. Fialka. "North Korean Nuclear Effort Tests U.S.," *Wall Street Journal.* 14 November 1991, A10.

557. Richard Pipes. "Team B: The Reality Behind the Myth," *Commentary.* , October 1986, 25.

558. "Russia, China seek stronger partnership," *Brockton (Massachusetts) Sunday Enterprise.* 29 December 1996, 3.

559. Erik Eckholm, "China Says U.S. Missile Shield Could Force an Arms Buildup," *New York Times.* 11 May 2000, A.6.

560. Gar Alperovitz, "Questioning Hiroshima," *Boston Globe.* 20 August 1994, 15

561. Erik Eckholm, "China Says U.S. Missile Shield Could Force an Arms Buildup," *New York Times.* 11 May 2000, 1, A6.

562. Editorial, "To Curb China's Arms Trade," *New York Times.* 6 July 1991, 20.

563. Max Boot, "Victorian Soldiers Have Some Lessons for U.S.," *Wall Street Journal.* 25 August 1998, A14.

564. Skinner, *Contingencies of Reinforcement.* 7.

Index